LEGION

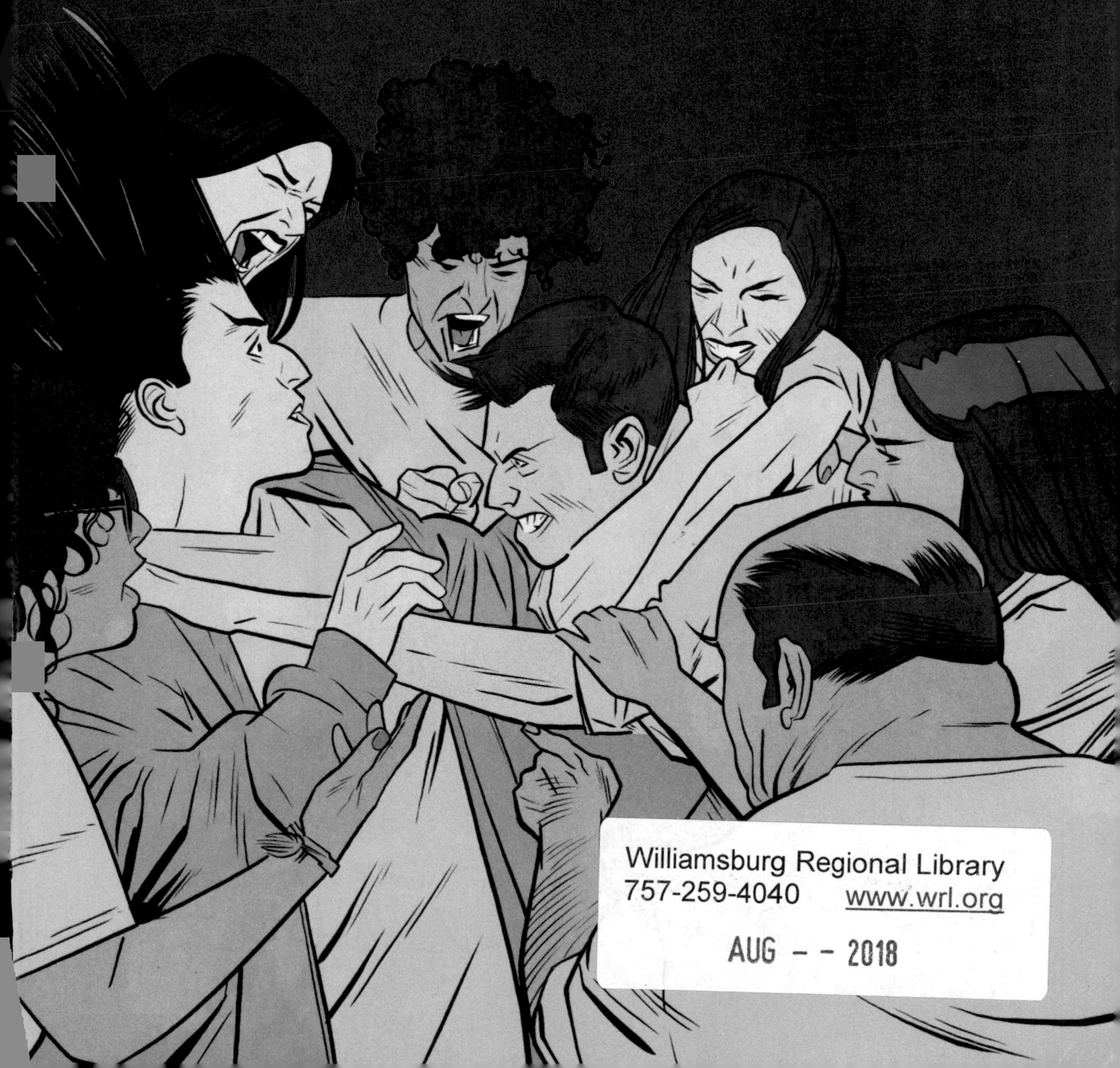

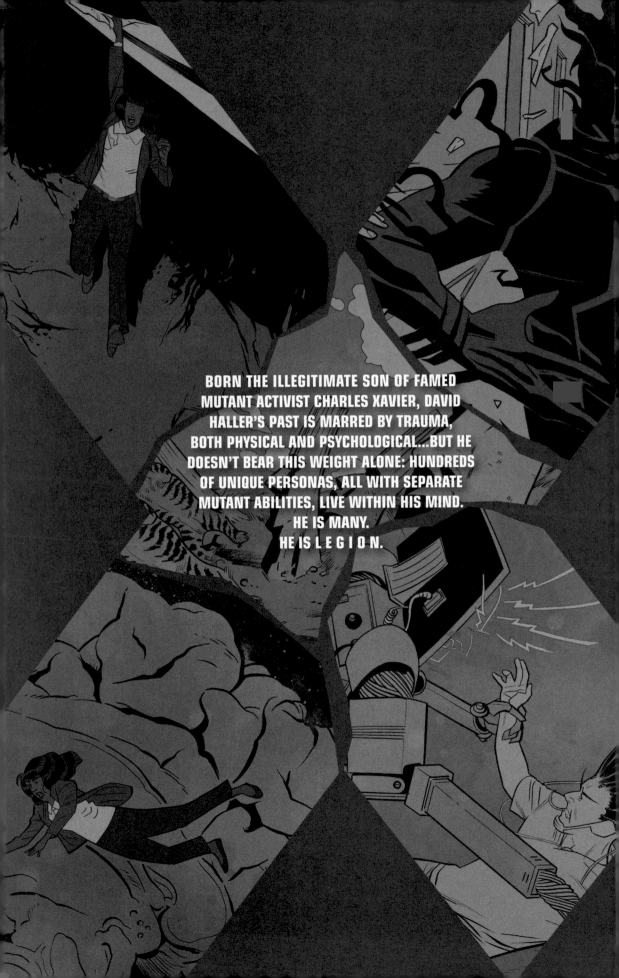

BORN THE ILLEGITIMATE SON OF FAMED
MUTANT ACTIVIST CHARLES XAVIER, DAVID
HALLER'S PAST IS MARRED BY TRAUMA,
BOTH PHYSICAL AND PSYCHOLOGICAL...BUT HE
DOESN'T BEAR THIS WEIGHT ALONE: HUNDREDS
OF UNIQUE PERSONAS, ALL WITH SEPARATE
MUTANT ABILITIES, LIVE WITHIN HIS MIND.
HE IS MANY.
HE IS L E G I O N.

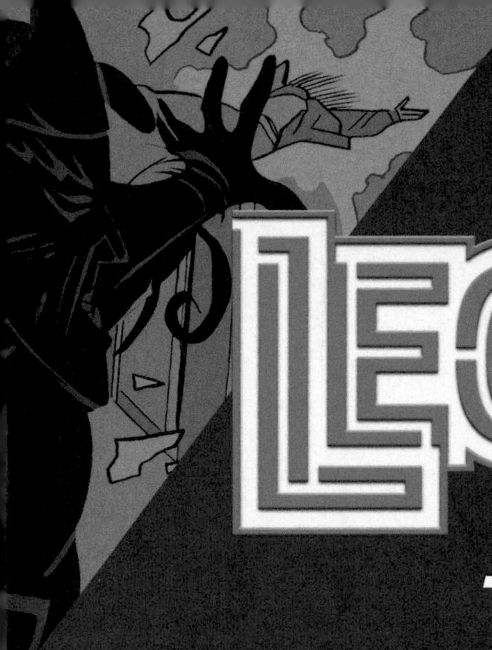

LEGION

TRAUMA

Writer/**PETER MILLIGAN**

Artists/**WILFREDO TORRES** (#1-3 & #5)
& **LEE M. FERGUSON** (#4-5)

Inkers/**WILFREDO TORRES** (#1-3) & **LEE M. FERGUSON** (#4-5)
with **MARC DEERING** (#3 & #5) & **BELARDINO BRABO** (#5)

Color Artist/**DAN BROWN**

Letterer/**VC's TRAVIS LANHAM**

Cover Artist/**Javier Rodríguez**

Assistant Editors/**CHRIS ROBINSON** & **ANNALISE BISSA**

Editor/**DARREN SHAN**

X-Men Group Editor/**MARK PANICCIA**

Collection Editor/**JENNIFER GRÜNWALD** • Assistant Editor/**CAITLIN O'CONNELL**
Associate Managing Editor/**KATERI WOODY** • Editor, Special Projects/**MARK D. BEAZLEY**
VP Production & Special Projects/**JEFF YOUNGQUIST** • SVP Print, Sales & Marketing/**DAVID GABRIEL**
Book Designer/**JAY BOWEN**

Editor in Chief/**C.B. CEBULSKI** • Chief Creative Officer/**JOE QUESADA**
President/**DAN BUCKLEY** • Executive Producer/**ALAN FINE**

LEGION: TRAUMA. Contains material originally published in magazine form as LEGION #1-5. First printing 2018. ISBN 978-1-302-91162-1. Published by MARVEL WORLDWIDE, INC., a subsidiary of MARVEL ENTERTAINMENT, LLC. OFFICE OF PUBLICATION: 135 West 50th Street, New York, NY 10020. **Printed in the U.S.A.** DAN BUCKLEY, President, Marvel Entertainment; JOHN NEE, Publisher; JOE QUESADA, Chief Creative Officer; TOM BREVOORT, SVP of Publishing; DAVID BOGART, SVP of Business Affairs & Operations, Publishing & Partnership; DAVID GABRIEL, SVP of Sales & Marketing, Publishing; JEFF YOUNGQUIST, VP of Production & Special Projects; DAN CARR, Executive Director of Publishing Technology; ALEX MORALES, Director of Publishing Operations; DAN EDINGTON, Managing Editor; SUSAN CRESPI, Production Manager; STAN LEE, Chairman Emeritus. For information regarding advertising in Marvel Comics or on Marvel.com, please contact Vit DeBellis, Custom Solutions & Integrated Advertising Manager, at vdebellis@marvel.com. For Marvel subscription inquiries, please call 888-511-5480. **Manufactured between 5/25/2018 and 6/26/2018 by QUAD GRAPHICS SARATOGA, SARATOGA SPRINGS, NY, USA.**

10 9 8 7 6 5 4 3 2 1

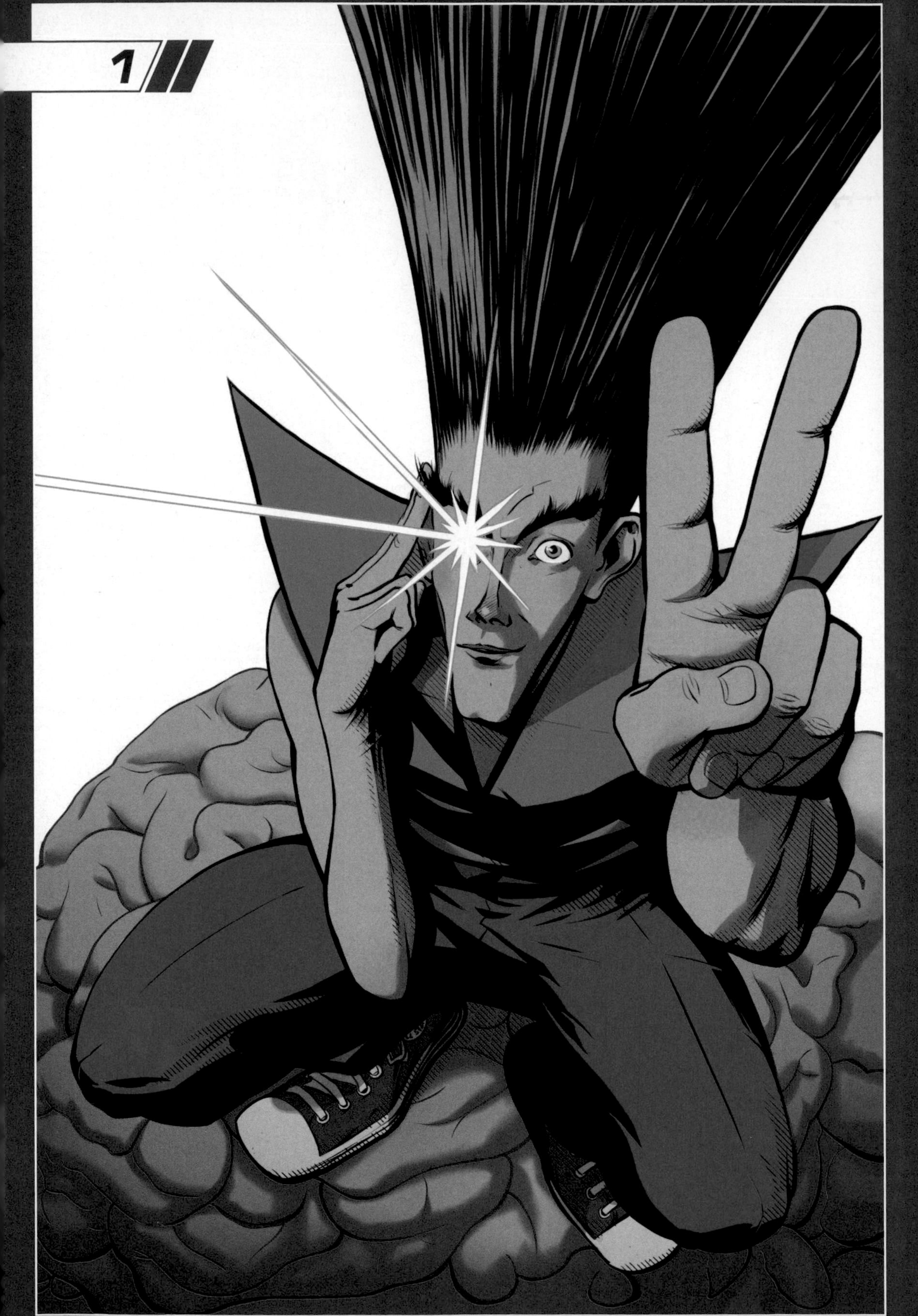
1

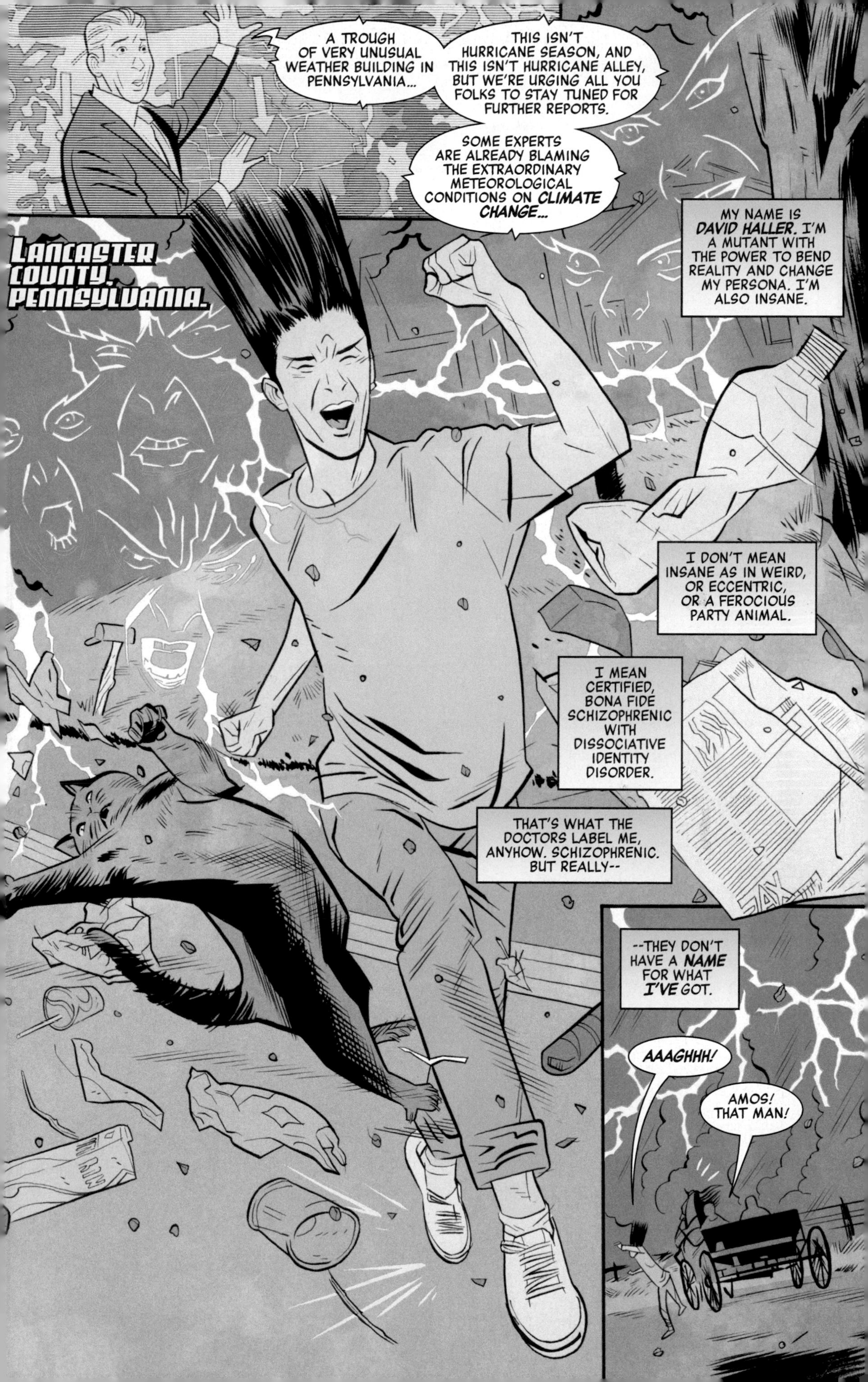
A TROUGH OF VERY UNUSUAL WEATHER BUILDING IN PENNSYLVANIA...
THIS ISN'T HURRICANE SEASON, AND THIS ISN'T HURRICANE ALLEY, BUT WE'RE URGING ALL YOU FOLKS TO STAY TUNED FOR FURTHER REPORTS.
SOME EXPERTS ARE ALREADY BLAMING THE EXTRAORDINARY METEOROLOGICAL CONDITIONS ON *CLIMATE CHANGE*...
LANCASTER COUNTY, PENNSYLVANIA.
MY NAME IS *DAVID HALLER*. I'M A MUTANT WITH THE POWER TO BEND REALITY AND CHANGE MY PERSONA. I'M ALSO INSANE.
I DON'T MEAN INSANE AS IN WEIRD, OR ECCENTRIC, OR A FEROCIOUS PARTY ANIMAL.
I MEAN CERTIFIED, BONA FIDE SCHIZOPHRENIC WITH DISSOCIATIVE IDENTITY DISORDER.
THAT'S WHAT THE DOCTORS LABEL ME, ANYHOW. SCHIZOPHRENIC. BUT REALLY--
--THEY DON'T HAVE A *NAME* FOR WHAT *I'VE* GOT.
AAAGHHH!
AMOS! THAT MAN!

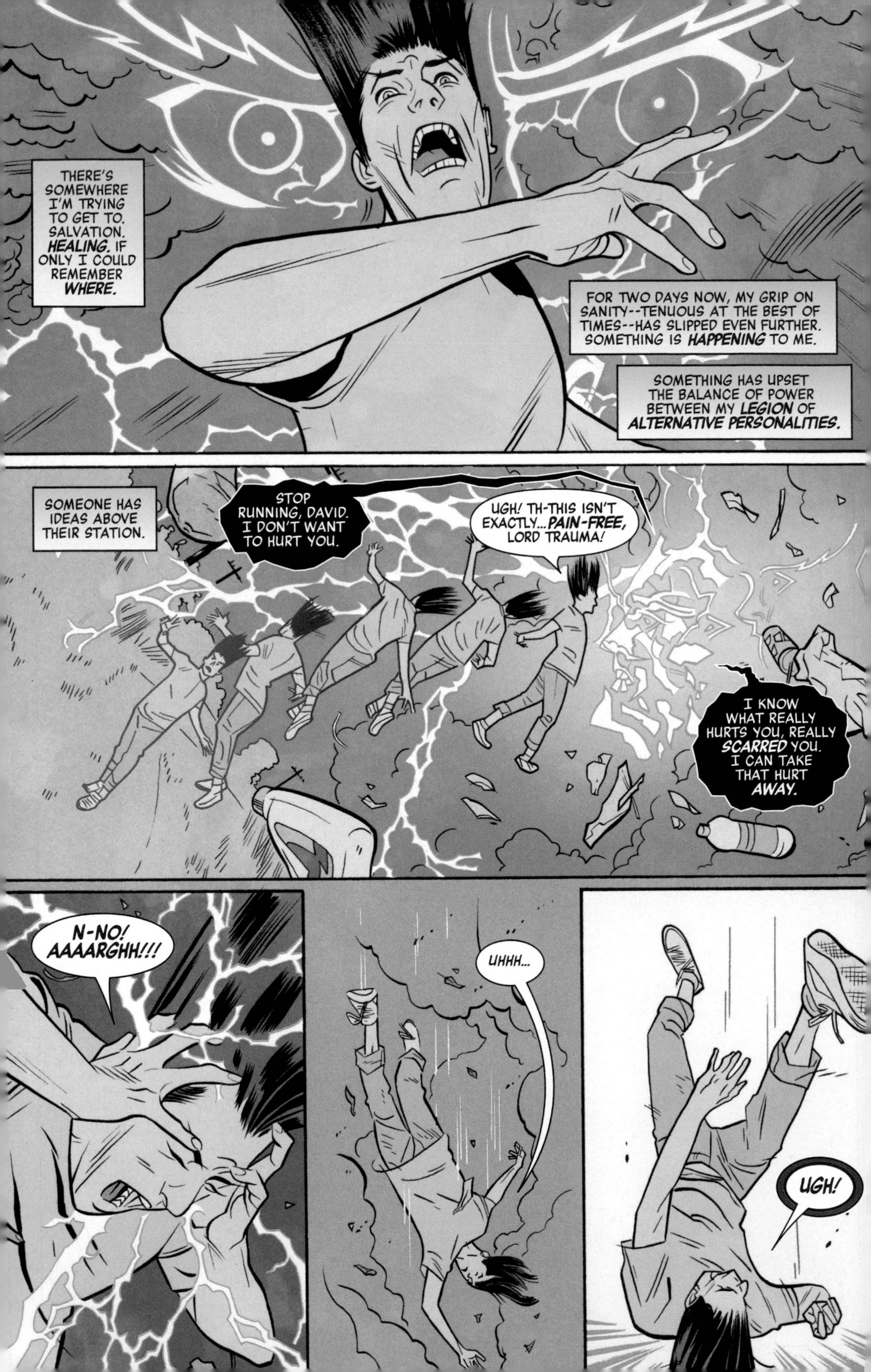
THERE'S SOMEWHERE I'M TRYING TO GET TO. SALVATION. HEALING. IF ONLY I COULD REMEMBER WHERE.
FOR TWO DAYS NOW, MY GRIP ON SANITY--TENUOUS AT THE BEST OF TIMES--HAS SLIPPED EVEN FURTHER. SOMETHING IS HAPPENING TO ME.
SOMETHING HAS UPSET THE BALANCE OF POWER BETWEEN MY LEGION OF ALTERNATIVE PERSONALITIES.
SOMEONE HAS IDEAS ABOVE THEIR STATION.
STOP RUNNING, DAVID. I DON'T WANT TO HURT YOU.
UGH! TH-THIS ISN'T EXACTLY...PAIN-FREE, LORD TRAUMA!
I KNOW WHAT REALLY HURTS YOU, REALLY SCARRED YOU. I CAN TAKE THAT HURT AWAY.
N-NO! AAAARGHH!!!
UHHH...
UGH!

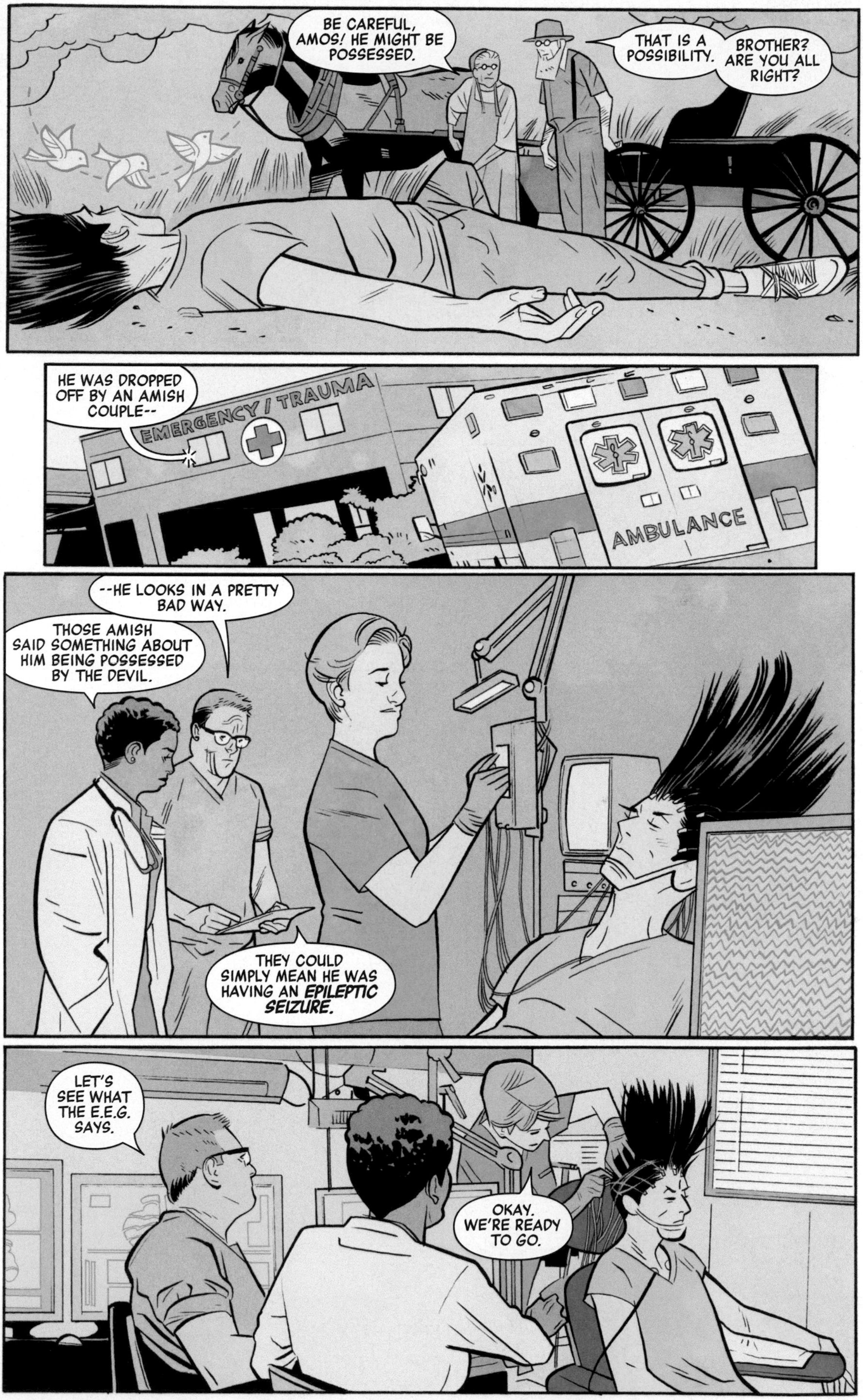
BE CAREFUL, AMOS! HE MIGHT BE POSSESSED.
THAT IS A POSSIBILITY.
BROTHER? ARE YOU ALL RIGHT?
HE WAS DROPPED OFF BY AN AMISH COUPLE--
EMERGENCY / TRAUMA
AMBULANCE
--HE LOOKS IN A PRETTY BAD WAY.
THOSE AMISH SAID SOMETHING ABOUT HIM BEING POSSESSED BY THE DEVIL.
THEY COULD SIMPLY MEAN HE WAS HAVING AN EPILEPTIC SEIZURE.
LET'S SEE WHAT THE E.E.G. SAYS.
OKAY. WE'RE READY TO GO.

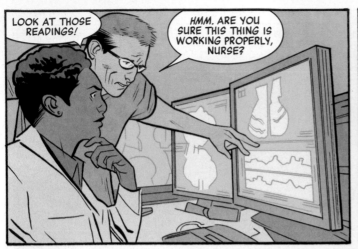

LOOK AT THOSE READINGS!

HMM. ARE YOU SURE THIS THING IS WORKING PROPERLY, NURSE?

ABSOLUTELY.

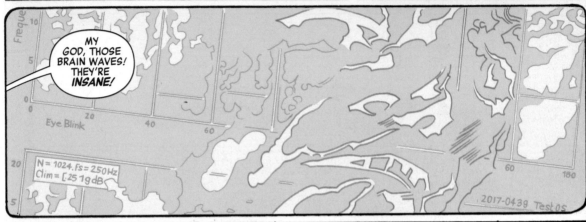

MY GOD, THOSE BRAIN WAVES! THEY'RE *INSANE!*

Freque

Eye Blink

N = 1024. fs = 250Hz
Clim = [-25 19 dB

2017-0439 Test 05

WITH SIGNALS LIKE THESE, HE MUST BE HAVING A MASSIVE SEIZURE *AT THIS VERY MINUTE.*

SEDATIVES, NURSE, QUICK!

NO! NO SEDATION!

D-DID YOU *HEAR* THAT?!

PUT THE PATIENT UNDER, NURSE, FOR THE L-LOVE OF GOD...

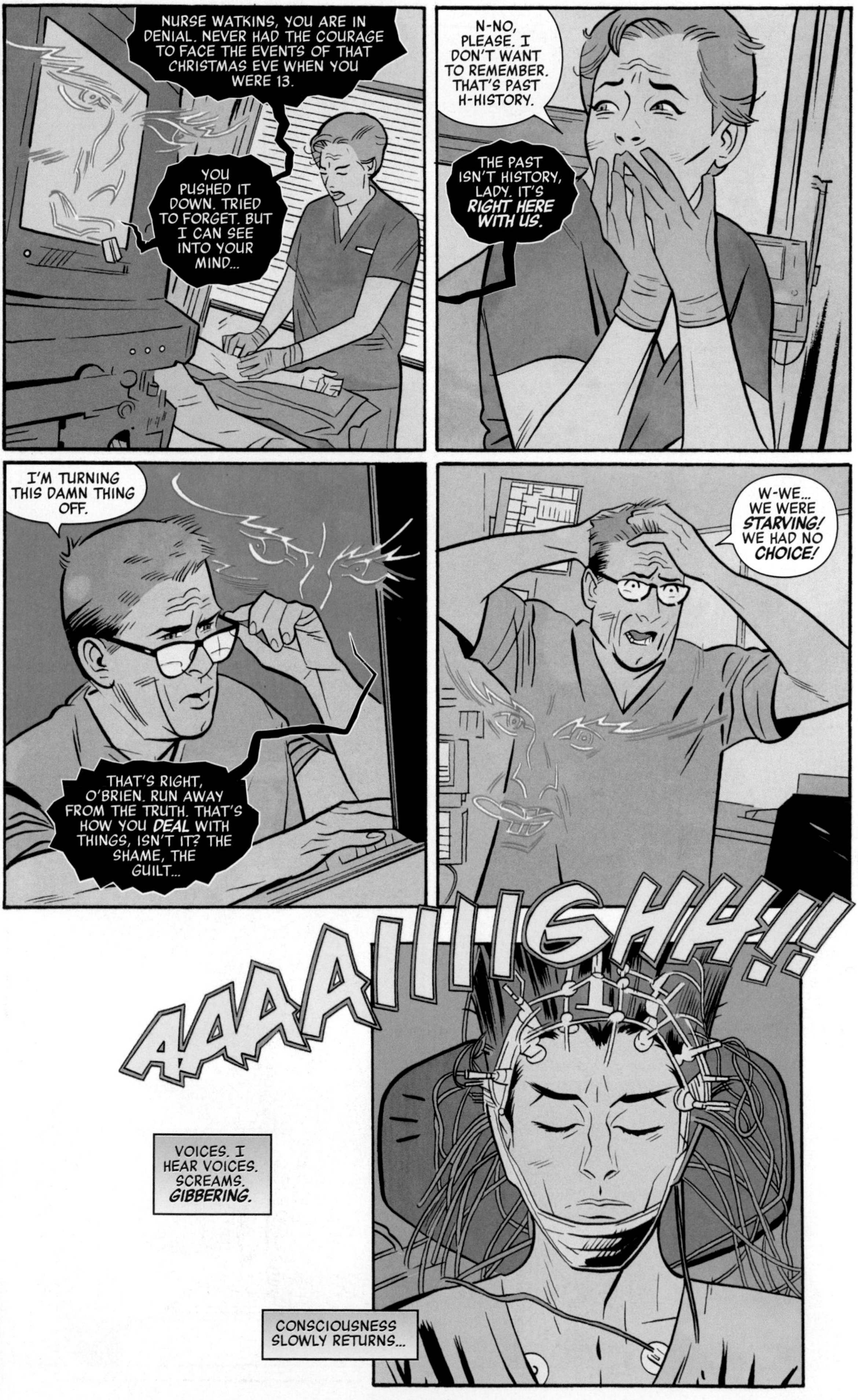
NURSE WATKINS, YOU ARE IN DENIAL. NEVER HAD THE COURAGE TO FACE THE EVENTS OF THAT CHRISTMAS EVE WHEN YOU WERE 13.
YOU PUSHED IT DOWN. TRIED TO FORGET. BUT I CAN SEE INTO YOUR MIND...
N-NO, PLEASE. I DON'T WANT TO REMEMBER. THAT'S PAST H-HISTORY.
THE PAST ISN'T HISTORY, LADY. IT'S RIGHT HERE WITH US.
I'M TURNING THIS DAMN THING OFF.
THAT'S RIGHT, O'BRIEN. RUN AWAY FROM THE TRUTH. THAT'S HOW YOU DEAL WITH THINGS, ISN'T IT? THE SHAME, THE GUILT...
W-WE... WE WERE STARVING! WE HAD NO CHOICE!
AAAIIIIGHH!!
VOICES. I HEAR VOICES. SCREAMS. GIBBERING.
CONSCIOUSNESS SLOWLY RETURNS...

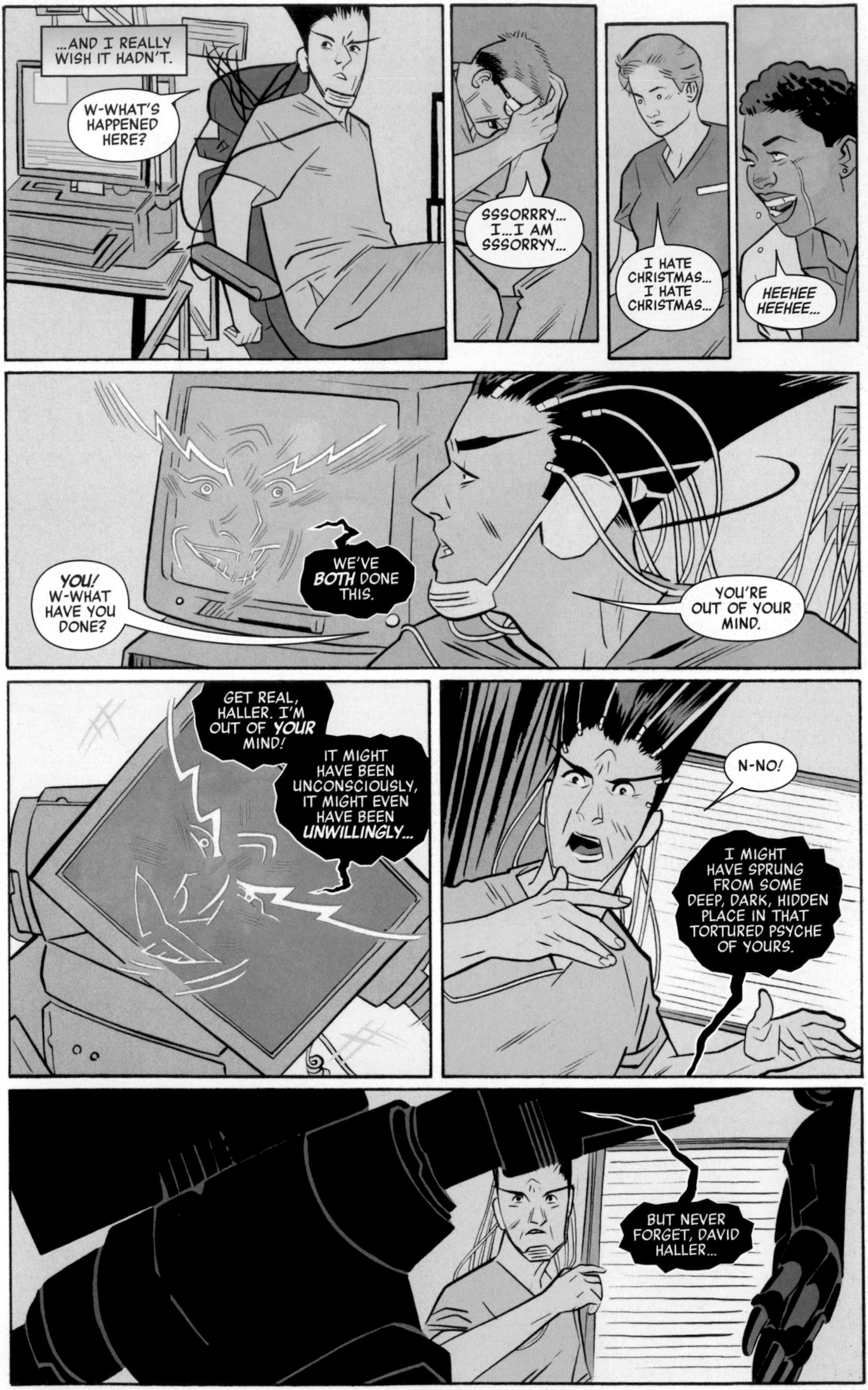
...AND I REALLY WISH IT HADN'T.
W-WHAT'S HAPPENED HERE?
SSSORRRY... I...I AM SSSORRYY...
I HATE CHRISTMAS... I HATE CHRISTMAS...
HEEHEE HEEHEE...
YOU! W-WHAT HAVE YOU DONE?
WE'VE BOTH DONE THIS.
YOU'RE OUT OF YOUR MIND.
GET REAL, HALLER. I'M OUT OF YOUR MIND!
IT MIGHT HAVE BEEN UNCONSCIOUSLY, IT MIGHT EVEN HAVE BEEN UNWILLINGLY...
N-NO!
I MIGHT HAVE SPRUNG FROM SOME DEEP, DARK, HIDDEN PLACE IN THAT TORTURED PSYCHE OF YOURS.
BUT NEVER FORGET, DAVID HALLER...

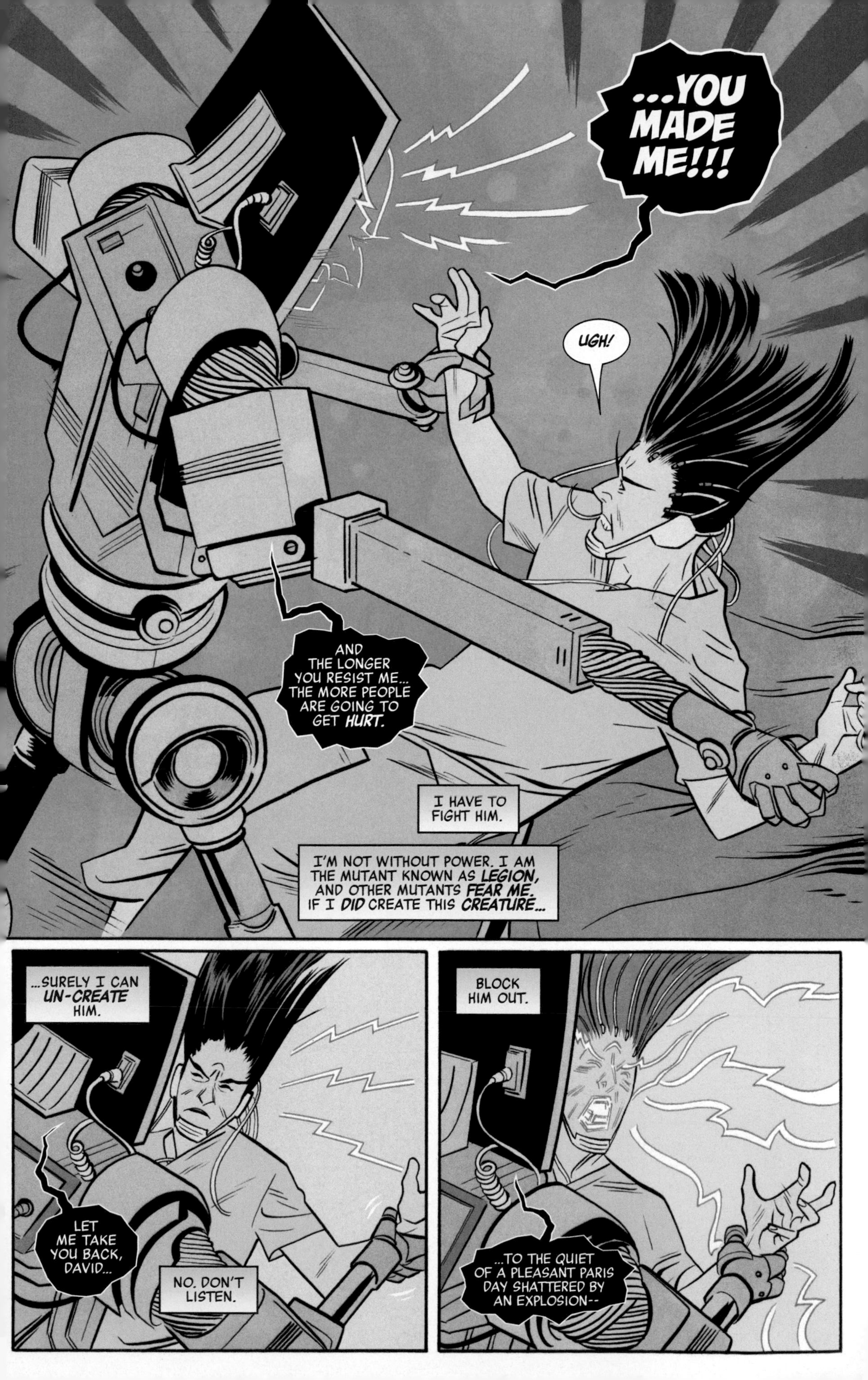
...YOU MADE ME!!!
UGH!
AND THE LONGER YOU RESIST ME... THE MORE PEOPLE ARE GOING TO GET HURT.
I HAVE TO FIGHT HIM.
I'M NOT WITHOUT POWER. I AM THE MUTANT KNOWN AS LEGION, AND OTHER MUTANTS FEAR ME. IF I DID CREATE THIS CREATURE...
...SURELY I CAN UN-CREATE HIM.
LET ME TAKE YOU BACK, DAVID...
NO. DON'T LISTEN.
BLOCK HIM OUT.
...TO THE QUIET OF A PLEASANT PARIS DAY SHATTERED BY AN EXPLOSION--

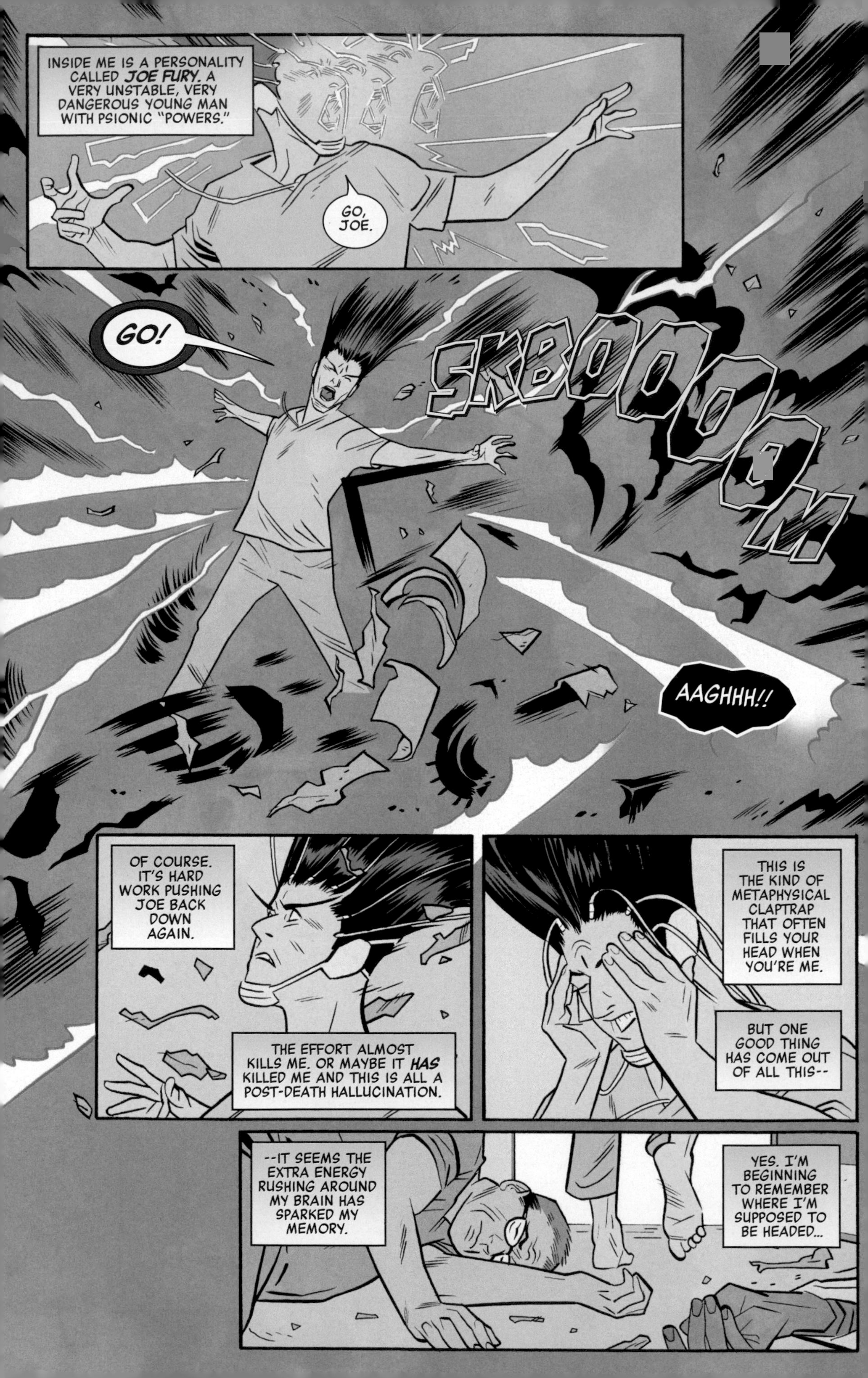
INSIDE ME IS A PERSONALITY CALLED JOE FURY. A VERY UNSTABLE, VERY DANGEROUS YOUNG MAN WITH PSIONIC "POWERS."
GO, JOE.
GO!
SKBOOOOOM
AAGHHH!!
OF COURSE. IT'S HARD WORK PUSHING JOE BACK DOWN AGAIN.
THE EFFORT ALMOST KILLS ME. OR MAYBE IT HAS KILLED ME AND THIS IS ALL A POST-DEATH HALLUCINATION.
THIS IS THE KIND OF METAPHYSICAL CLAPTRAP THAT OFTEN FILLS YOUR HEAD WHEN YOU'RE ME.
BUT ONE GOOD THING HAS COME OUT OF ALL THIS--
--IT SEEMS THE EXTRA ENERGY RUSHING AROUND MY BRAIN HAS SPARKED MY MEMORY.
YES. I'M BEGINNING TO REMEMBER WHERE I'M SUPPOSED TO BE HEADED...

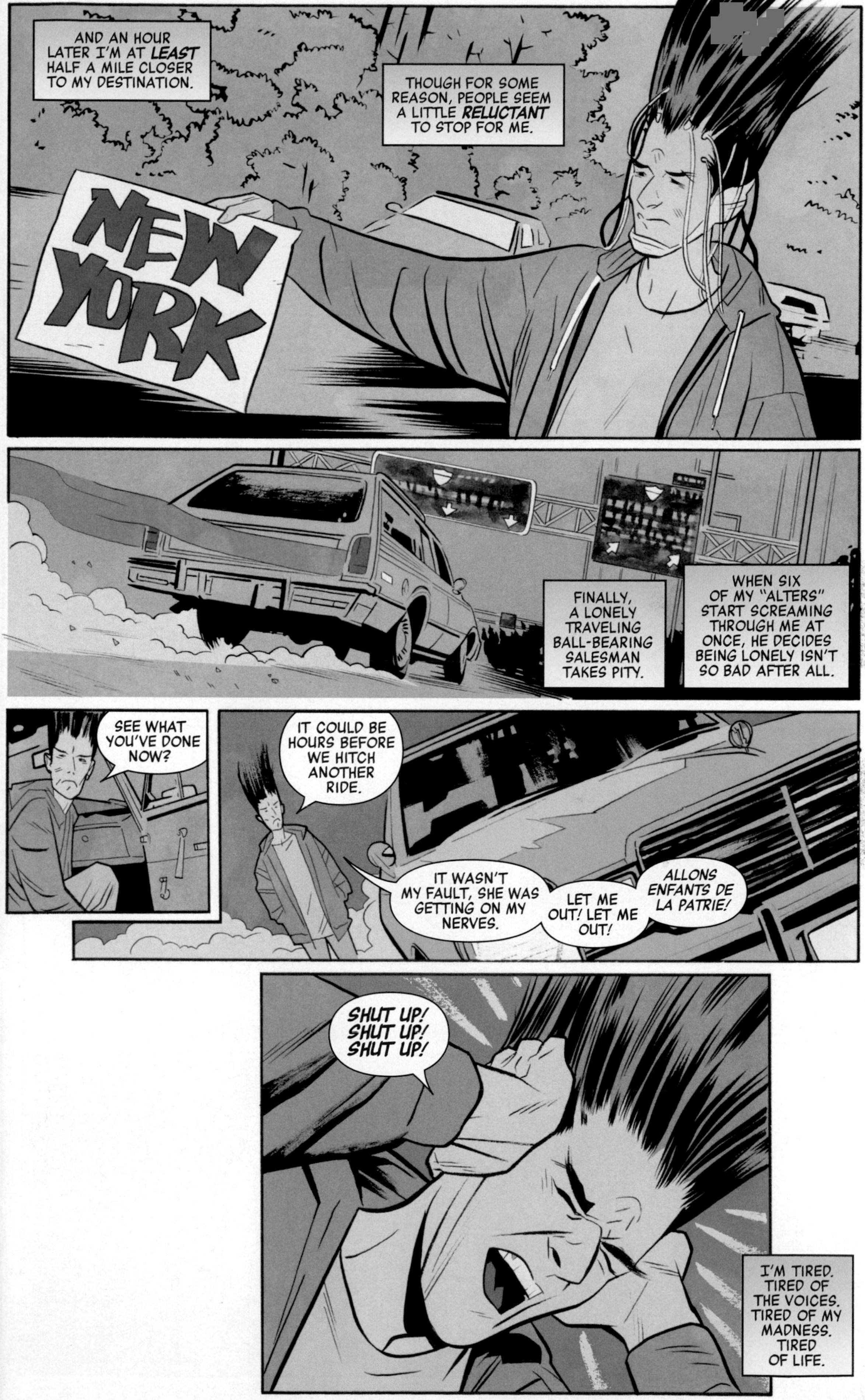
AND AN HOUR LATER I'M AT LEAST HALF A MILE CLOSER TO MY DESTINATION.
THOUGH FOR SOME REASON, PEOPLE SEEM A LITTLE RELUCTANT TO STOP FOR ME.
NEW YORK
FINALLY, A LONELY TRAVELING BALL-BEARING SALESMAN TAKES PITY.
WHEN SIX OF MY "ALTERS" START SCREAMING THROUGH ME AT ONCE, HE DECIDES BEING LONELY ISN'T SO BAD AFTER ALL.
SEE WHAT YOU'VE DONE NOW?
IT COULD BE HOURS BEFORE WE HITCH ANOTHER RIDE.
IT WASN'T MY FAULT, SHE WAS GETTING ON MY NERVES.
LET ME OUT! LET ME OUT!
ALLONS ENFANTS DE LA PATRIE!
SHUT UP! SHUT UP! SHUT UP!
I'M TIRED. TIRED OF THE VOICES. TIRED OF MY MADNESS. TIRED OF LIFE.

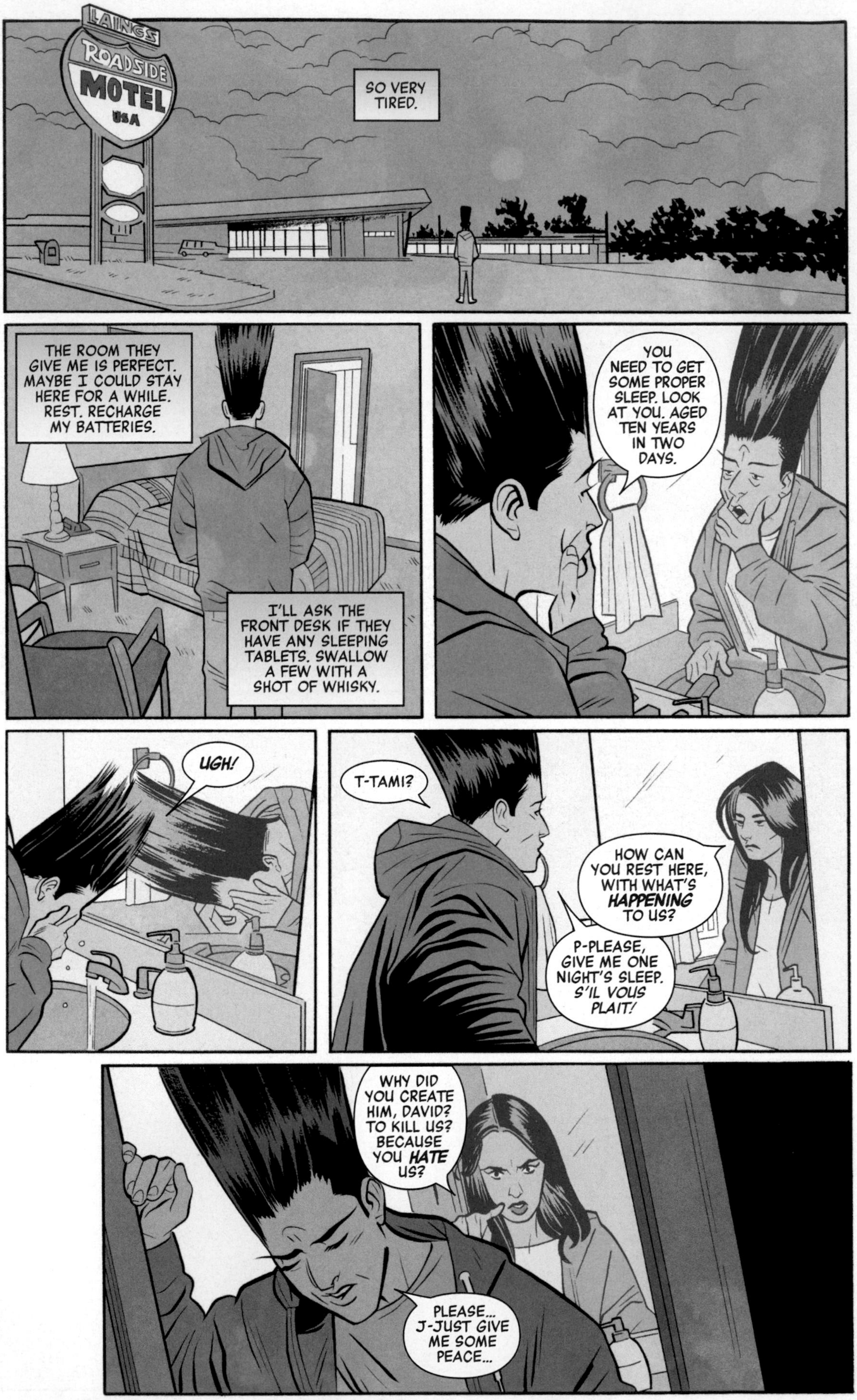
LAINGS
ROADSIDE
MOTEL
USA
SO VERY TIRED.
THE ROOM THEY GIVE ME IS PERFECT. MAYBE I COULD STAY HERE FOR A WHILE. REST. RECHARGE MY BATTERIES.
I'LL ASK THE FRONT DESK IF THEY HAVE ANY SLEEPING TABLETS. SWALLOW A FEW WITH A SHOT OF WHISKY.
YOU NEED TO GET SOME PROPER SLEEP. LOOK AT YOU. AGED TEN YEARS IN TWO DAYS.
UGH!
T-TAMI?
HOW CAN YOU REST HERE, WITH WHAT'S HAPPENING TO US?
P-PLEASE, GIVE ME ONE NIGHT'S SLEEP. S'IL VOUS PLAIT!
WHY DID YOU CREATE HIM, DAVID? TO KILL US? BECAUSE YOU HATE US?
PLEASE... J-JUST GIVE ME SOME PEACE...

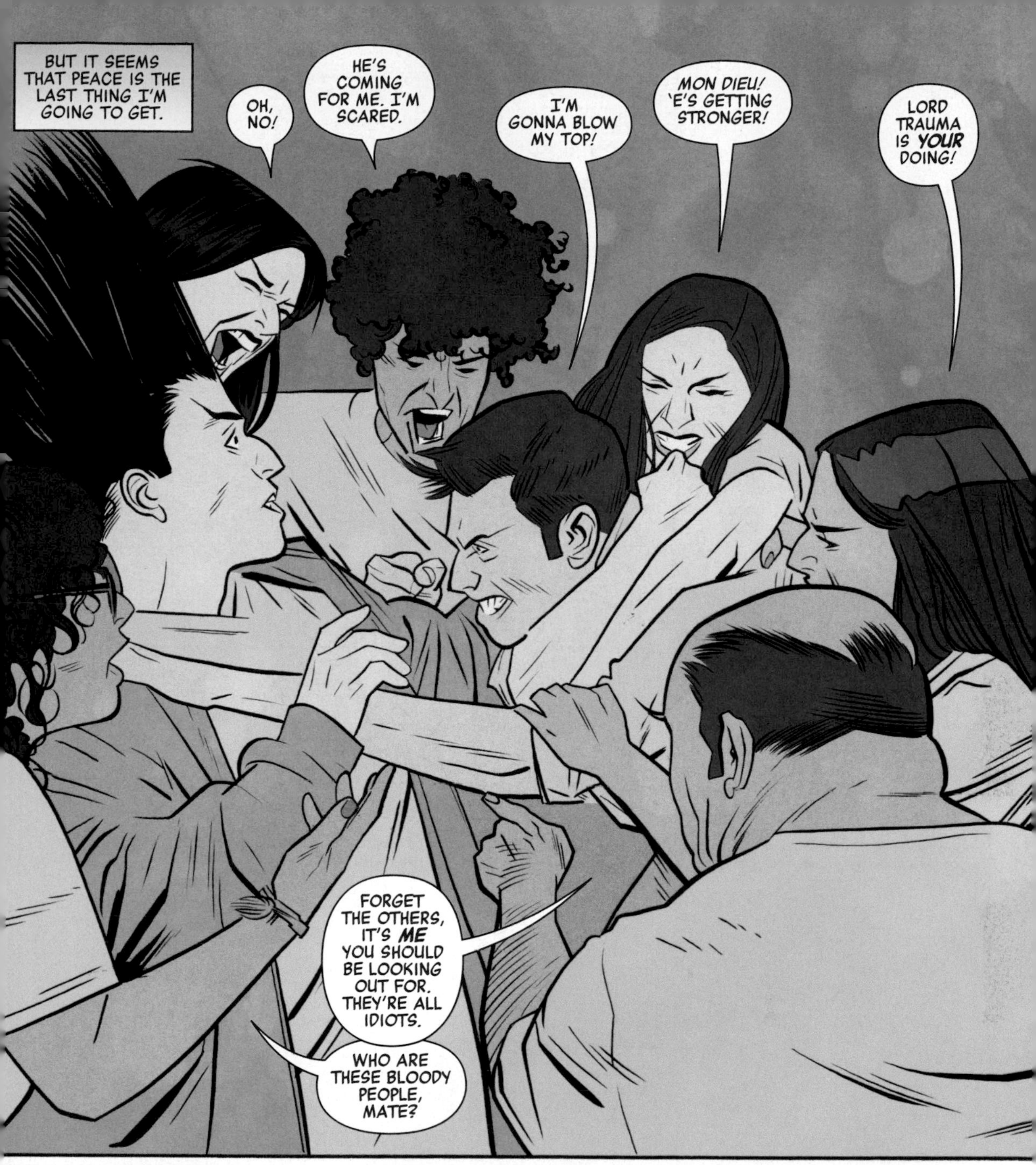
BUT IT SEEMS THAT PEACE IS THE LAST THING I'M GOING TO GET.
OH, NO!
HE'S COMING FOR ME. I'M SCARED.
I'M GONNA BLOW MY TOP!
MON DIEU! 'E'S GETTING STRONGER!
LORD TRAUMA IS YOUR DOING!
FORGET THE OTHERS, IT'S ME YOU SHOULD BE LOOKING OUT FOR. THEY'RE ALL IDIOTS.
WHO ARE THESE BLOODY PEOPLE, MATE?

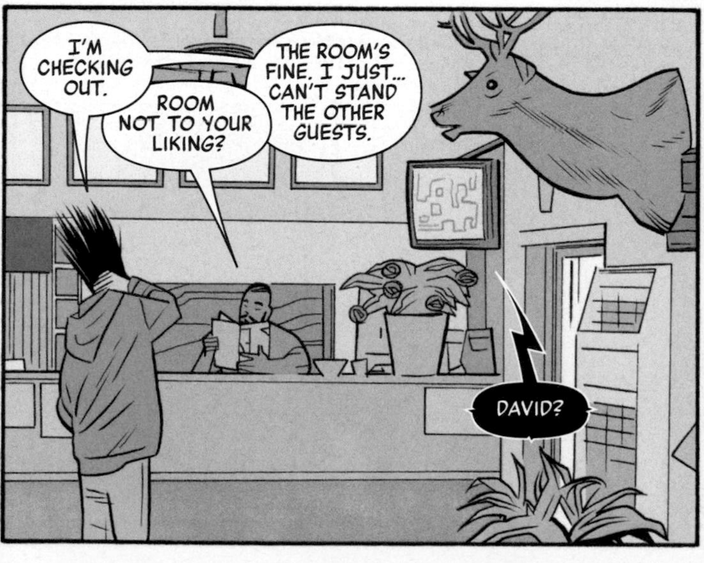
I'M CHECKING OUT.
ROOM NOT TO YOUR LIKING?
THE ROOM'S FINE. I JUST... CAN'T STAND THE OTHER GUESTS.
DAVID?

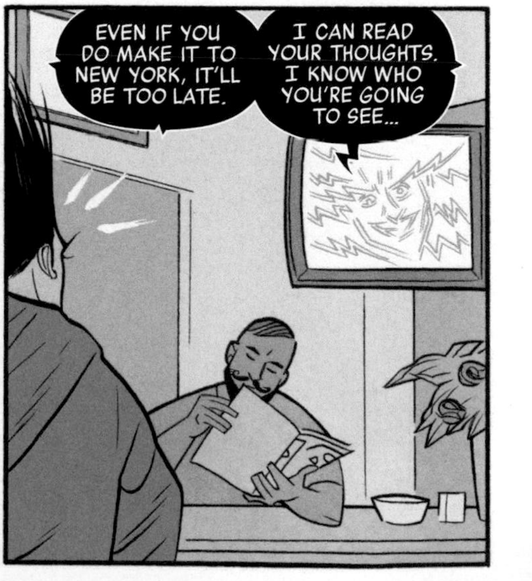
EVEN IF YOU DO MAKE IT TO NEW YORK, IT'LL BE TOO LATE.
I CAN READ YOUR THOUGHTS. I KNOW WHO YOU'RE GOING TO SEE...

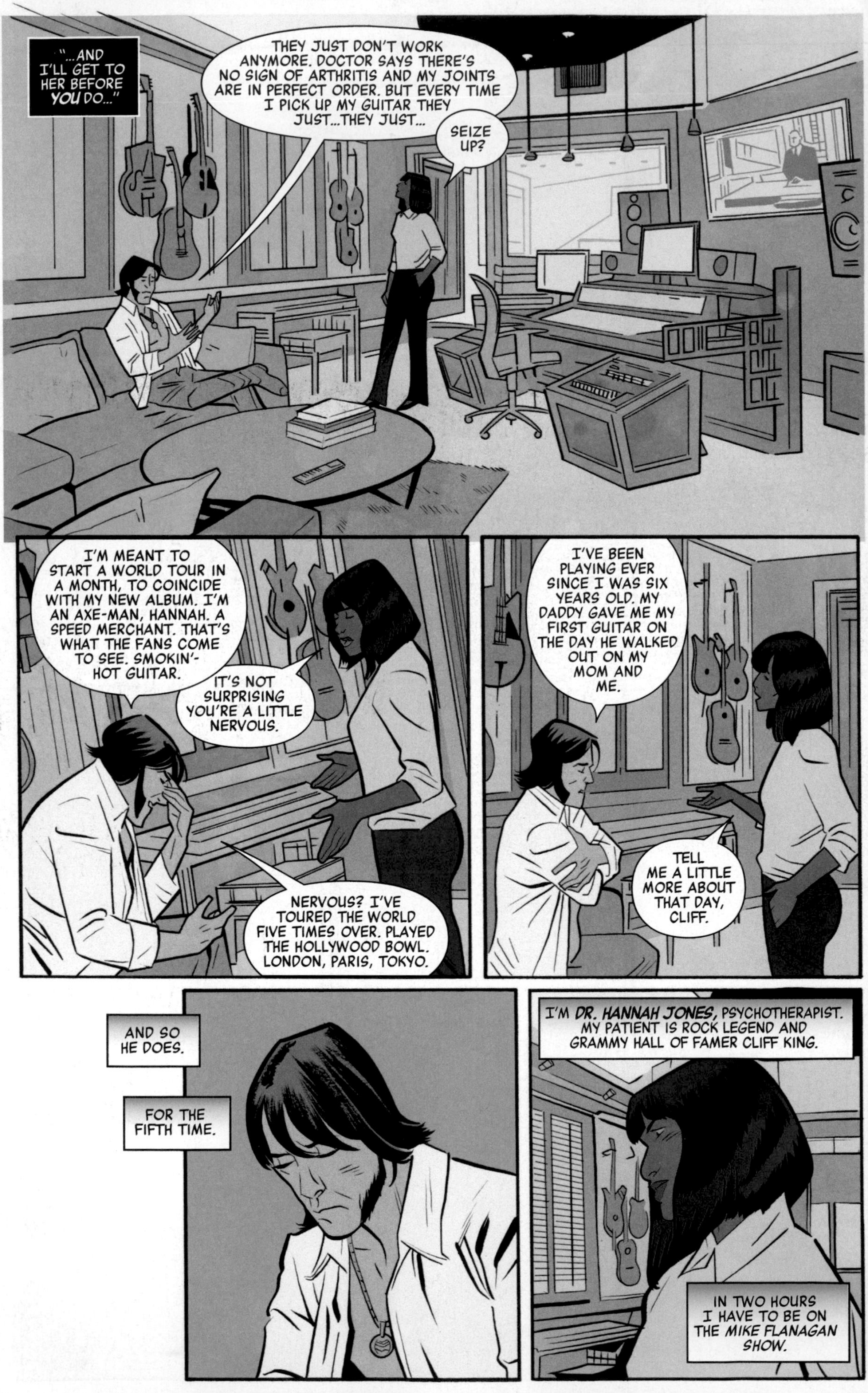

"...AND I'LL GET TO HER BEFORE *YOU* DO..."
THEY JUST DON'T WORK ANYMORE. DOCTOR SAYS THERE'S NO SIGN OF ARTHRITIS AND MY JOINTS ARE IN PERFECT ORDER. BUT EVERY TIME I PICK UP MY GUITAR THEY JUST...THEY JUST...
SEIZE UP?
I'M MEANT TO START A WORLD TOUR IN A MONTH, TO COINCIDE WITH MY NEW ALBUM. I'M AN AXE-MAN, HANNAH. A SPEED MERCHANT. THAT'S WHAT THE FANS COME TO SEE. SMOKIN'-HOT GUITAR.
IT'S NOT SURPRISING YOU'RE A LITTLE NERVOUS.
NERVOUS? I'VE TOURED THE WORLD FIVE TIMES OVER. PLAYED THE HOLLYWOOD BOWL. LONDON, PARIS, TOKYO.
I'VE BEEN PLAYING EVER SINCE I WAS SIX YEARS OLD. MY DADDY GAVE ME MY FIRST GUITAR ON THE DAY HE WALKED OUT ON MY MOM AND ME.
TELL ME A LITTLE MORE ABOUT THAT DAY, CLIFF.
AND SO HE DOES.
FOR THE FIFTH TIME.
I'M *DR. HANNAH JONES,* PSYCHOTHERAPIST. MY PATIENT IS ROCK LEGEND AND GRAMMY HALL OF FAMER CLIFF KING.
IN TWO HOURS I HAVE TO BE ON THE *MIKE FLANAGAN SHOW.*

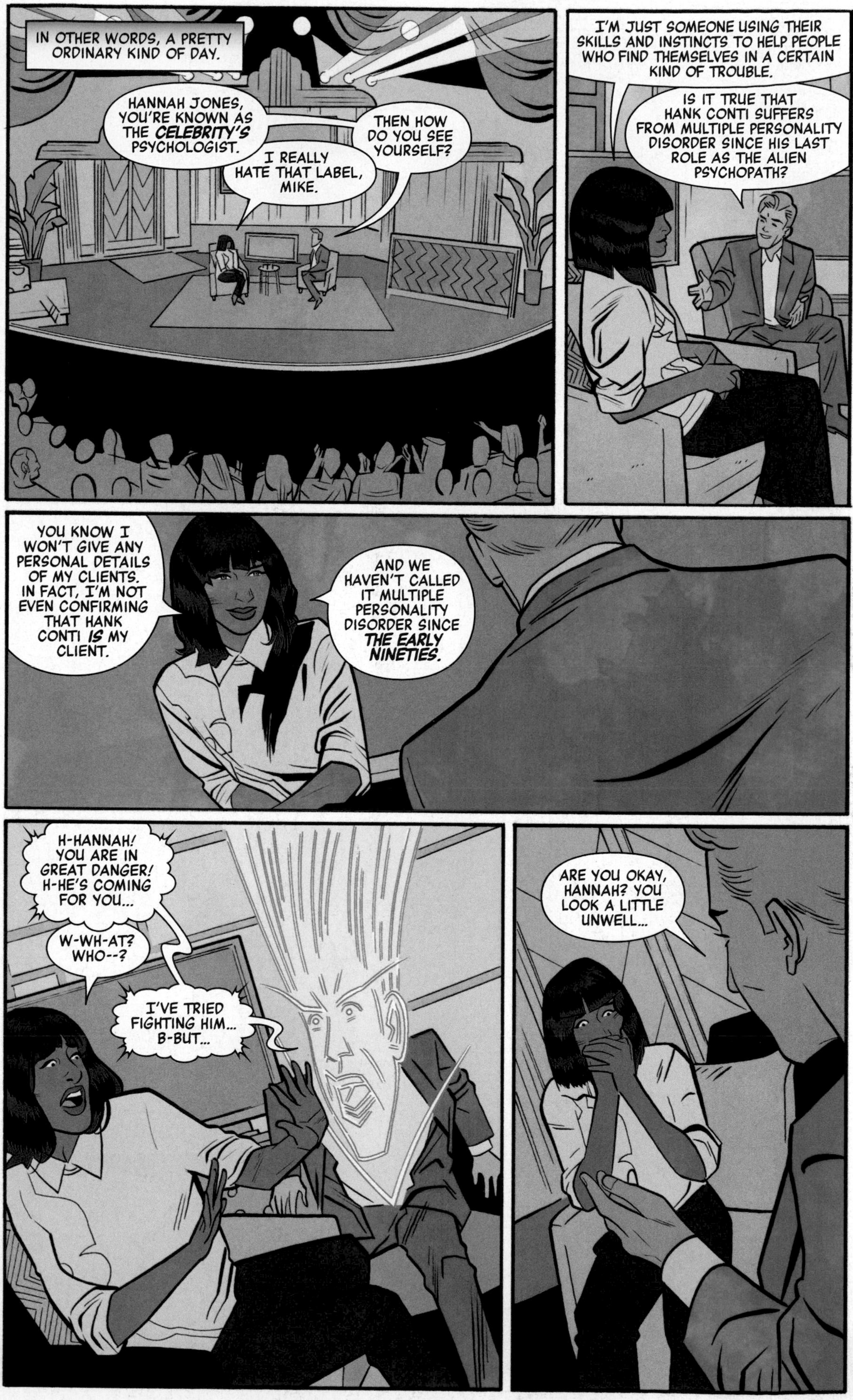
IN OTHER WORDS, A PRETTY ORDINARY KIND OF DAY.
HANNAH JONES, YOU'RE KNOWN AS THE CELEBRITY'S PSYCHOLOGIST.
I REALLY HATE THAT LABEL, MIKE.
THEN HOW DO YOU SEE YOURSELF?
I'M JUST SOMEONE USING THEIR SKILLS AND INSTINCTS TO HELP PEOPLE WHO FIND THEMSELVES IN A CERTAIN KIND OF TROUBLE.
IS IT TRUE THAT HANK CONTI SUFFERS FROM MULTIPLE PERSONALITY DISORDER SINCE HIS LAST ROLE AS THE ALIEN PSYCHOPATH?
YOU KNOW I WON'T GIVE ANY PERSONAL DETAILS OF MY CLIENTS. IN FACT, I'M NOT EVEN CONFIRMING THAT HANK CONTI IS MY CLIENT.
AND WE HAVEN'T CALLED IT MULTIPLE PERSONALITY DISORDER SINCE THE EARLY NINETIES.
H-HANNAH! YOU ARE IN GREAT DANGER! H-HE'S COMING FOR YOU...
W-WH-AT? WHO--?
I'VE TRIED FIGHTING HIM... B-BUT...
ARE YOU OKAY, HANNAH? YOU LOOK A LITTLE UNWELL...

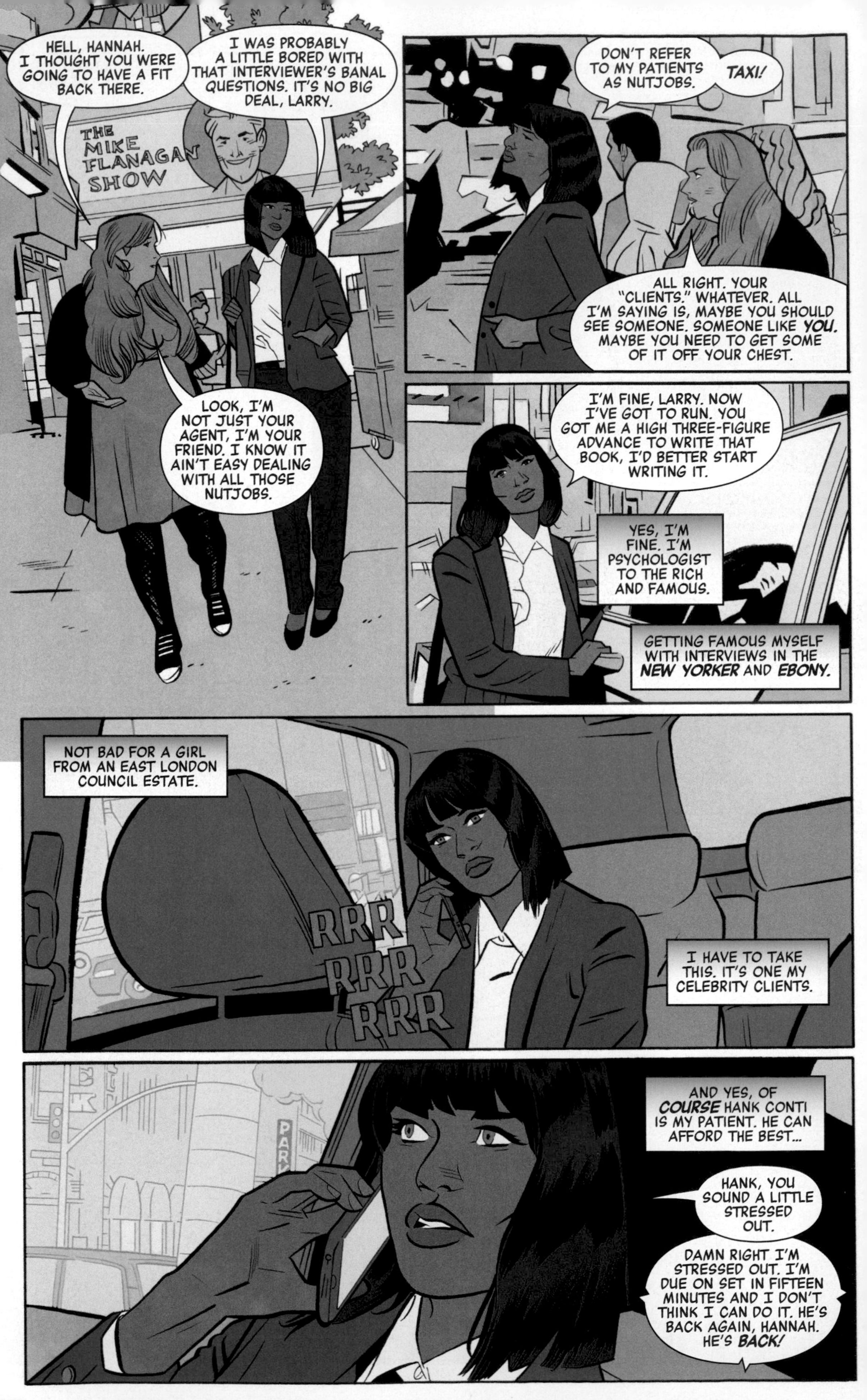
HELL, HANNAH. I THOUGHT YOU WERE GOING TO HAVE A FIT BACK THERE.
I WAS PROBABLY A LITTLE BORED WITH THAT INTERVIEWER'S BANAL QUESTIONS. IT'S NO BIG DEAL, LARRY.
THE MIKE FLANAGAN SHOW
LOOK, I'M NOT JUST YOUR AGENT, I'M YOUR FRIEND. I KNOW IT AIN'T EASY DEALING WITH ALL THOSE NUTJOBS.
DON'T REFER TO MY PATIENTS AS NUTJOBS.
TAXI!
ALL RIGHT. YOUR "CLIENTS." WHATEVER. ALL I'M SAYING IS, MAYBE YOU SHOULD SEE SOMEONE. SOMEONE LIKE YOU. MAYBE YOU NEED TO GET SOME OF IT OFF YOUR CHEST.
I'M FINE, LARRY. NOW I'VE GOT TO RUN. YOU GOT ME A HIGH THREE-FIGURE ADVANCE TO WRITE THAT BOOK, I'D BETTER START WRITING IT.
YES, I'M FINE. I'M PSYCHOLOGIST TO THE RICH AND FAMOUS.
GETTING FAMOUS MYSELF WITH INTERVIEWS IN THE NEW YORKER AND EBONY.
NOT BAD FOR A GIRL FROM AN EAST LONDON COUNCIL ESTATE.
RRR RRR RRR
I HAVE TO TAKE THIS. IT'S ONE MY CELEBRITY CLIENTS.
AND YES, OF COURSE HANK CONTI IS MY PATIENT. HE CAN AFFORD THE BEST...
HANK, YOU SOUND A LITTLE STRESSED OUT.
DAMN RIGHT I'M STRESSED OUT. I'M DUE ON SET IN FIFTEEN MINUTES AND I DON'T THINK I CAN DO IT. HE'S BACK AGAIN, HANNAH. HE'S BACK!

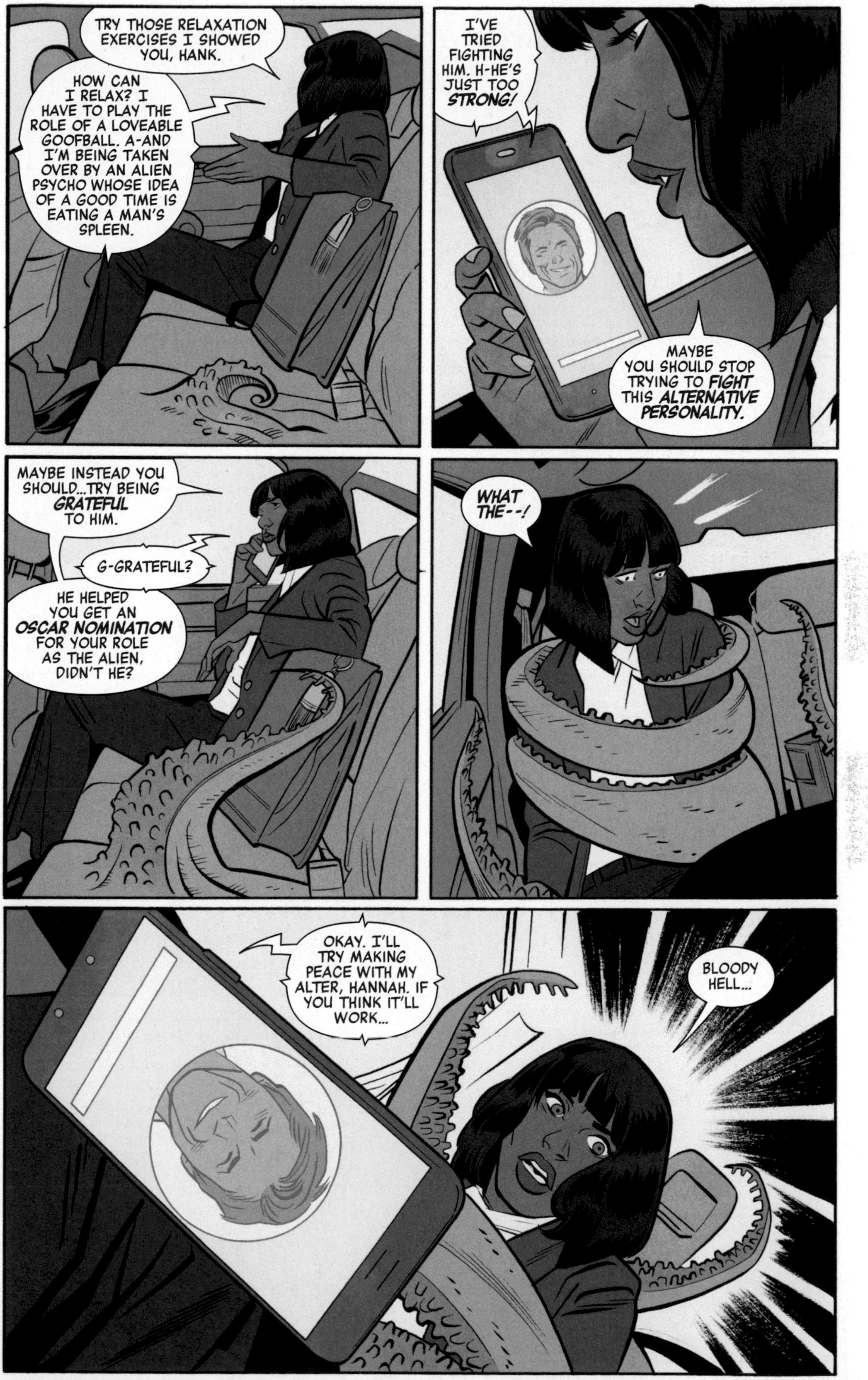
TRY THOSE RELAXATION EXERCISES I SHOWED YOU, HANK.
HOW CAN I RELAX? I HAVE TO PLAY THE ROLE OF A LOVEABLE GOOFBALL. A-AND I'M BEING TAKEN OVER BY AN ALIEN PSYCHO WHOSE IDEA OF A GOOD TIME IS EATING A MAN'S SPLEEN.
I'VE TRIED FIGHTING HIM. H-HE'S JUST TOO STRONG!
MAYBE YOU SHOULD STOP TRYING TO FIGHT THIS ALTERNATIVE PERSONALITY.
MAYBE INSTEAD YOU SHOULD...TRY BEING GRATEFUL TO HIM.
G-GRATEFUL?
HE HELPED YOU GET AN OSCAR NOMINATION FOR YOUR ROLE AS THE ALIEN, DIDN'T HE?
WHAT THE--!
OKAY. I'LL TRY MAKING PEACE WITH MY ALTER, HANNAH. IF YOU THINK IT'LL WORK...
BLOODY HELL...

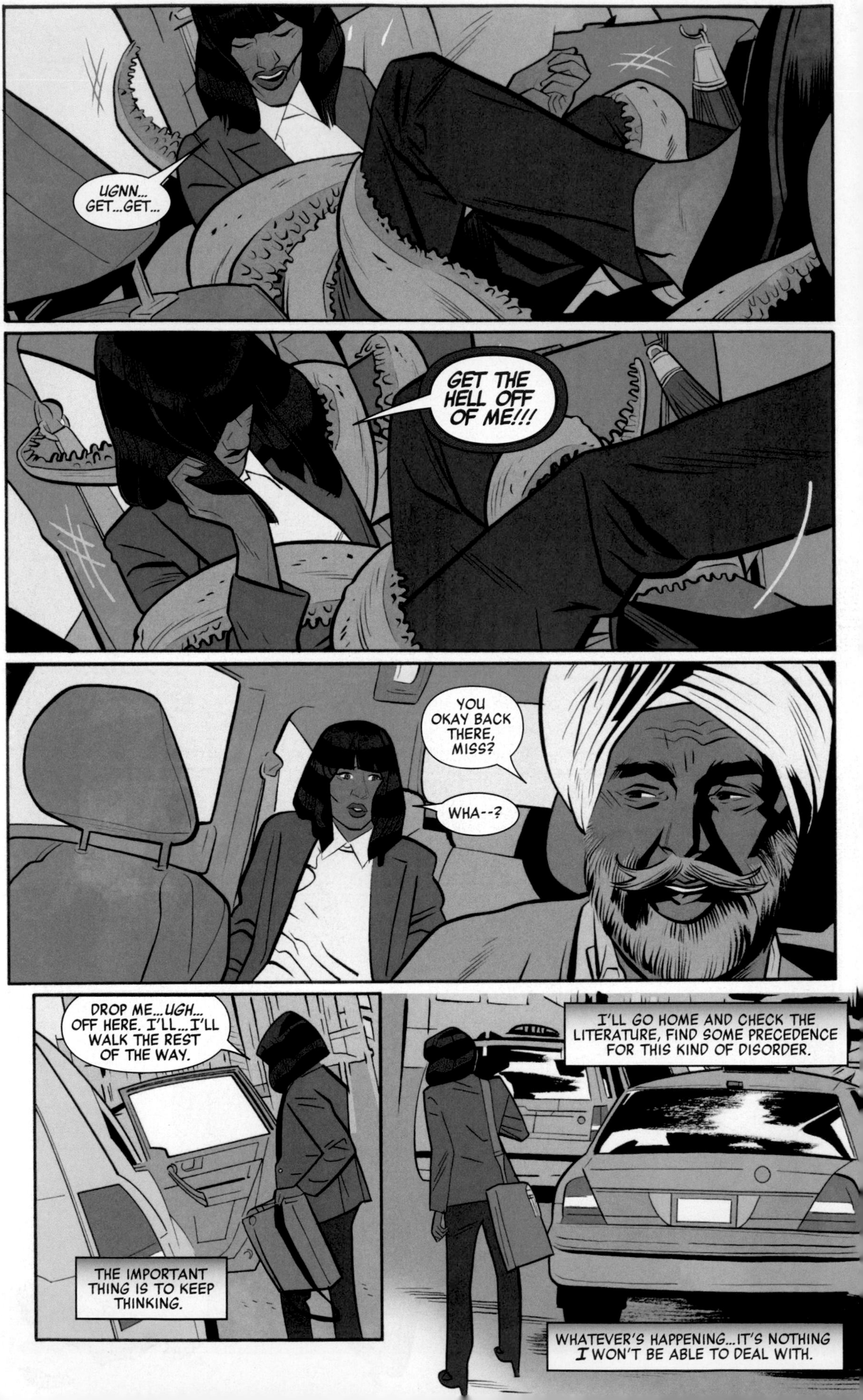
UGNN... GET...GET...
GET THE HELL OFF OF ME!!!
YOU OKAY BACK THERE, MISS?
WHA--?
DROP ME...UGH... OFF HERE. I'LL...I'LL WALK THE REST OF THE WAY.
THE IMPORTANT THING IS TO KEEP THINKING.
I'LL GO HOME AND CHECK THE LITERATURE, FIND SOME PRECEDENCE FOR THIS KIND OF DISORDER.
WHATEVER'S HAPPENING...IT'S NOTHING I WON'T BE ABLE TO DEAL WITH.

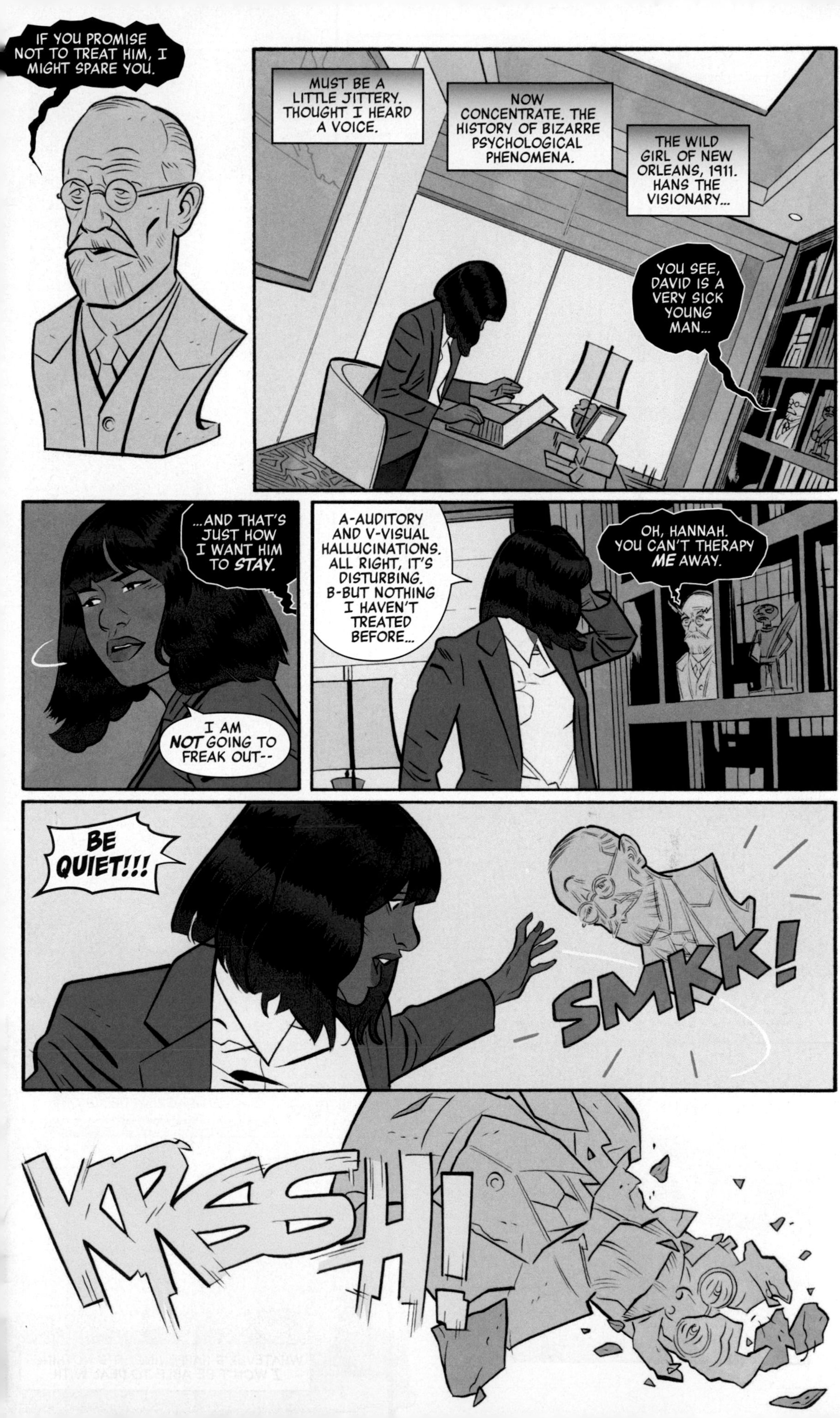
IF YOU PROMISE NOT TO TREAT HIM, I MIGHT SPARE YOU.
MUST BE A LITTLE JITTERY. THOUGHT I HEARD A VOICE.
NOW CONCENTRATE. THE HISTORY OF BIZARRE PSYCHOLOGICAL PHENOMENA.
THE WILD GIRL OF NEW ORLEANS, 1911. HANS THE VISIONARY...
YOU SEE, DAVID IS A VERY SICK YOUNG MAN...
...AND THAT'S JUST HOW I WANT HIM TO STAY.
I AM NOT GOING TO FREAK OUT--
A-AUDITORY AND V-VISUAL HALLUCINATIONS. ALL RIGHT, IT'S DISTURBING. B-BUT NOTHING I HAVEN'T TREATED BEFORE...
OH, HANNAH. YOU CAN'T THERAPY ME AWAY.
BE QUIET!!!
SMKK!
KRSSH!

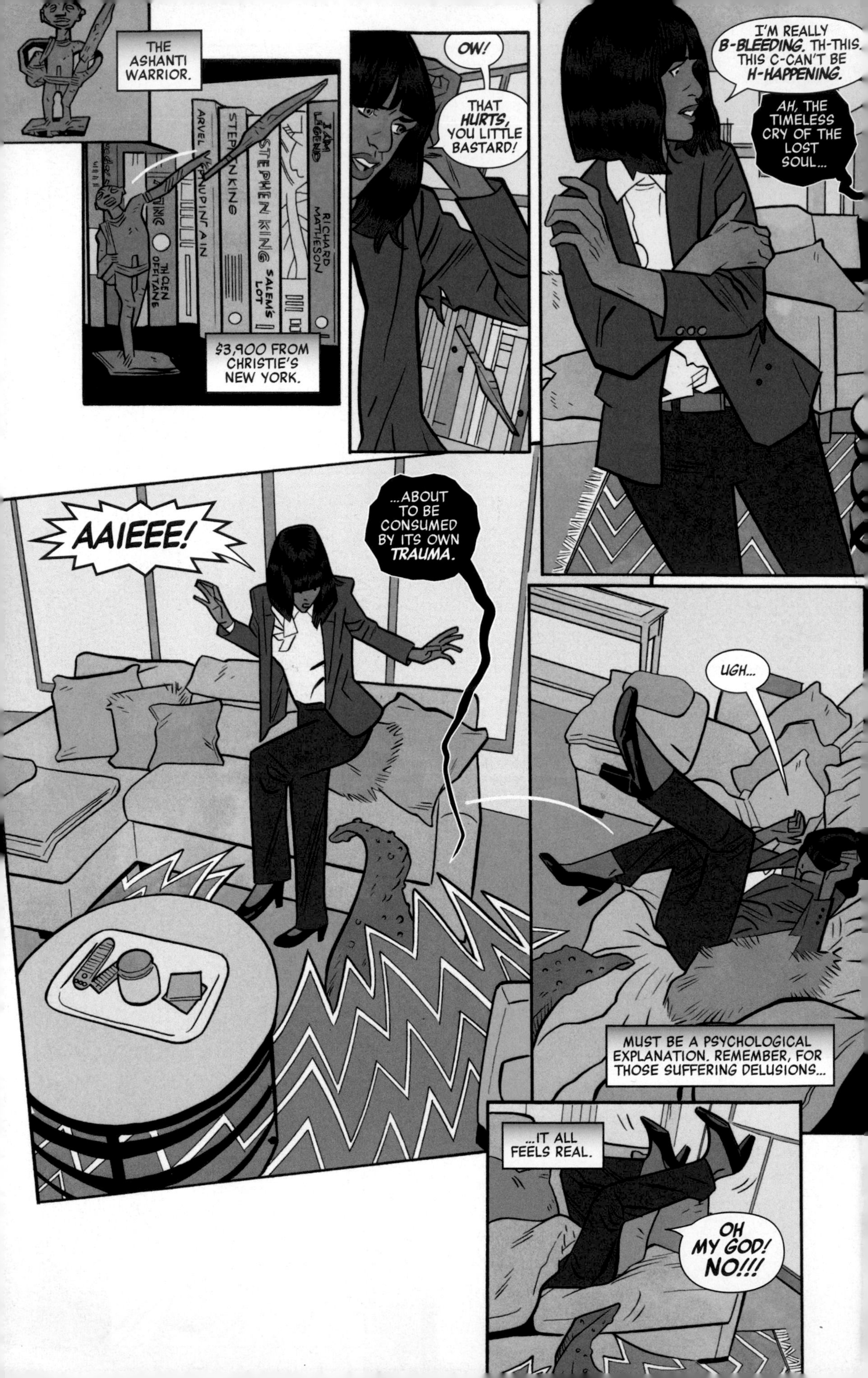

THE ASHANTI WARRIOR.
$3,900 FROM CHRISTIE'S NEW YORK.
OW!
THAT HURTS, YOU LITTLE BASTARD!
I'M REALLY B-BLEEDING. TH-THIS. THIS C-CAN'T BE H-HAPPENING.
AH, THE TIMELESS CRY OF THE LOST SOUL...
AAIEEE!
...ABOUT TO BE CONSUMED BY ITS OWN TRAUMA.
UGH...
MUST BE A PSYCHOLOGICAL EXPLANATION. REMEMBER, FOR THOSE SUFFERING DELUSIONS...
...IT ALL FEELS REAL.
OH MY GOD! NO!!!

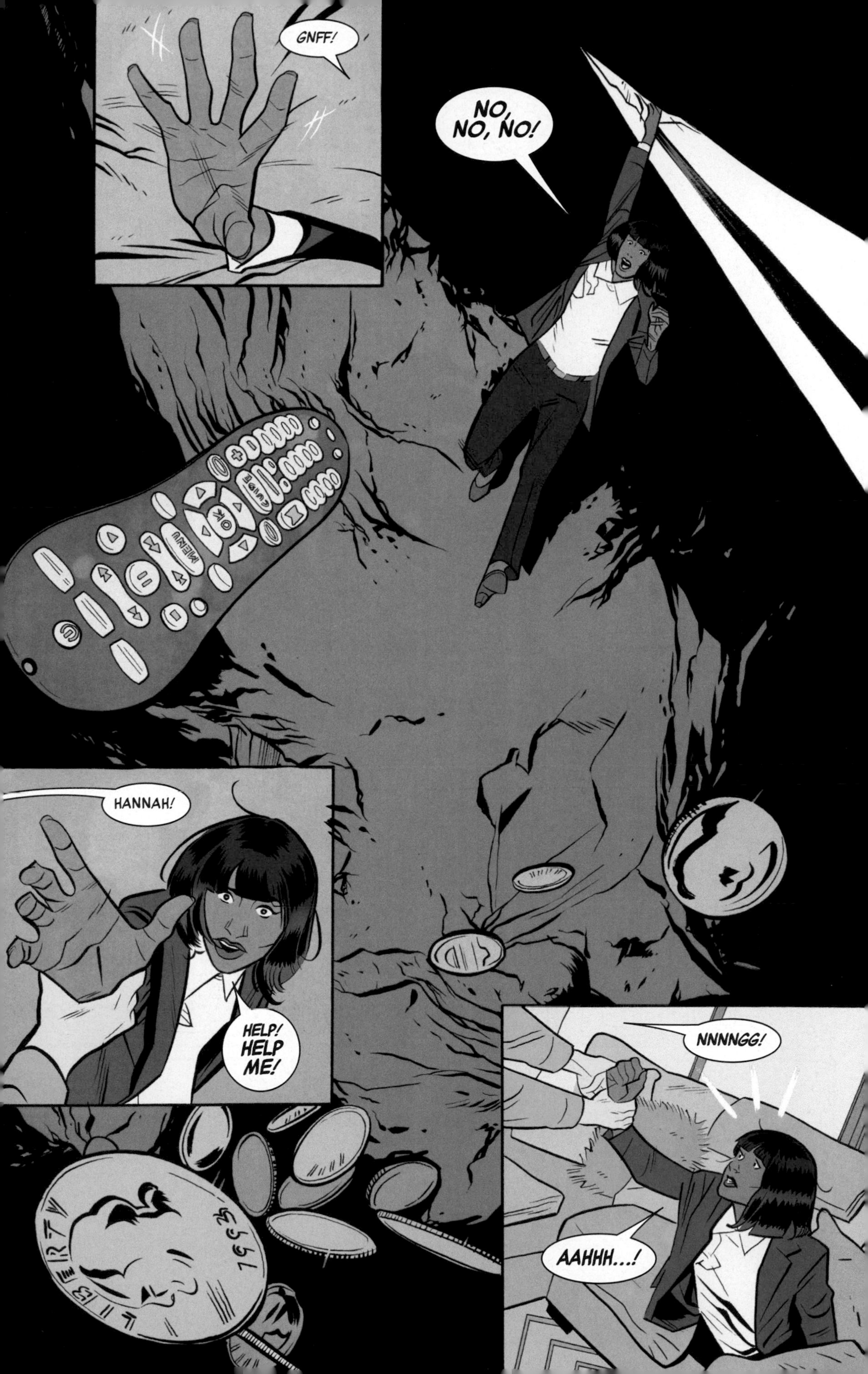
GNFF!
NO, NO, NO!
HANNAH!
HELP! HELP ME!
NNNNGG!
AAHHH...!

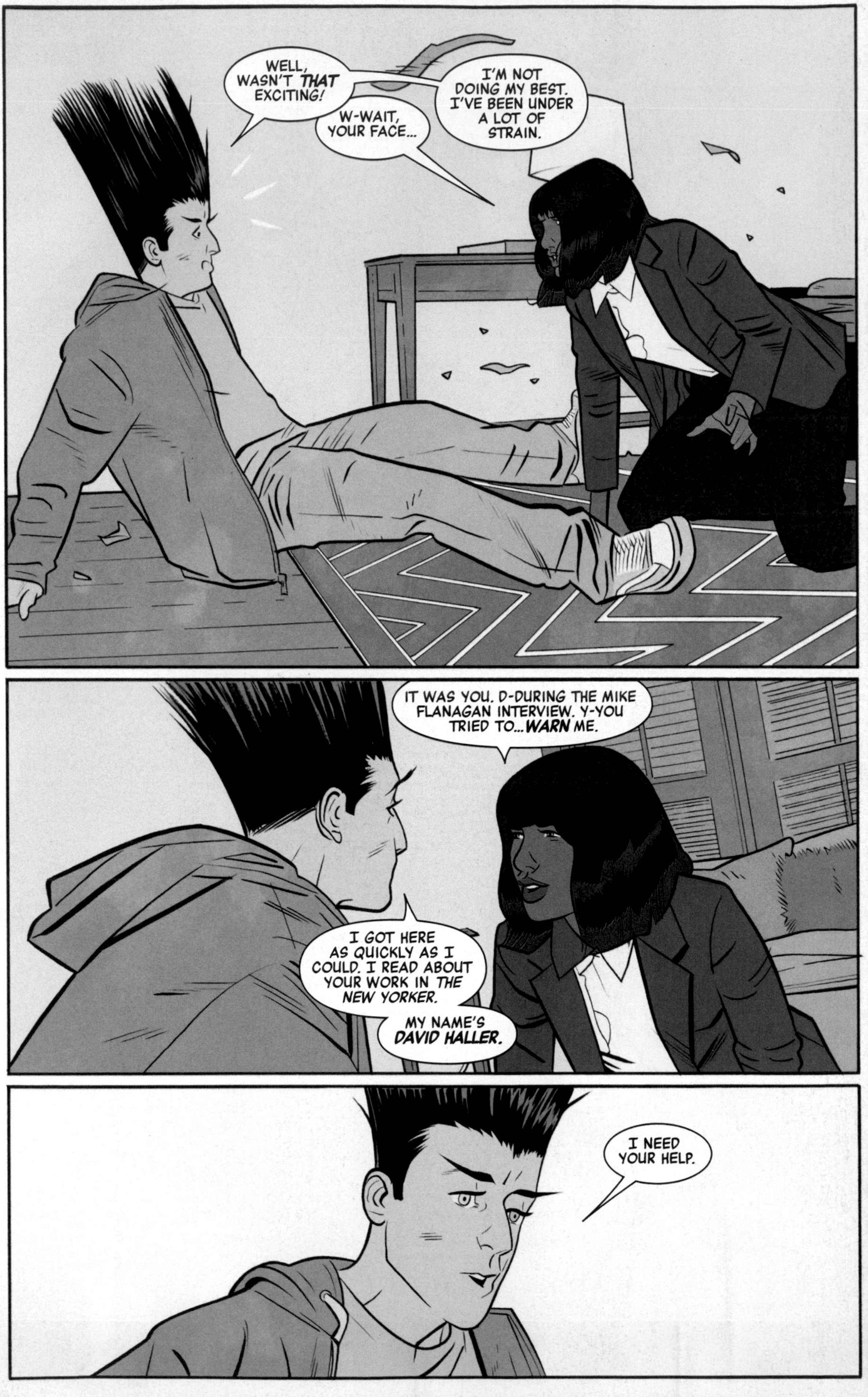
WELL, WASN'T THAT EXCITING!
W-WAIT, YOUR FACE...
I'M NOT DOING MY BEST. I'VE BEEN UNDER A LOT OF STRAIN.
IT WAS YOU. D-DURING THE MIKE FLANAGAN INTERVIEW. Y-YOU TRIED TO...WARN ME.
I GOT HERE AS QUICKLY AS I COULD. I READ ABOUT YOUR WORK IN THE NEW YORKER.
MY NAME'S DAVID HALLER.
I NEED YOUR HELP.

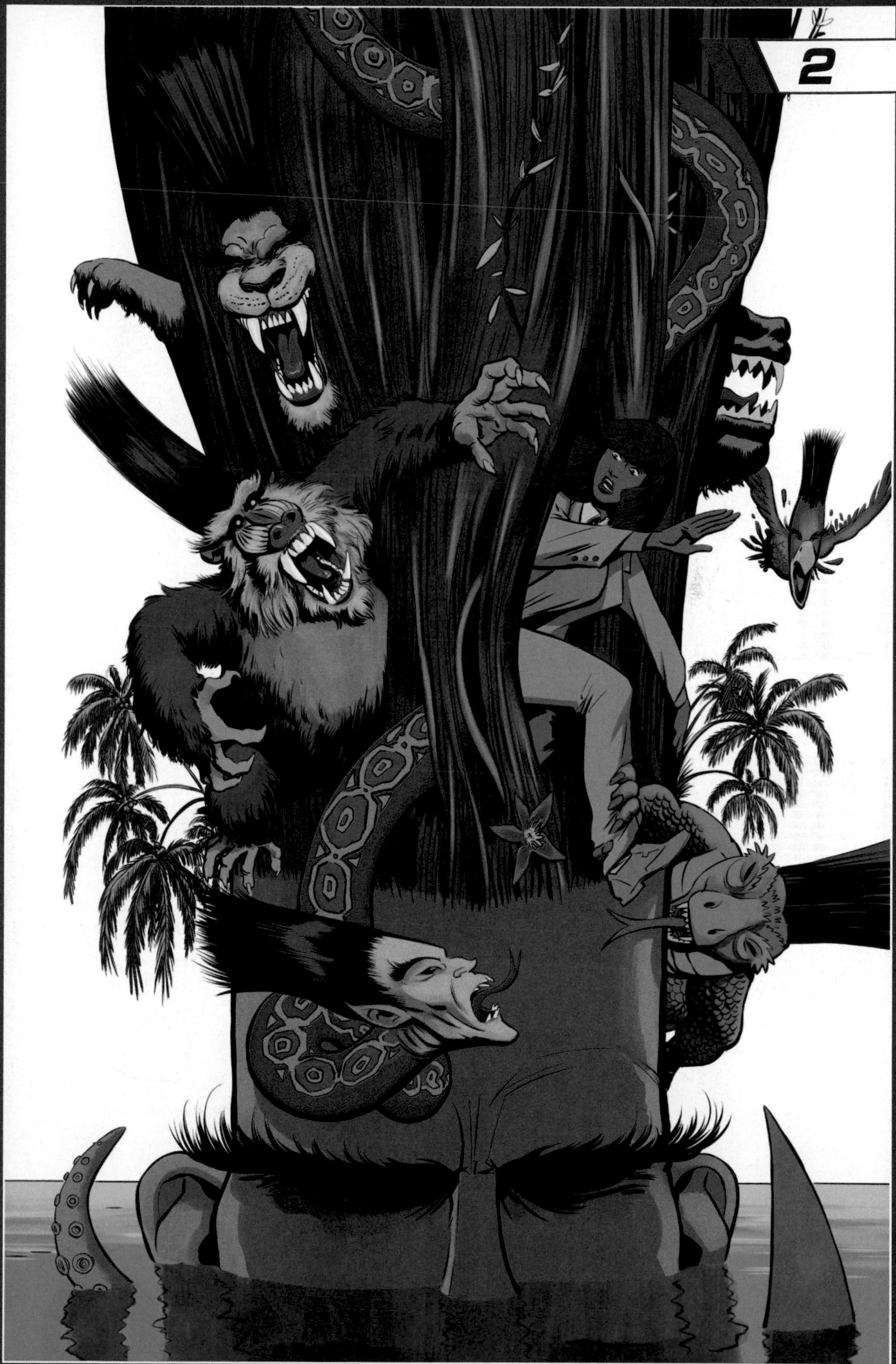
2

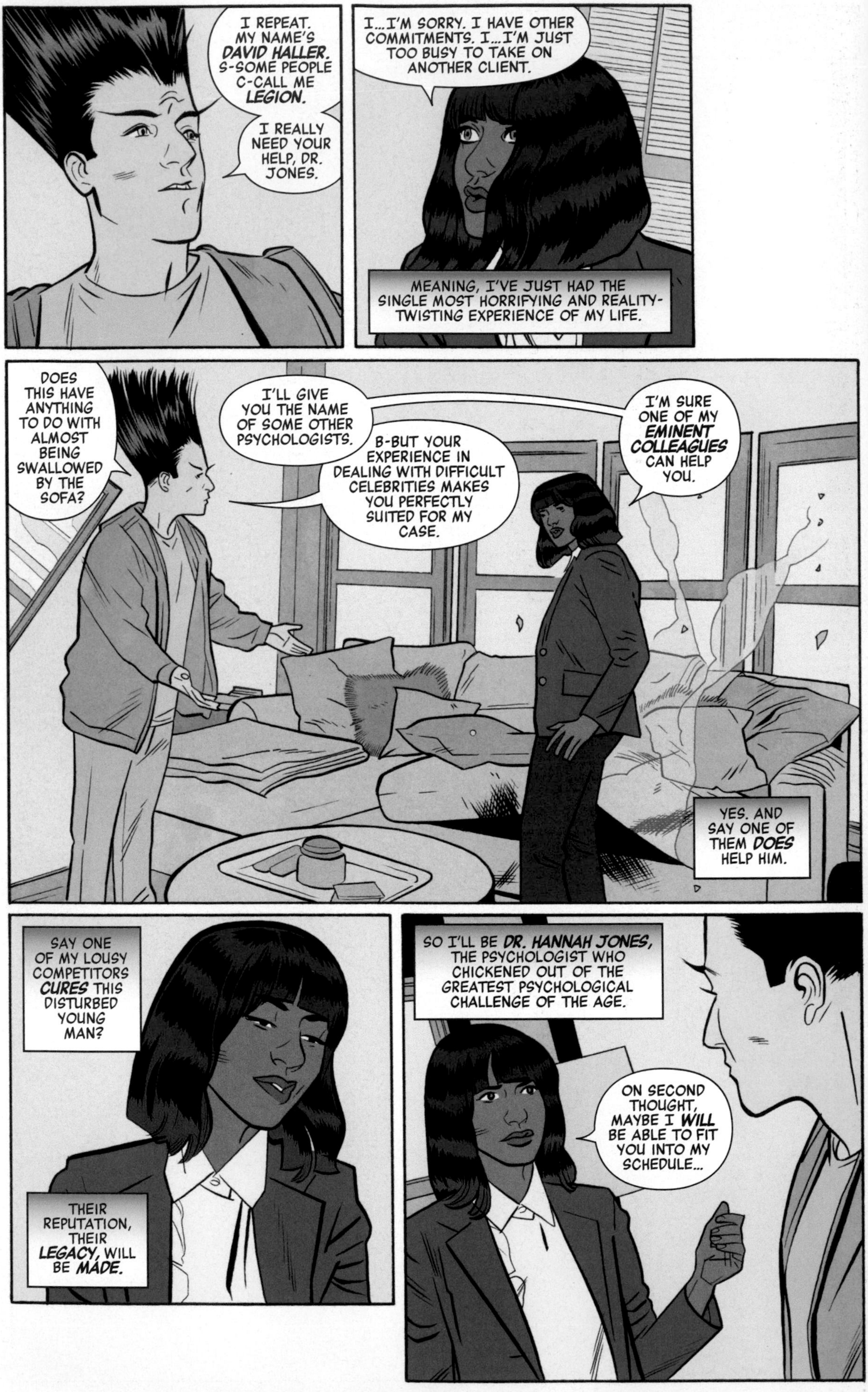
I REPEAT. MY NAME'S DAVID HALLER. S-SOME PEOPLE C-CALL ME LEGION.
I REALLY NEED YOUR HELP, DR. JONES.
I...I'M SORRY. I HAVE OTHER COMMITMENTS. I...I'M JUST TOO BUSY TO TAKE ON ANOTHER CLIENT.
MEANING, I'VE JUST HAD THE SINGLE MOST HORRIFYING AND REALITY-TWISTING EXPERIENCE OF MY LIFE.
DOES THIS HAVE ANYTHING TO DO WITH ALMOST BEING SWALLOWED BY THE SOFA?
I'LL GIVE YOU THE NAME OF SOME OTHER PSYCHOLOGISTS.
I'M SURE ONE OF MY EMINENT COLLEAGUES CAN HELP YOU.
B-BUT YOUR EXPERIENCE IN DEALING WITH DIFFICULT CELEBRITIES MAKES YOU PERFECTLY SUITED FOR MY CASE.
YES. AND SAY ONE OF THEM DOES HELP HIM.
SAY ONE OF MY LOUSY COMPETITORS CURES THIS DISTURBED YOUNG MAN?
THEIR REPUTATION, THEIR LEGACY, WILL BE MADE.
SO I'LL BE DR. HANNAH JONES, THE PSYCHOLOGIST WHO CHICKENED OUT OF THE GREATEST PSYCHOLOGICAL CHALLENGE OF THE AGE.
ON SECOND THOUGHT, MAYBE I WILL BE ABLE TO FIT YOU INTO MY SCHEDULE...

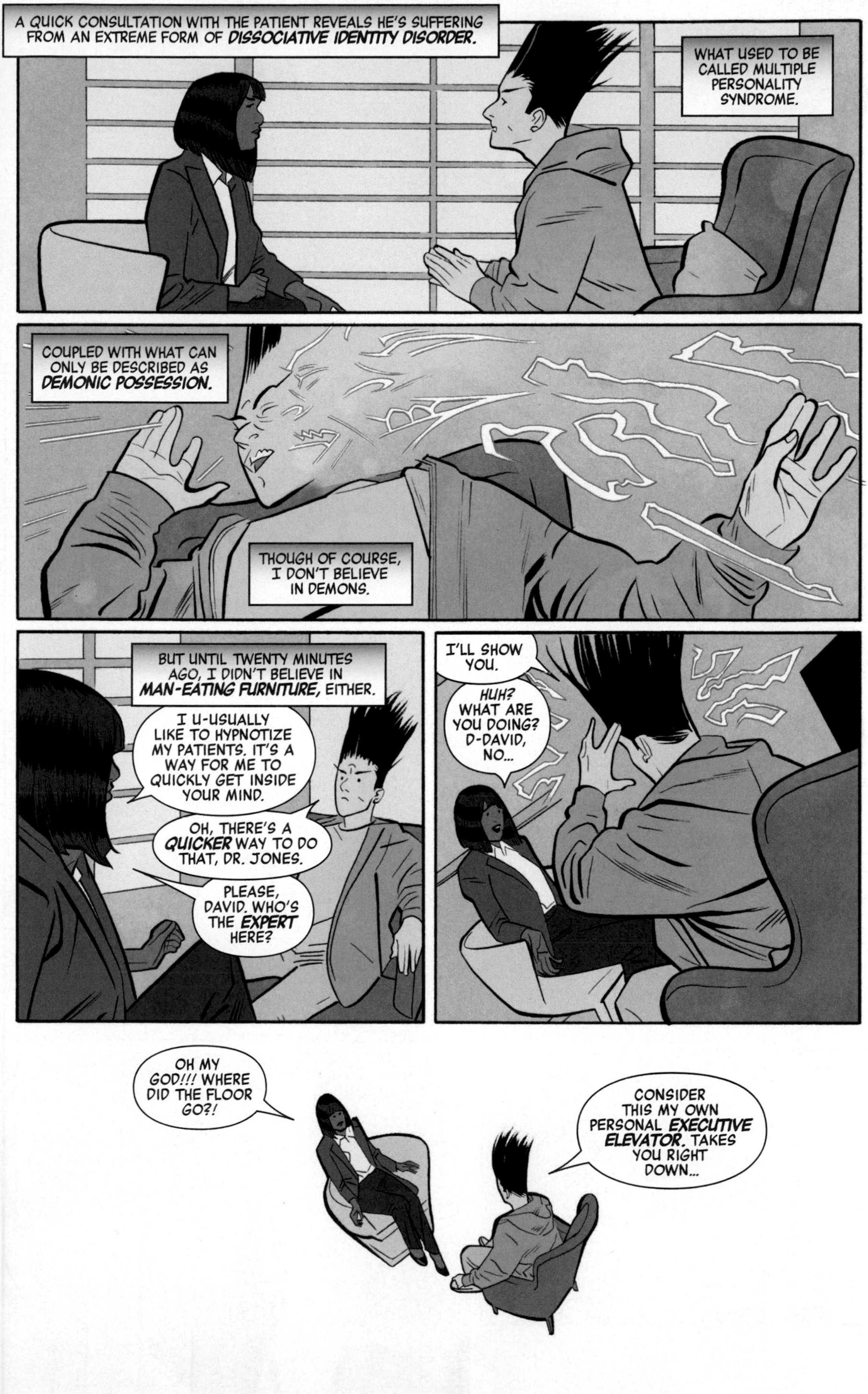
A QUICK CONSULTATION WITH THE PATIENT REVEALS HE'S SUFFERING FROM AN EXTREME FORM OF DISSOCIATIVE IDENTITY DISORDER.
WHAT USED TO BE CALLED MULTIPLE PERSONALITY SYNDROME.
COUPLED WITH WHAT CAN ONLY BE DESCRIBED AS DEMONIC POSSESSION.
THOUGH OF COURSE, I DON'T BELIEVE IN DEMONS.
BUT UNTIL TWENTY MINUTES AGO, I DIDN'T BELIEVE IN MAN-EATING FURNITURE, EITHER.
I U-USUALLY LIKE TO HYPNOTIZE MY PATIENTS. IT'S A WAY FOR ME TO QUICKLY GET INSIDE YOUR MIND.
OH, THERE'S A QUICKER WAY TO DO THAT, DR. JONES.
PLEASE, DAVID. WHO'S THE EXPERT HERE?
I'LL SHOW YOU.
HUH? WHAT ARE YOU DOING? D-DAVID, NO...
OH MY GOD!!! WHERE DID THE FLOOR GO?!
CONSIDER THIS MY OWN PERSONAL EXECUTIVE ELEVATOR. TAKES YOU RIGHT DOWN...

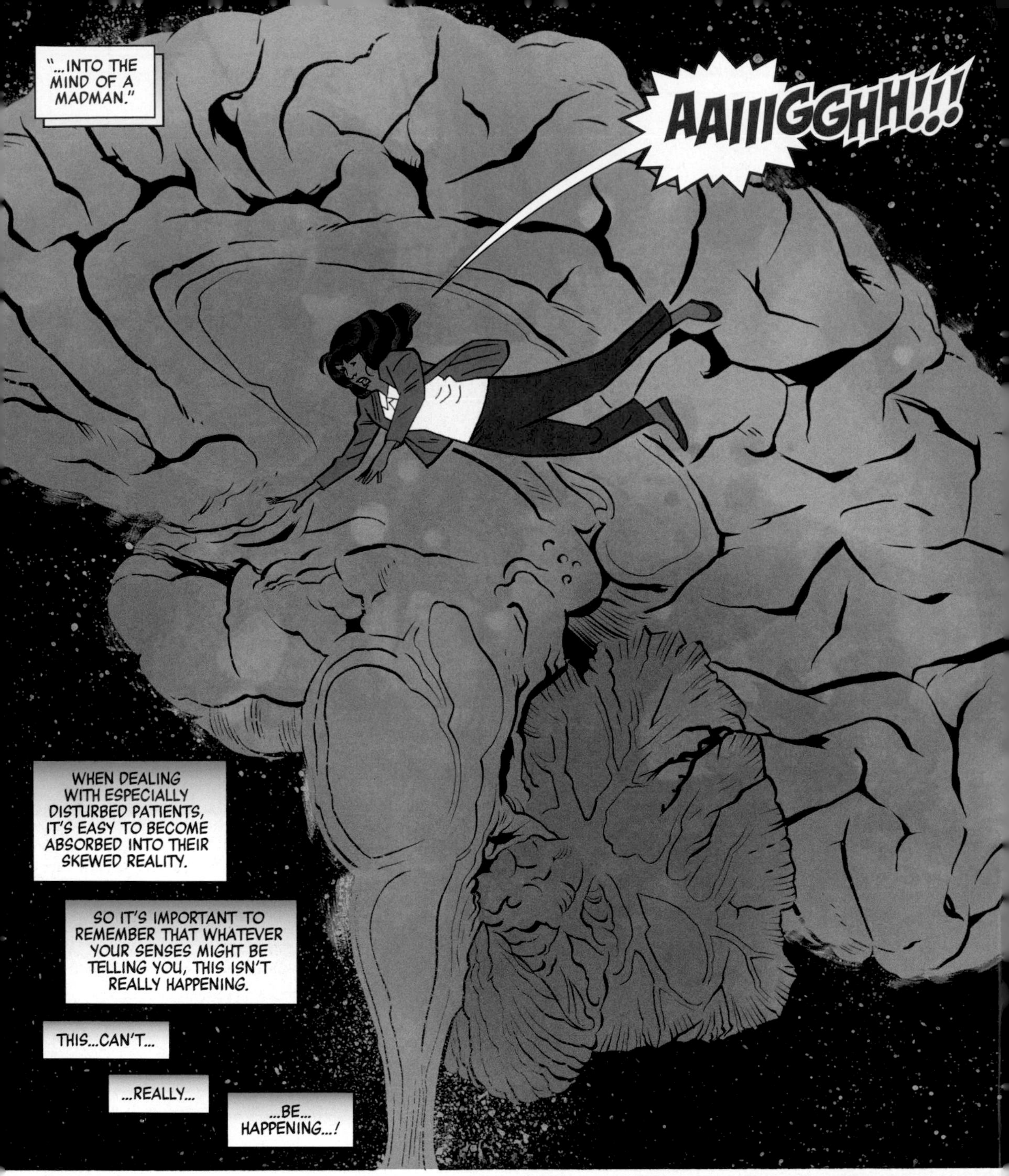
"...INTO THE MIND OF A MADMAN."
AAIIIGGHH!!!
WHEN DEALING WITH ESPECIALLY DISTURBED PATIENTS, IT'S EASY TO BECOME ABSORBED INTO THEIR SKEWED REALITY.
SO IT'S IMPORTANT TO REMEMBER THAT WHATEVER YOUR SENSES MIGHT BE TELLING YOU, THIS ISN'T REALLY HAPPENING.
THIS...CAN'T...
...REALLY...
...BE... HAPPENING...!
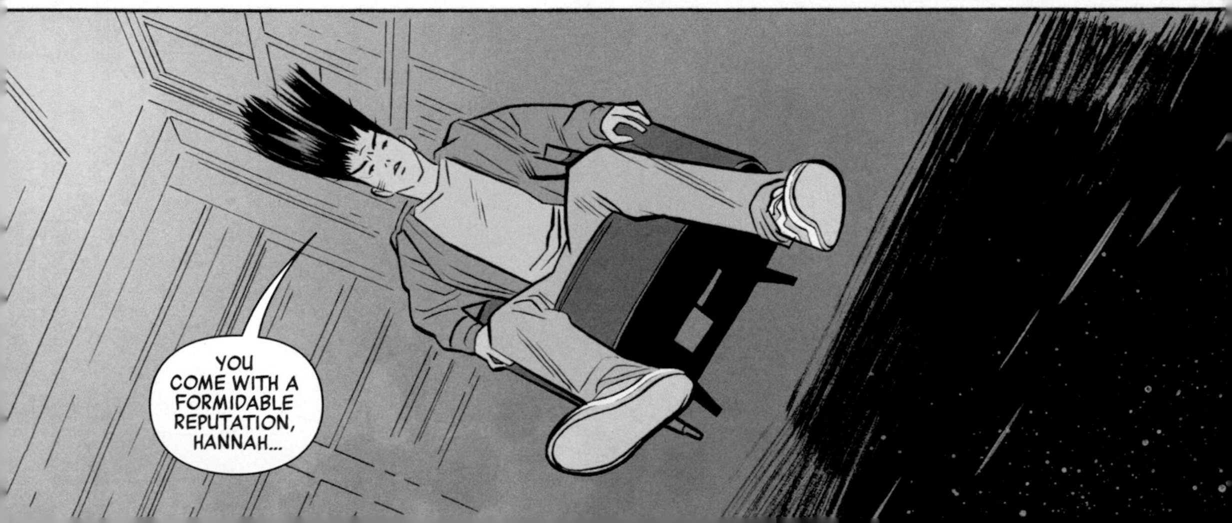
YOU COME WITH A FORMIDABLE REPUTATION, HANNAH...

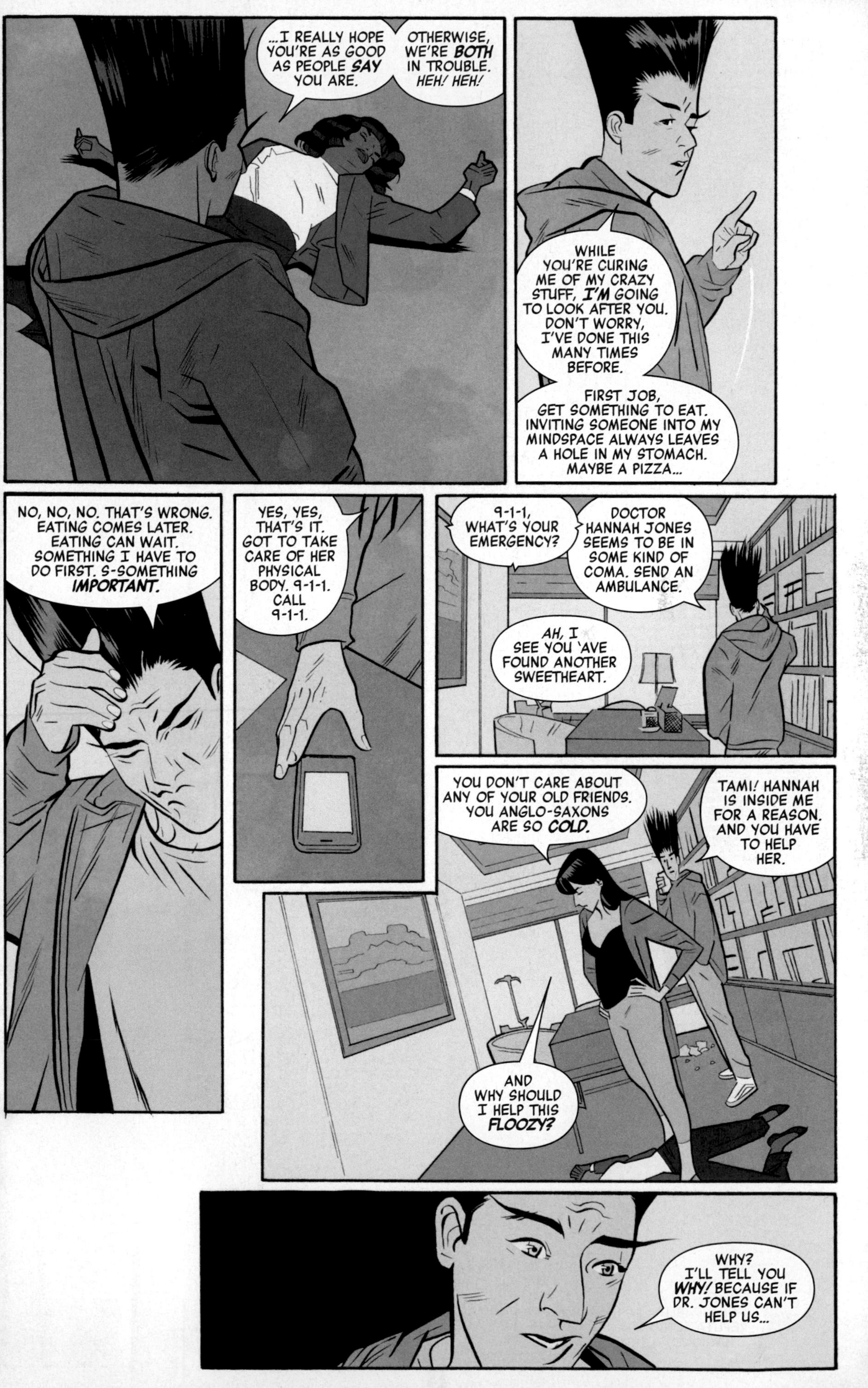
...I REALLY HOPE YOU'RE AS GOOD AS PEOPLE SAY YOU ARE.
OTHERWISE, WE'RE BOTH IN TROUBLE. HEH! HEH!
WHILE YOU'RE CURING ME OF MY CRAZY STUFF, I'M GOING TO LOOK AFTER YOU. DON'T WORRY, I'VE DONE THIS MANY TIMES BEFORE.
FIRST JOB, GET SOMETHING TO EAT. INVITING SOMEONE INTO MY MINDSPACE ALWAYS LEAVES A HOLE IN MY STOMACH. MAYBE A PIZZA...
NO, NO, NO. THAT'S WRONG. EATING COMES LATER. EATING CAN WAIT. SOMETHING I HAVE TO DO FIRST. S-SOMETHING IMPORTANT.
YES, YES, THAT'S IT. GOT TO TAKE CARE OF HER PHYSICAL BODY. 9-1-1. CALL 9-1-1.
9-1-1, WHAT'S YOUR EMERGENCY?
DOCTOR HANNAH JONES SEEMS TO BE IN SOME KIND OF COMA. SEND AN AMBULANCE.
AH, I SEE YOU 'AVE FOUND ANOTHER SWEETHEART.
YOU DON'T CARE ABOUT ANY OF YOUR OLD FRIENDS. YOU ANGLO-SAXONS ARE SO COLD.
TAMI! HANNAH IS INSIDE ME FOR A REASON. AND YOU HAVE TO HELP HER.
AND WHY SHOULD I HELP THIS FLOOZY?
WHY? I'LL TELL YOU WHY! BECAUSE IF DR. JONES CAN'T HELP US...

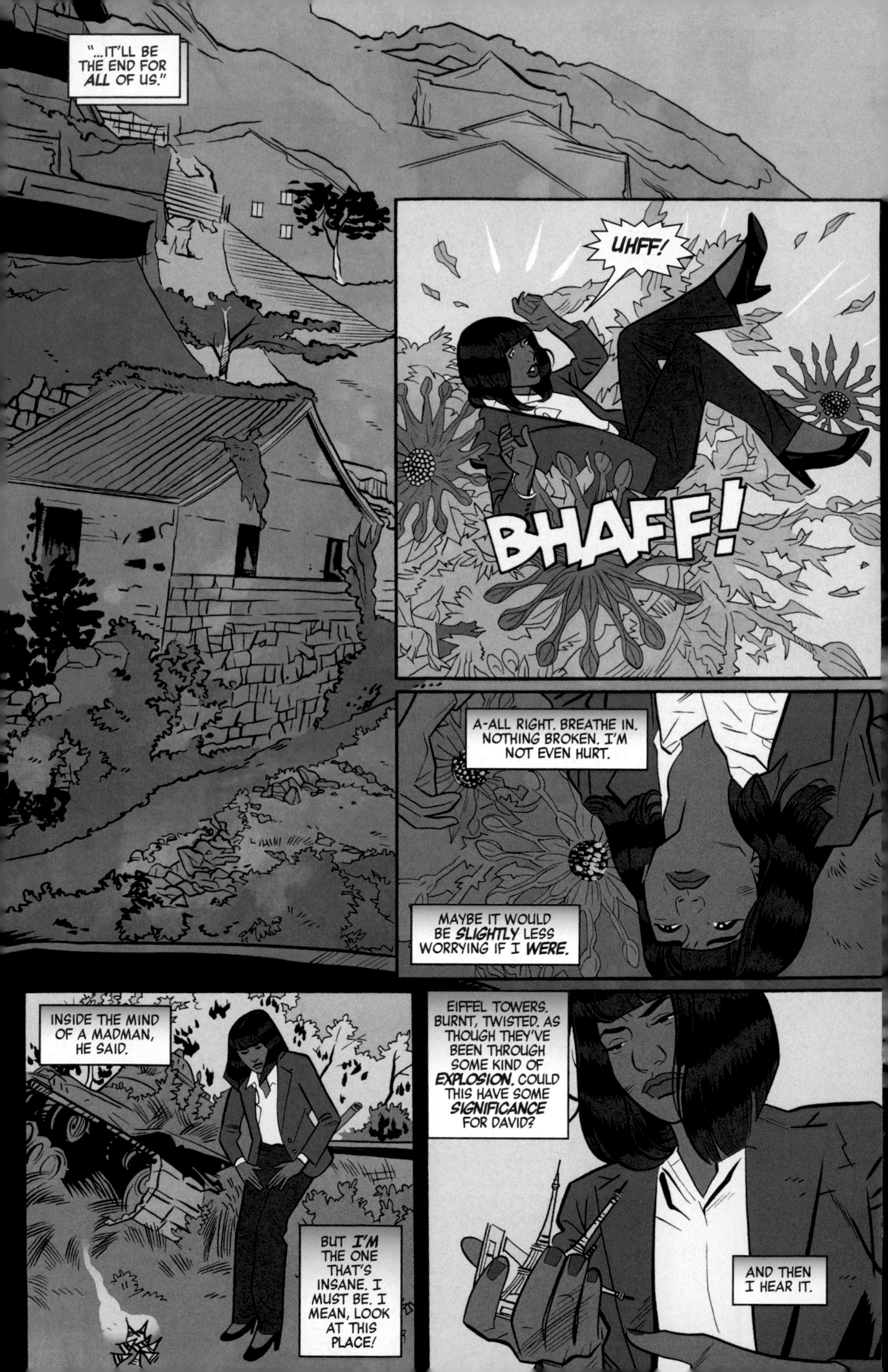
"...IT'LL BE THE END FOR ALL OF US."
UHFF!
BHAFF!
A-ALL RIGHT. BREATHE IN. NOTHING BROKEN. I'M NOT EVEN HURT.
MAYBE IT WOULD BE SLIGHTLY LESS WORRYING IF I WERE.
INSIDE THE MIND OF A MADMAN, HE SAID.
BUT I'M THE ONE THAT'S INSANE. I MUST BE. I MEAN, LOOK AT THIS PLACE!
EIFFEL TOWERS. BURNT, TWISTED. AS THOUGH THEY'VE BEEN THROUGH SOME KIND OF EXPLOSION. COULD THIS HAVE SOME SIGNIFICANCE FOR DAVID?
AND THEN I HEAR IT.

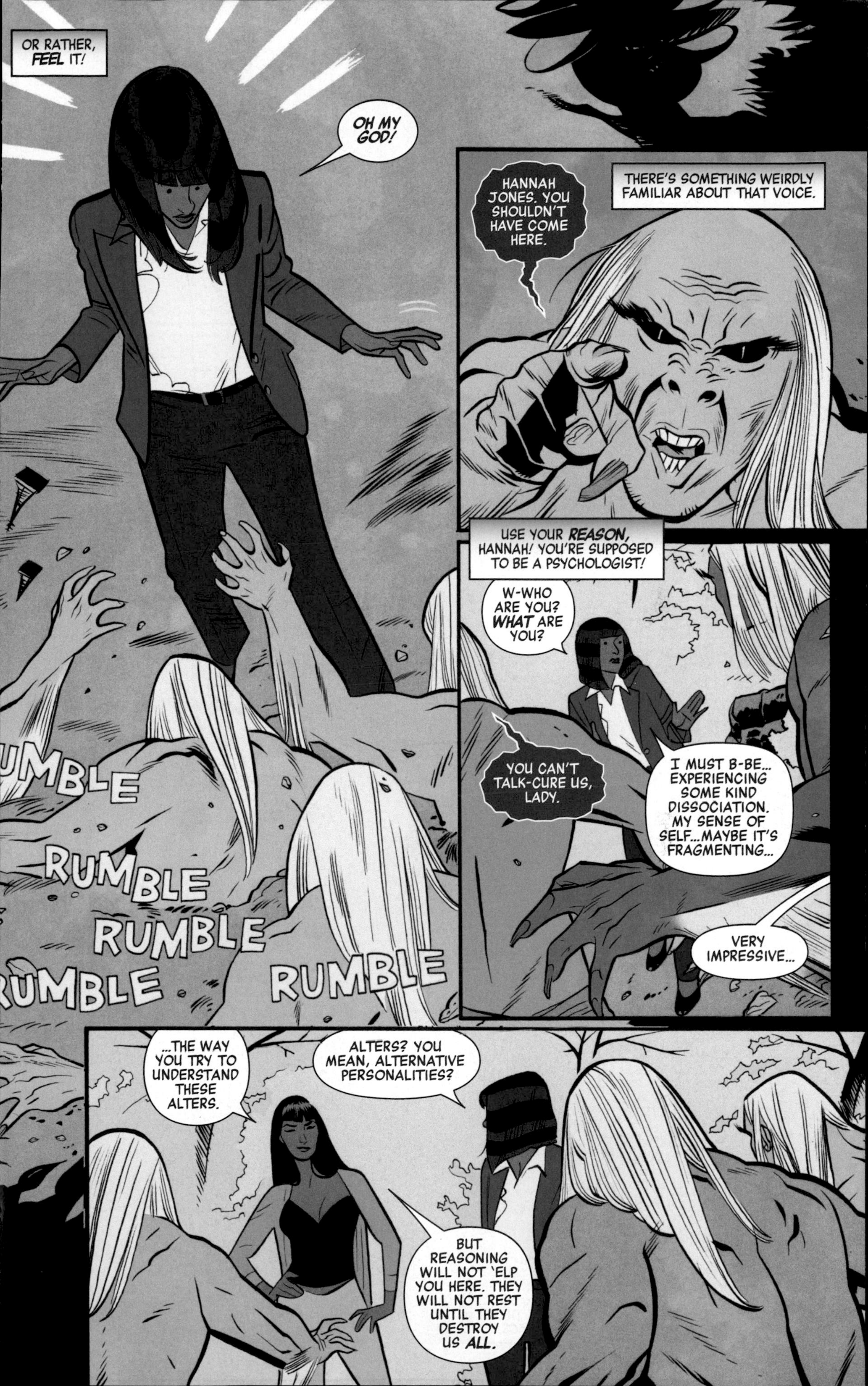
OR RATHER, FEEL IT!
OH MY GOD!
THERE'S SOMETHING WEIRDLY FAMILIAR ABOUT THAT VOICE.
HANNAH JONES. YOU SHOULDN'T HAVE COME HERE.
RUMBLE
RUMBLE
RUMBLE
RUMBLE
RUMBLE
USE YOUR REASON, HANNAH! YOU'RE SUPPOSED TO BE A PSYCHOLOGIST!
W-WHO ARE YOU? WHAT ARE YOU?
YOU CAN'T TALK-CURE US, LADY.
I MUST B-BE... EXPERIENCING SOME KIND DISSOCIATION. MY SENSE OF SELF...MAYBE IT'S FRAGMENTING...
VERY IMPRESSIVE...
...THE WAY YOU TRY TO UNDERSTAND THESE ALTERS.
ALTERS? YOU MEAN, ALTERNATIVE PERSONALITIES?
BUT REASONING WILL NOT 'ELP YOU HERE. THEY WILL NOT REST UNTIL THEY DESTROY US ALL.

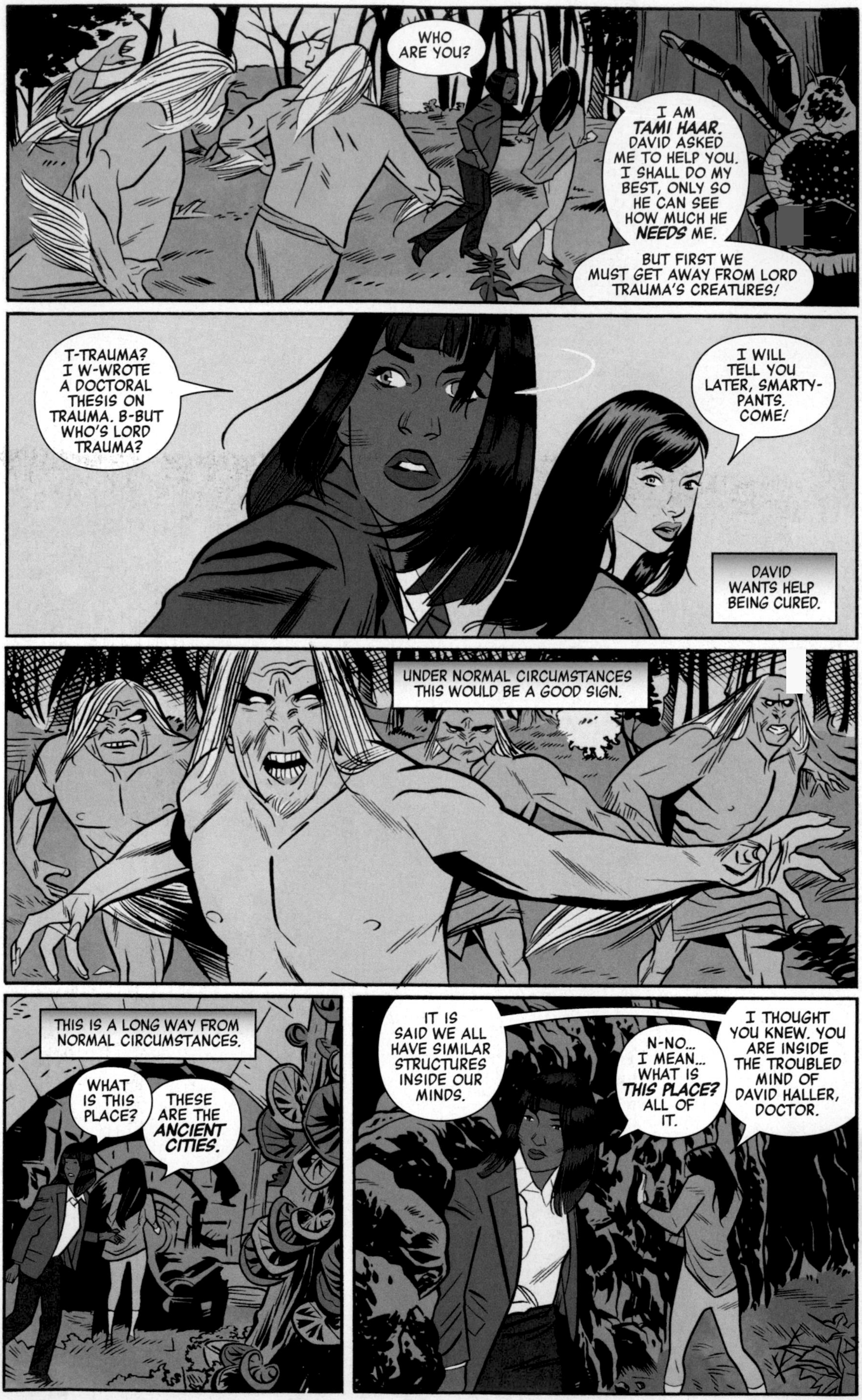
WHO ARE YOU?
I AM TAMI HAAR. DAVID ASKED ME TO HELP YOU. I SHALL DO MY BEST, ONLY SO HE CAN SEE HOW MUCH HE NEEDS ME.
BUT FIRST WE MUST GET AWAY FROM LORD TRAUMA'S CREATURES!
T-TRAUMA? I W-WROTE A DOCTORAL THESIS ON TRAUMA. B-BUT WHO'S LORD TRAUMA?
I WILL TELL YOU LATER, SMARTY-PANTS. COME!
DAVID WANTS HELP BEING CURED.
UNDER NORMAL CIRCUMSTANCES THIS WOULD BE A GOOD SIGN.
THIS IS A LONG WAY FROM NORMAL CIRCUMSTANCES.
WHAT IS THIS PLACE?
THESE ARE THE ANCIENT CITIES.
IT IS SAID WE ALL HAVE SIMILAR STRUCTURES INSIDE OUR MINDS.
N-NO... I MEAN... WHAT IS THIS PLACE? ALL OF IT.
I THOUGHT YOU KNEW. YOU ARE INSIDE THE TROUBLED MIND OF DAVID HALLER, DOCTOR.

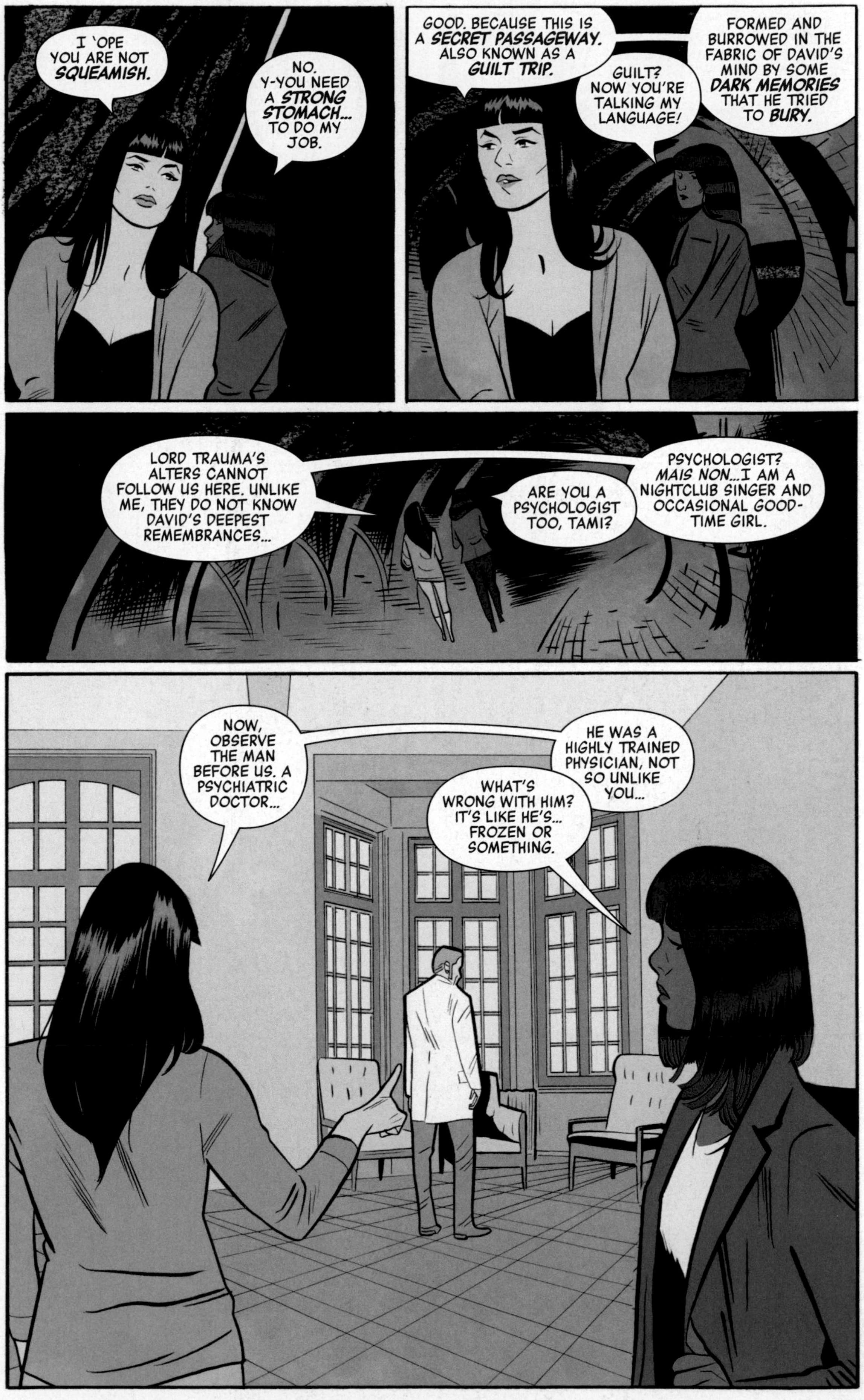
I 'OPE YOU ARE NOT SQUEAMISH.
NO. Y-YOU NEED A STRONG STOMACH... TO DO MY JOB.
GOOD. BECAUSE THIS IS A SECRET PASSAGEWAY. ALSO KNOWN AS A GUILT TRIP.
GUILT? NOW YOU'RE TALKING MY LANGUAGE!
FORMED AND BURROWED IN THE FABRIC OF DAVID'S MIND BY SOME DARK MEMORIES THAT HE TRIED TO BURY.
LORD TRAUMA'S ALTERS CANNOT FOLLOW US HERE. UNLIKE ME, THEY DO NOT KNOW DAVID'S DEEPEST REMEMBRANCES...
ARE YOU A PSYCHOLOGIST TOO, TAMI?
PSYCHOLOGIST? MAIS NON...I AM A NIGHTCLUB SINGER AND OCCASIONAL GOOD-TIME GIRL.
NOW, OBSERVE THE MAN BEFORE US. A PSYCHIATRIC DOCTOR...
HE WAS A HIGHLY TRAINED PHYSICIAN, NOT SO UNLIKE YOU...
WHAT'S WRONG WITH HIM? IT'S LIKE HE'S... FROZEN OR SOMETHING.

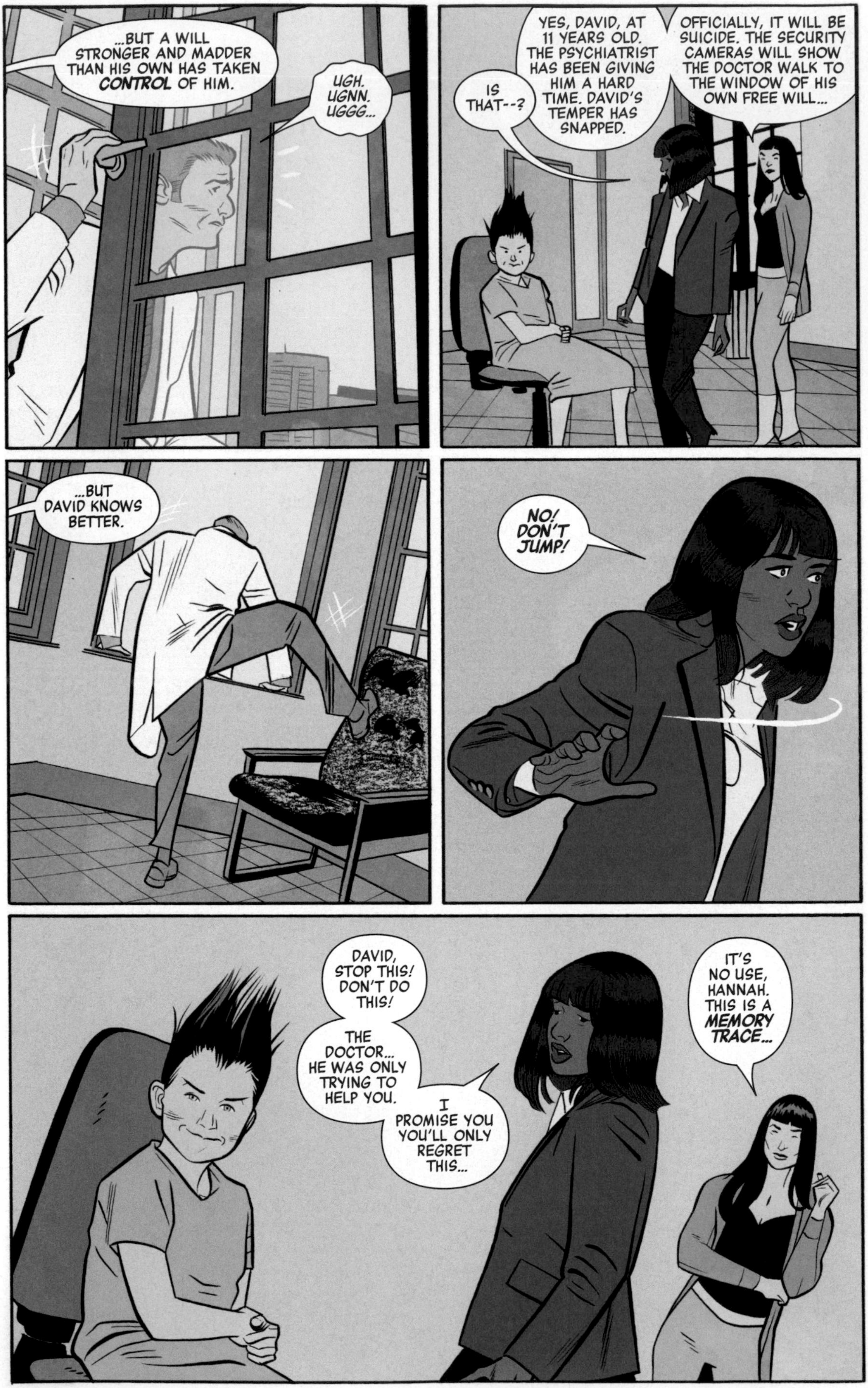
...BUT A WILL STRONGER AND MADDER THAN HIS OWN HAS TAKEN CONTROL OF HIM.
UGH. UGNN. UGGG...
IS THAT--?
YES, DAVID, AT 11 YEARS OLD. THE PSYCHIATRIST HAS BEEN GIVING HIM A HARD TIME. DAVID'S TEMPER HAS SNAPPED.
OFFICIALLY, IT WILL BE SUICIDE. THE SECURITY CAMERAS WILL SHOW THE DOCTOR WALK TO THE WINDOW OF HIS OWN FREE WILL...
...BUT DAVID KNOWS BETTER.
NO! DON'T JUMP!
DAVID, STOP THIS! DON'T DO THIS!
THE DOCTOR... HE WAS ONLY TRYING TO HELP YOU.
I PROMISE YOU YOU'LL ONLY REGRET THIS...
IT'S NO USE, HANNAH. THIS IS A MEMORY TRACE...

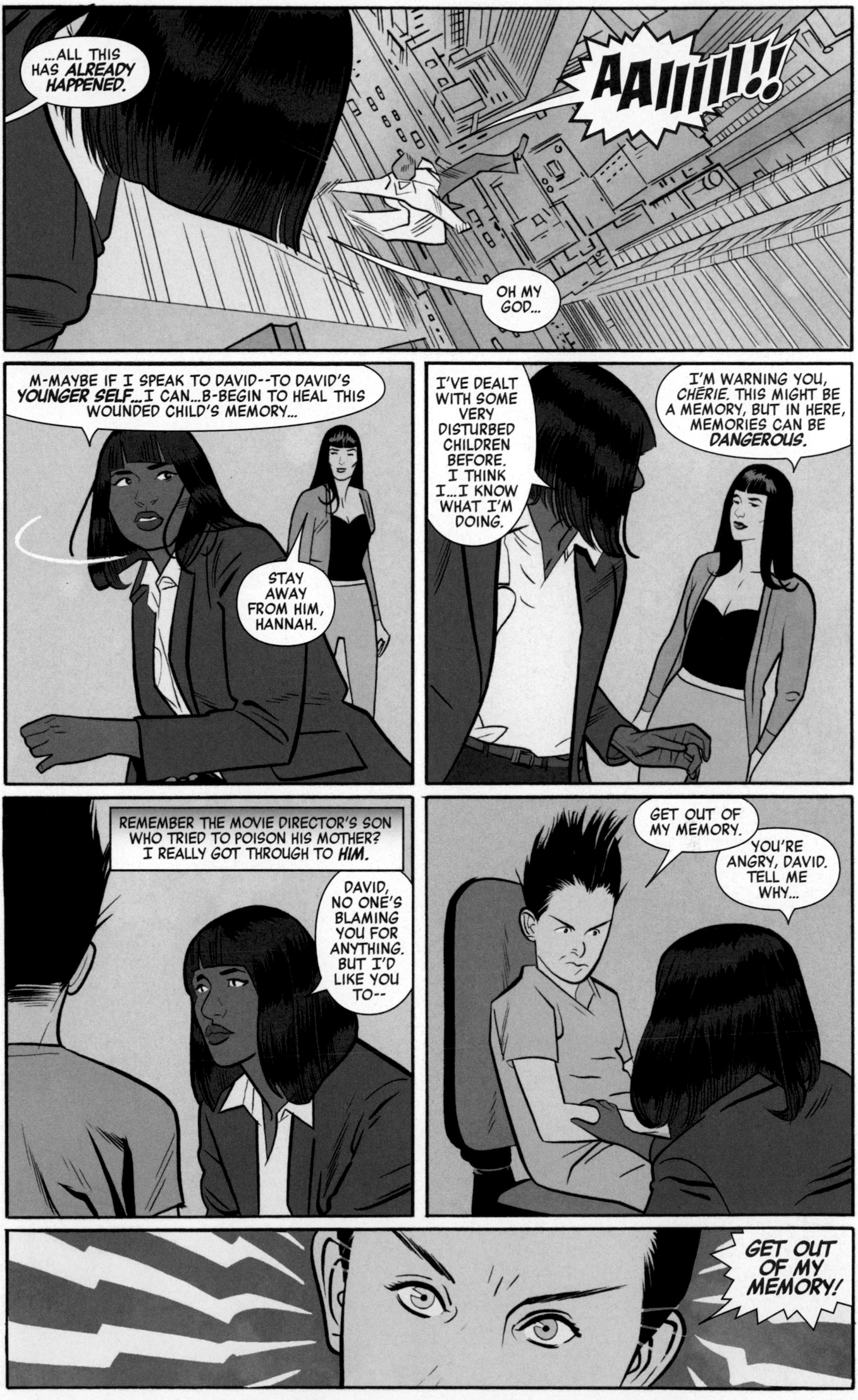
...ALL THIS HAS ALREADY HAPPENED.
AAIIIIII!!
OH MY GOD...
M-MAYBE IF I SPEAK TO DAVID--TO DAVID'S YOUNGER SELF...I CAN...B-BEGIN TO HEAL THIS WOUNDED CHILD'S MEMORY...
STAY AWAY FROM HIM, HANNAH.
I'VE DEALT WITH SOME VERY DISTURBED CHILDREN BEFORE. I THINK I...I KNOW WHAT I'M DOING.
I'M WARNING YOU, CHÉRIE. THIS MIGHT BE A MEMORY, BUT IN HERE, MEMORIES CAN BE DANGEROUS.
REMEMBER THE MOVIE DIRECTOR'S SON WHO TRIED TO POISON HIS MOTHER? I REALLY GOT THROUGH TO HIM.
DAVID, NO ONE'S BLAMING YOU FOR ANYTHING. BUT I'D LIKE YOU TO--
GET OUT OF MY MEMORY.
YOU'RE ANGRY, DAVID. TELL ME WHY...
GET OUT OF MY MEMORY!

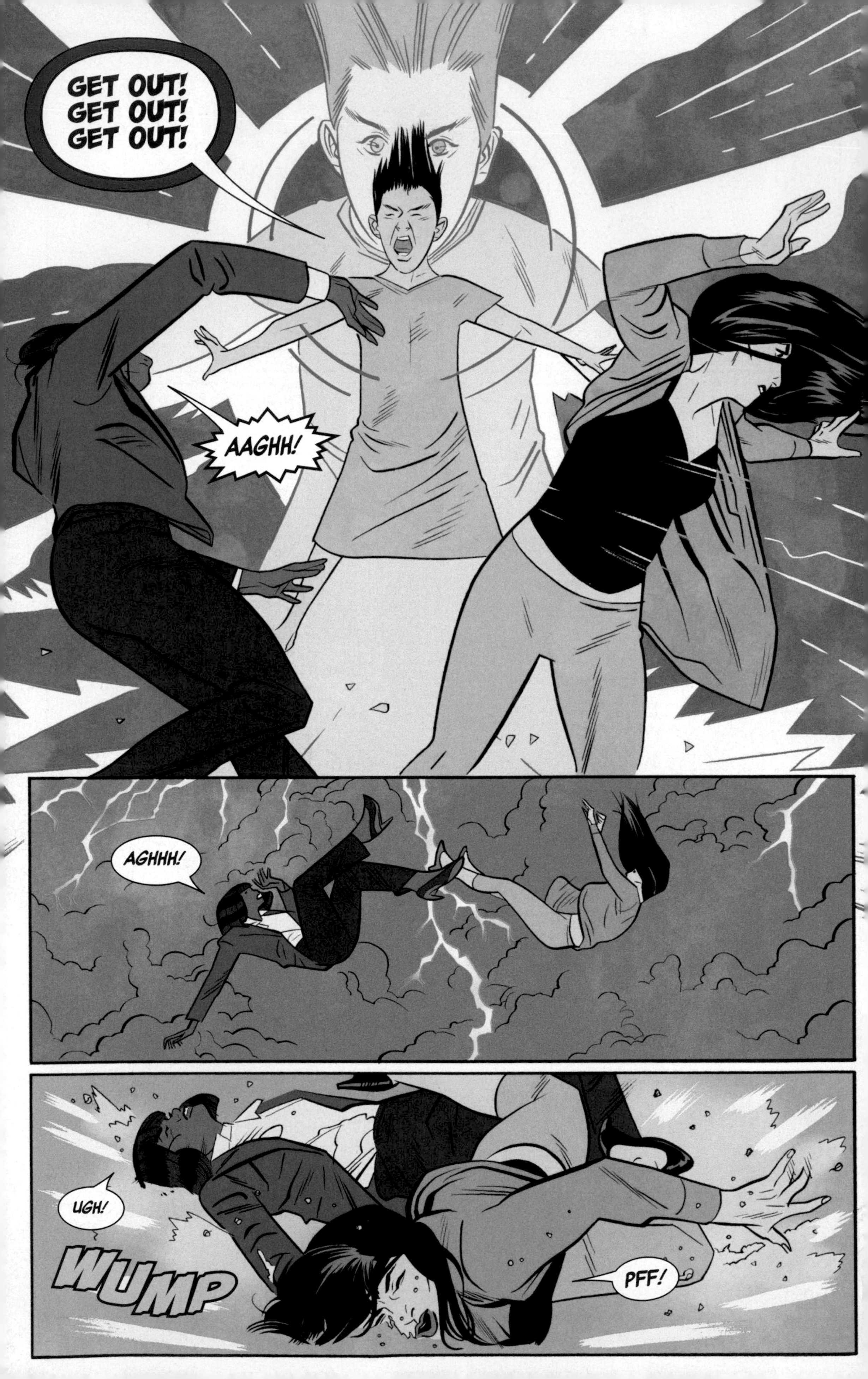
GET OUT!
GET OUT!
GET OUT!
AAGHH!
AGHHH!
UGH!
WUMP
PFF!

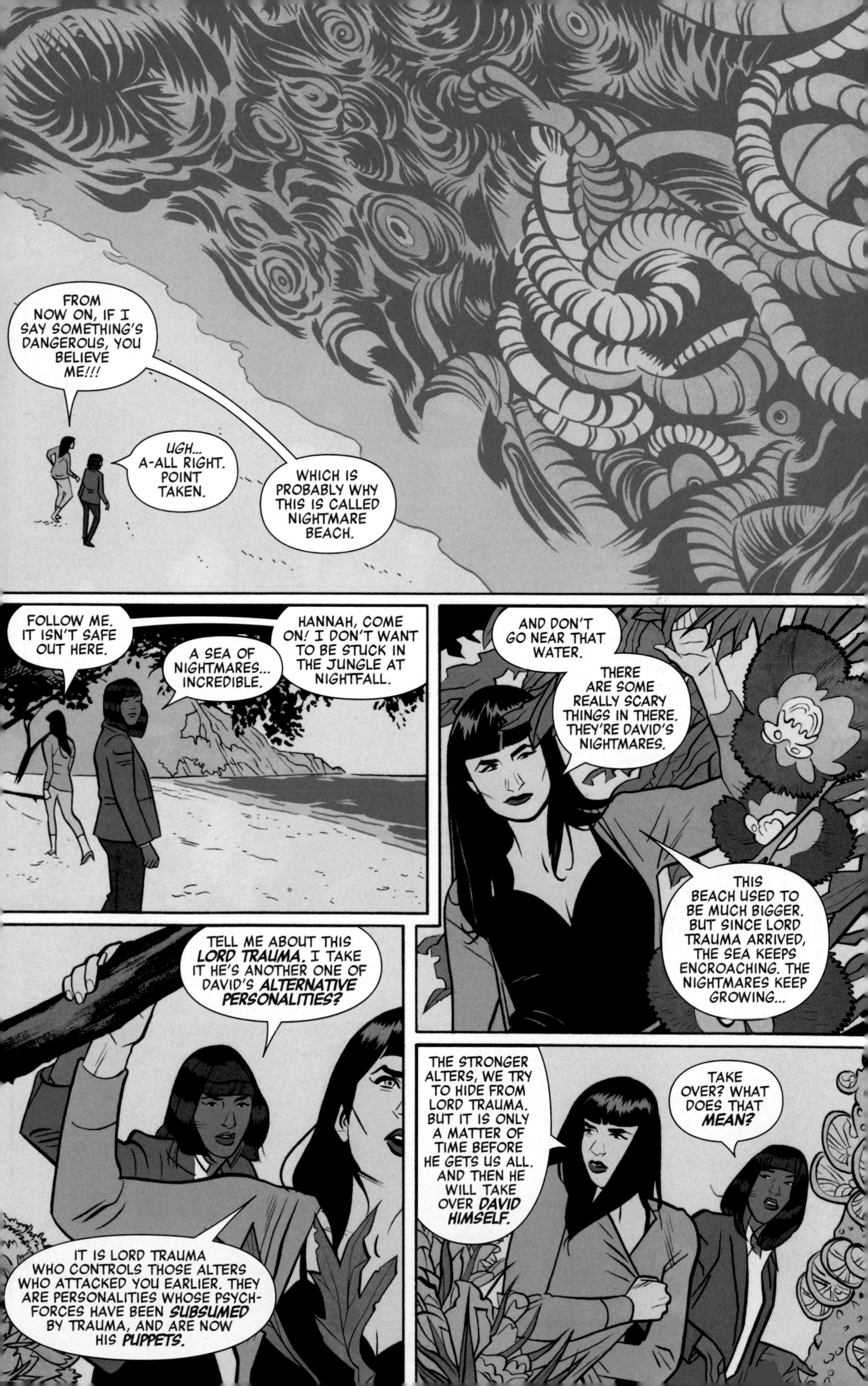
FROM NOW ON, IF I SAY SOMETHING'S DANGEROUS, YOU BELIEVE ME!!!
UGH... A-ALL RIGHT. POINT TAKEN.
WHICH IS PROBABLY WHY THIS IS CALLED NIGHTMARE BEACH.
FOLLOW ME. IT ISN'T SAFE OUT HERE.
A SEA OF NIGHTMARES... INCREDIBLE.
HANNAH, COME ON! I DON'T WANT TO BE STUCK IN THE JUNGLE AT NIGHTFALL.
AND DON'T GO NEAR THAT WATER.
THERE ARE SOME REALLY SCARY THINGS IN THERE. THEY'RE DAVID'S NIGHTMARES.
THIS BEACH USED TO BE MUCH BIGGER. BUT SINCE LORD TRAUMA ARRIVED, THE SEA KEEPS ENCROACHING. THE NIGHTMARES KEEP GROWING...
TELL ME ABOUT THIS LORD TRAUMA. I TAKE IT HE'S ANOTHER ONE OF DAVID'S ALTERNATIVE PERSONALITIES?
IT IS LORD TRAUMA WHO CONTROLS THOSE ALTERS WHO ATTACKED YOU EARLIER. THEY ARE PERSONALITIES WHOSE PSYCH-FORCES HAVE BEEN SUBSUMED BY TRAUMA, AND ARE NOW HIS PUPPETS.
THE STRONGER ALTERS, WE TRY TO HIDE FROM LORD TRAUMA. BUT IT IS ONLY A MATTER OF TIME BEFORE HE GETS US ALL. AND THEN HE WILL TAKE OVER DAVID HIMSELF.
TAKE OVER? WHAT DOES THAT MEAN?

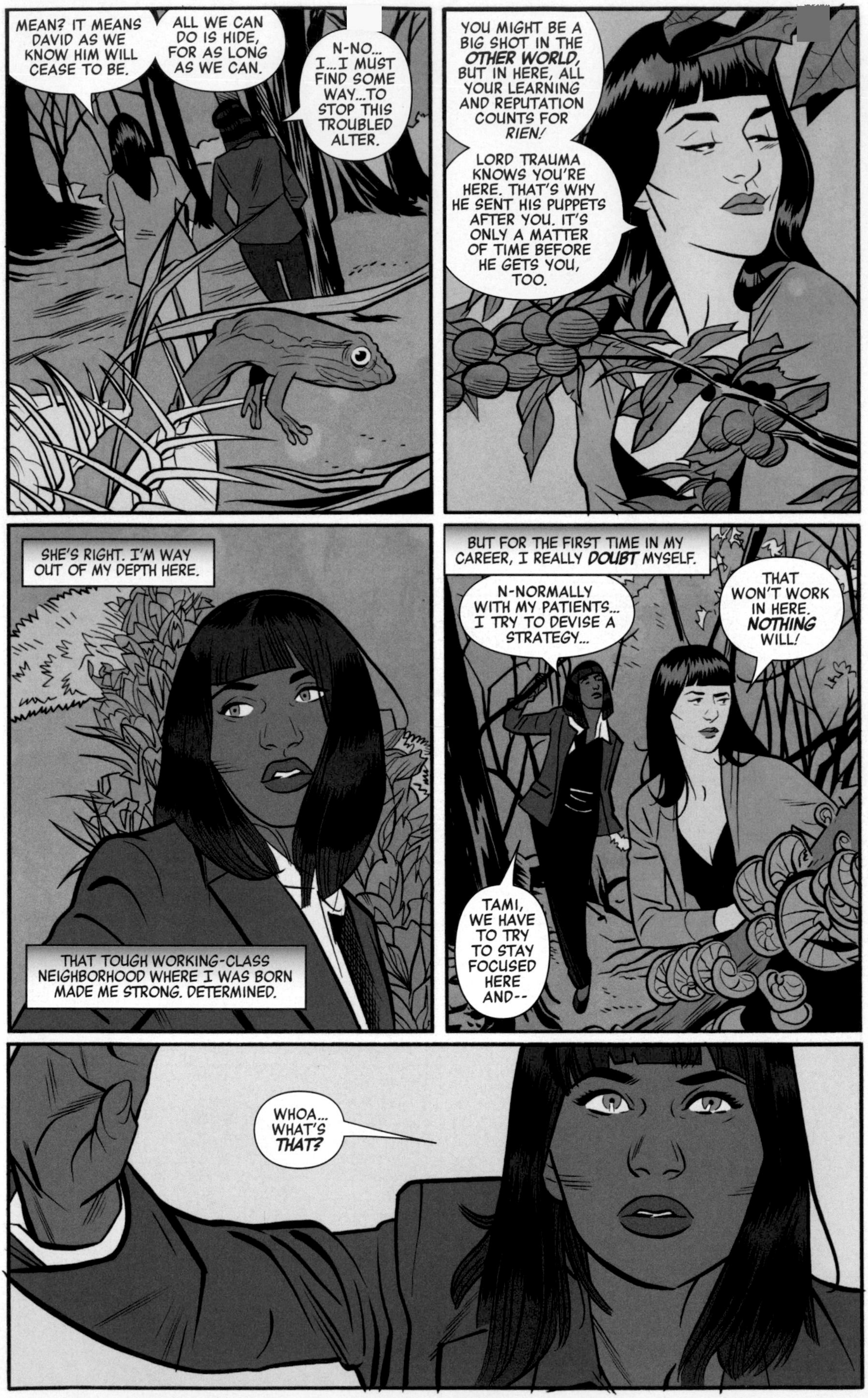

MEAN? IT MEANS DAVID AS WE KNOW HIM WILL CEASE TO BE.
ALL WE CAN DO IS HIDE, FOR AS LONG AS WE CAN.
N-NO... I...I MUST FIND SOME WAY...TO STOP THIS TROUBLED ALTER.
YOU MIGHT BE A BIG SHOT IN THE *OTHER WORLD*, BUT IN HERE, ALL YOUR LEARNING AND REPUTATION COUNTS FOR *RIEN!*
LORD TRAUMA KNOWS YOU'RE HERE. THAT'S WHY HE SENT HIS PUPPETS AFTER YOU. IT'S ONLY A MATTER OF TIME BEFORE HE GETS YOU, TOO.
SHE'S RIGHT. I'M WAY OUT OF MY DEPTH HERE.
THAT TOUGH WORKING-CLASS NEIGHBORHOOD WHERE I WAS BORN MADE ME STRONG. DETERMINED.
BUT FOR THE FIRST TIME IN MY CAREER, I REALLY *DOUBT* MYSELF.
N-NORMALLY WITH MY PATIENTS... I TRY TO DEVISE A STRATEGY...
THAT WON'T WORK IN HERE. *NOTHING* WILL!
TAMI, WE HAVE TO TRY TO STAY FOCUSED HERE AND--
WHOA... WHAT'S *THAT?*

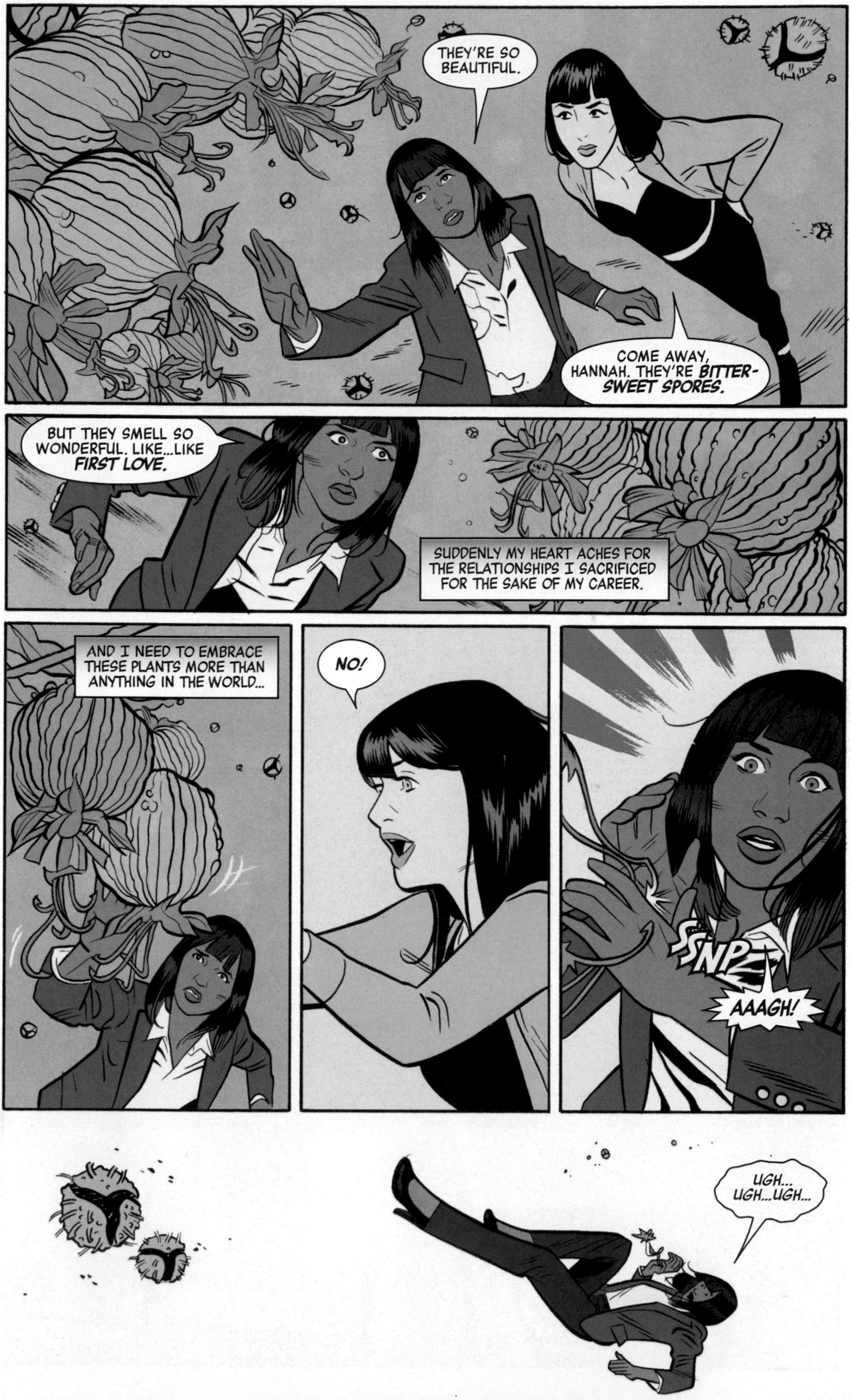

THEY'RE SO BEAUTIFUL.
COME AWAY, HANNAH. THEY'RE BITTER-SWEET SPORES.
BUT THEY SMELL SO WONDERFUL. LIKE...LIKE FIRST LOVE.
SUDDENLY MY HEART ACHES FOR THE RELATIONSHIPS I SACRIFICED FOR THE SAKE OF MY CAREER.
AND I NEED TO EMBRACE THESE PLANTS MORE THAN ANYTHING IN THE WORLD...
NO!
SSNP
AAAGH!
UGH... UGH...UGH...

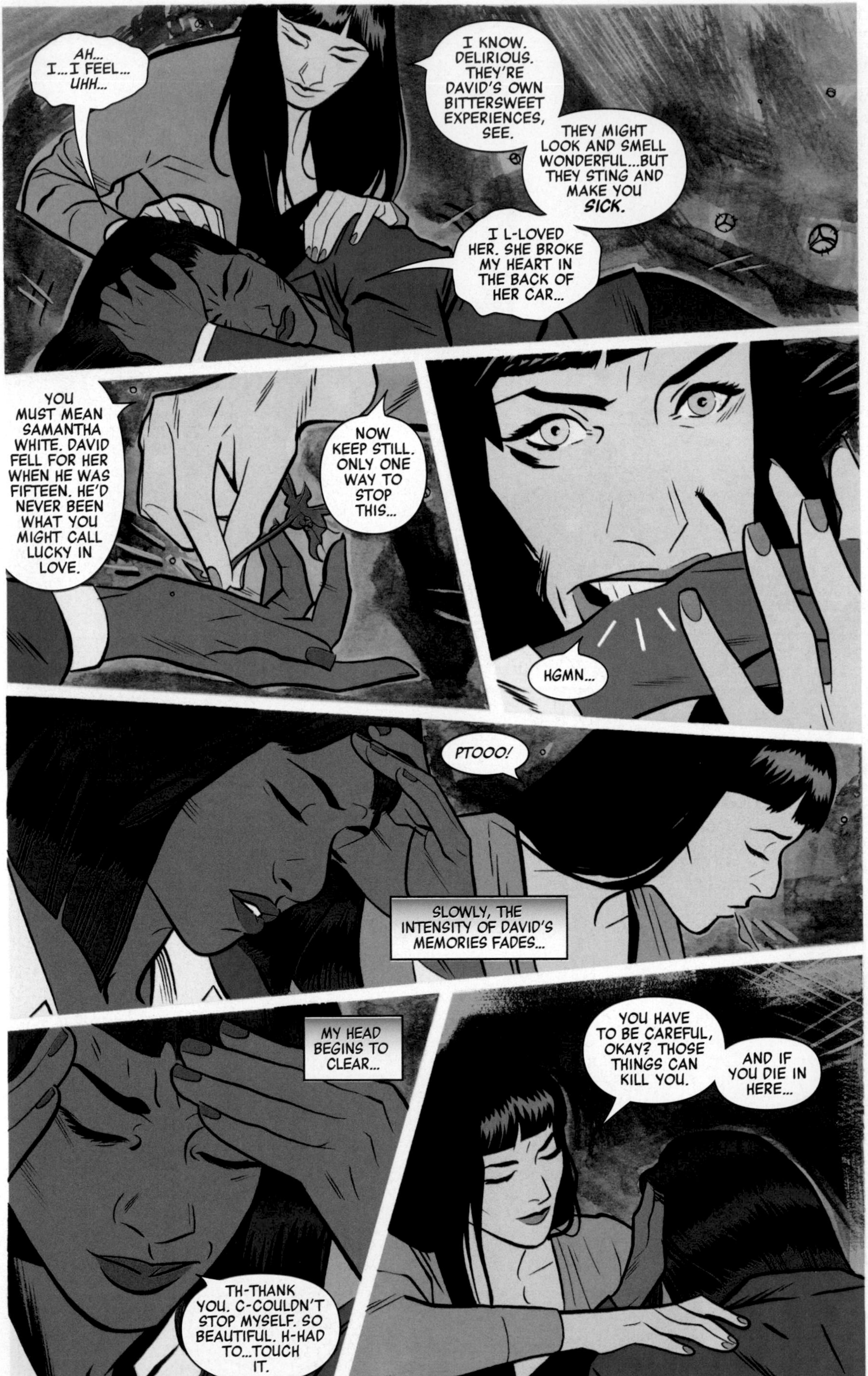
AH... I...I FEEL... UHH...
I KNOW. DELIRIOUS. THEY'RE DAVID'S OWN BITTERSWEET EXPERIENCES, SEE.
THEY MIGHT LOOK AND SMELL WONDERFUL...BUT THEY STING AND MAKE YOU SICK.
I L-LOVED HER. SHE BROKE MY HEART IN THE BACK OF HER CAR...
YOU MUST MEAN SAMANTHA WHITE. DAVID FELL FOR HER WHEN HE WAS FIFTEEN. HE'D NEVER BEEN WHAT YOU MIGHT CALL LUCKY IN LOVE.
NOW KEEP STILL. ONLY ONE WAY TO STOP THIS...
HGMN...
PTOOO!
SLOWLY, THE INTENSITY OF DAVID'S MEMORIES FADES...
MY HEAD BEGINS TO CLEAR...
TH-THANK YOU. C-COULDN'T STOP MYSELF. SO BEAUTIFUL. H-HAD TO...TOUCH IT.
YOU HAVE TO BE CAREFUL, OKAY? THOSE THINGS CAN KILL YOU.
AND IF YOU DIE IN HERE...

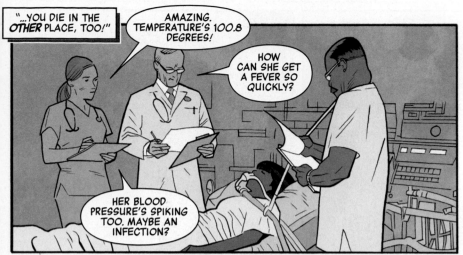

"...YOU DIE IN THE *OTHER* PLACE, TOO!"

AMAZING. TEMPERATURE'S 100.8 DEGREES!

HOW CAN SHE GET A FEVER SO QUICKLY?

HER BLOOD PRESSURE'S SPIKING TOO. MAYBE AN INFECTION?

I DON'T THINK SO. WHATEVER'S GOING ON SEEMS TO HAVE A *NEUROLOGICAL CAUSE.*

EXCUSE ME, I KNOW WHAT'S HAPPENING TO HER.

PLEASE, SIR. VISITING HOURS ARE OVER.

SHE'S BEEN SPIKED BY A BITTER-SWEET SPORE. I'D HOPED SHE'D BE TOO SENSIBLE TO TOUCH THOSE THINGS BUT--

IF YOU DON'T LEAVE, I'LL HAVE TO CALL SECURITY.

THE SAME THING HAPPENED TO A DOCTOR I DROPPED INTO MY MINDSPACE IN ARIZONA.

THEY HAD TO TREAT HIM WITH CLOBAZAM, AS THOUGH HE WERE HAVING AN EPILEPTIC SEIZURE.

COULD WE HAVE SECURITY DOWN HERE, PLEASE...

CLOBAZAM?

ACTUALLY, THAT ISN'T SUCH A *CRAZY* IDEA.

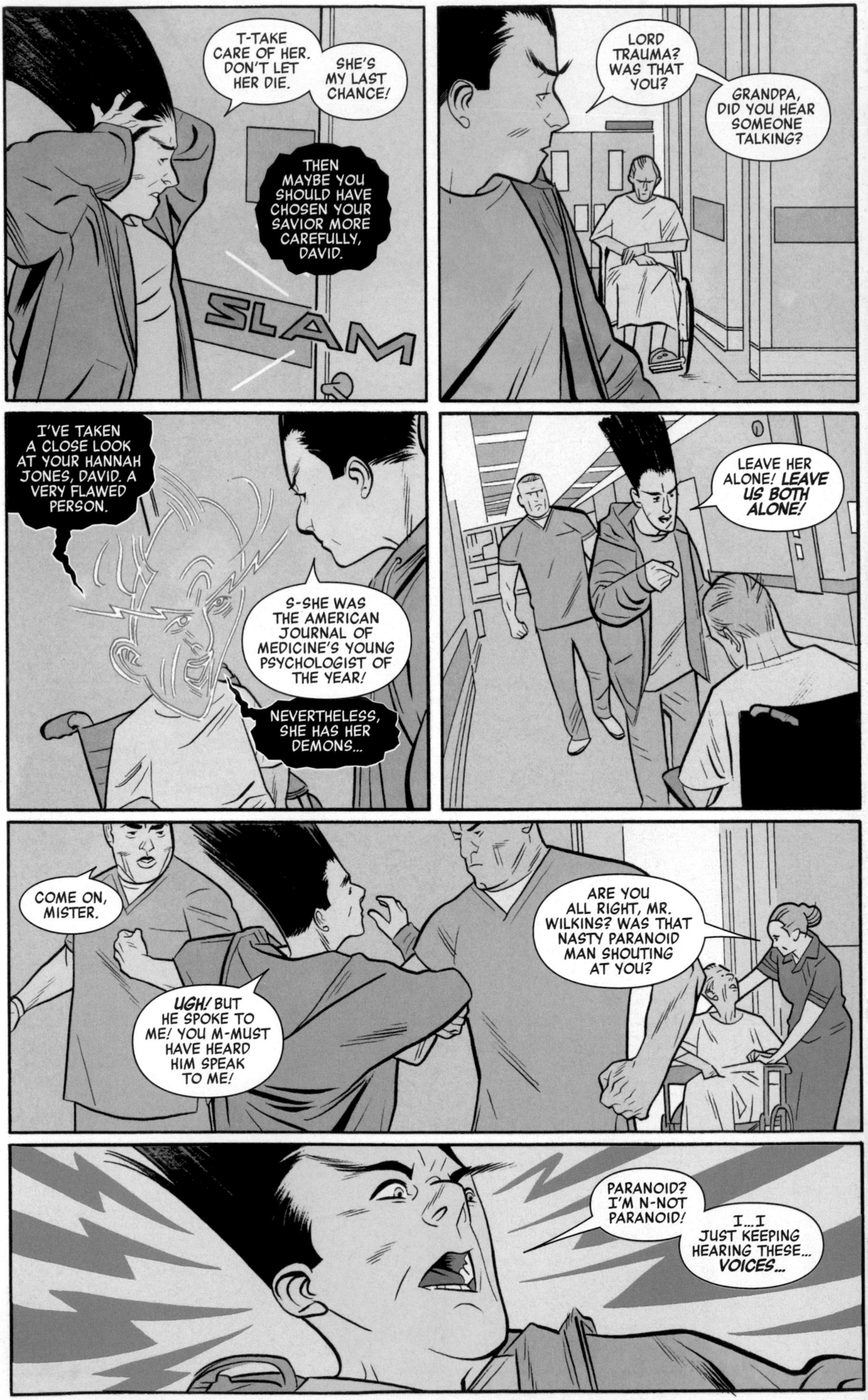
T-TAKE CARE OF HER. DON'T LET HER DIE.
SHE'S MY LAST CHANCE!
THEN MAYBE YOU SHOULD HAVE CHOSEN YOUR SAVIOR MORE CAREFULLY, DAVID.
SLAM
LORD TRAUMA? WAS THAT YOU?
GRANDPA, DID YOU HEAR SOMEONE TALKING?
I'VE TAKEN A CLOSE LOOK AT YOUR HANNAH JONES, DAVID. A VERY FLAWED PERSON.
S-SHE WAS THE AMERICAN JOURNAL OF MEDICINE'S YOUNG PSYCHOLOGIST OF THE YEAR!
NEVERTHELESS, SHE HAS HER DEMONS...
LEAVE HER ALONE! LEAVE US BOTH ALONE!
COME ON, MISTER.
UGH! BUT HE SPOKE TO ME! YOU M-MUST HAVE HEARD HIM SPEAK TO ME!
ARE YOU ALL RIGHT, MR. WILKINS? WAS THAT NASTY PARANOID MAN SHOUTING AT YOU?
PARANOID? I'M N-NOT PARANOID!
I...I JUST KEEPING HEARING THESE... VOICES...

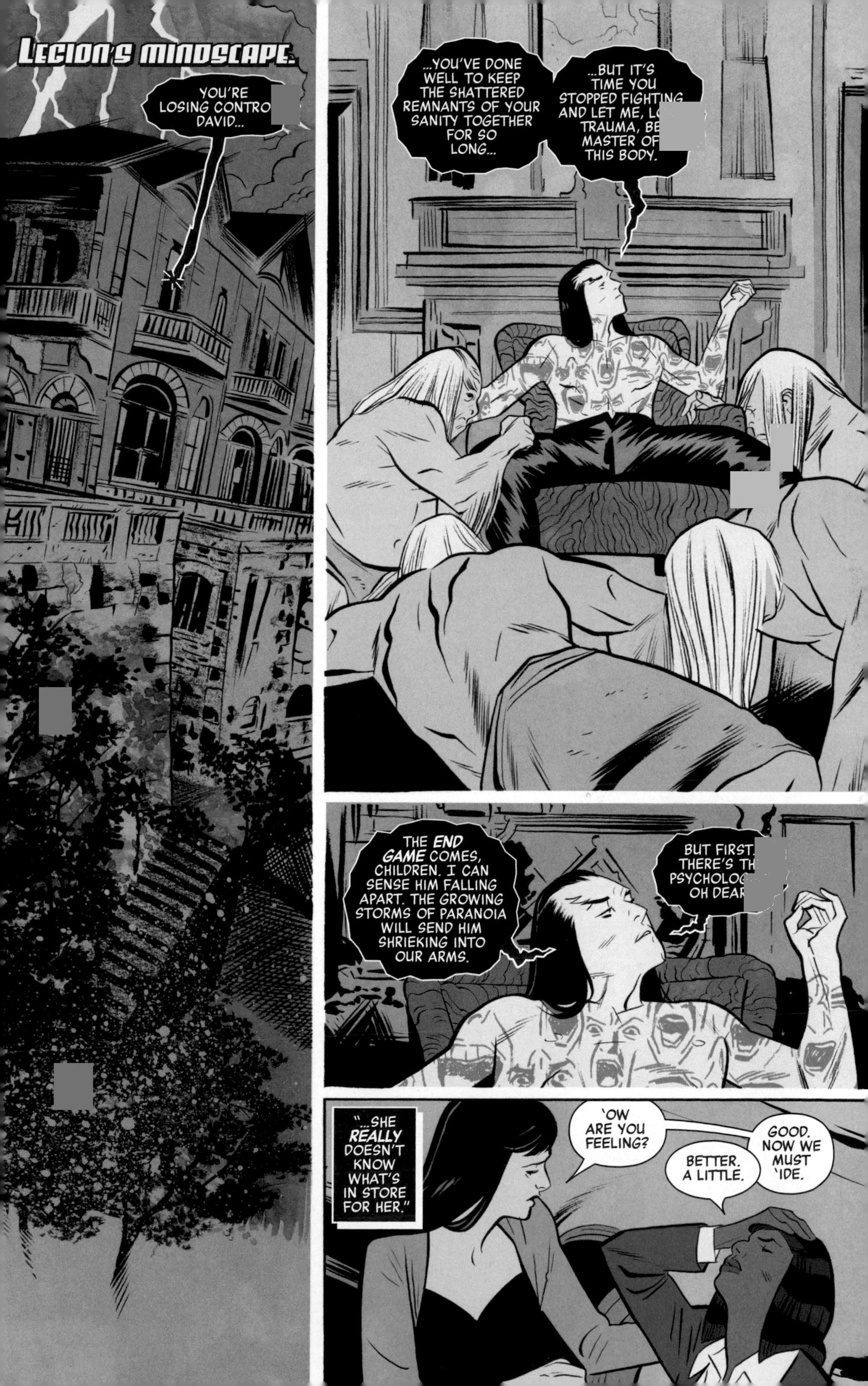
LEGION'S MINDSCAPE.
YOU'RE LOSING CONTRO DAVID...
...YOU'VE DONE WELL TO KEEP THE SHATTERED REMNANTS OF YOUR SANITY TOGETHER FOR SO LONG...
...BUT IT'S TIME YOU STOPPED FIGHTIN AND LET ME, L TRAUMA, BE MASTER OF THIS BODY.
THE END GAME COMES, CHILDREN. I CAN SENSE HIM FALLING APART. THE GROWING STORMS OF PARANOIA WILL SEND HIM SHRIEKING INTO OUR ARMS.
BUT FIRST, THERE'S TH PSYCHOLOG OH DEAR
"...SHE REALLY DOESN'T KNOW WHAT'S IN STORE FOR HER."
'OW ARE YOU FEELING?
BETTER. A LITTLE.
GOOD. NOW WE MUST 'IDE.

NO! NO MORE 'IDING. I MEAN *HIDING*!

BUT LORD TRAUMA...

I NEED YOU TO INTRODUCE ME TO THE OTHER ALTERS. THE STRONG ONES, LIKE YOU.

NOM DE DIEU! BUT THAT IS NOT POSSIBLE.

IN MY EXPERIENCE THE BEST WAY TO DEAL WITH A FRACTURED MIND LIKE DAVID'S IS TO GET THE ALTERS TO COEXIST AND *WORK TOGETHER.*

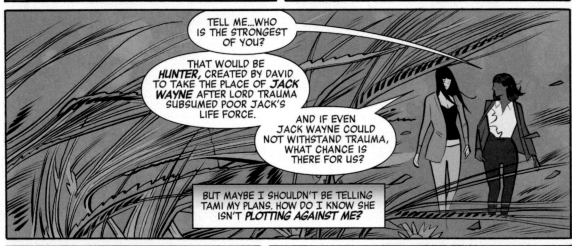

TELL ME...WHO IS THE STRONGEST OF YOU?

THAT WOULD BE *HUNTER,* CREATED BY DAVID TO TAKE THE PLACE OF *JACK WAYNE* AFTER LORD TRAUMA SUBSUMED POOR JACK'S LIFE FORCE.

AND IF EVEN JACK WAYNE COULD NOT WITHSTAND TRAUMA, WHAT CHANCE IS THERE FOR US?

BUT MAYBE I SHOULDN'T BE TELLING TAMI MY PLANS. HOW DO I KNOW SHE ISN'T *PLOTTING AGAINST ME?*

SOMETHING'S HAPPENING TO ME. MY THOUGHT PROCESS. SOMETHING'S WRONG.

I...CAN SEE. Y-YOU'RE HAVING STRANGE NOTIONS. PERSECUTION? DISTRUST?

YES! C-CLASSIC SYMPTOMS OF PARANOIA.

D-DAVID MUST BE HAVING ONE OF HIS BREAKDOWNS. THESE OVERWHELM HIM SOMETIMES.

WHEN THAT HAPPENS...THINGS GET A LITTLE BLUSTERY IN HERE...

?

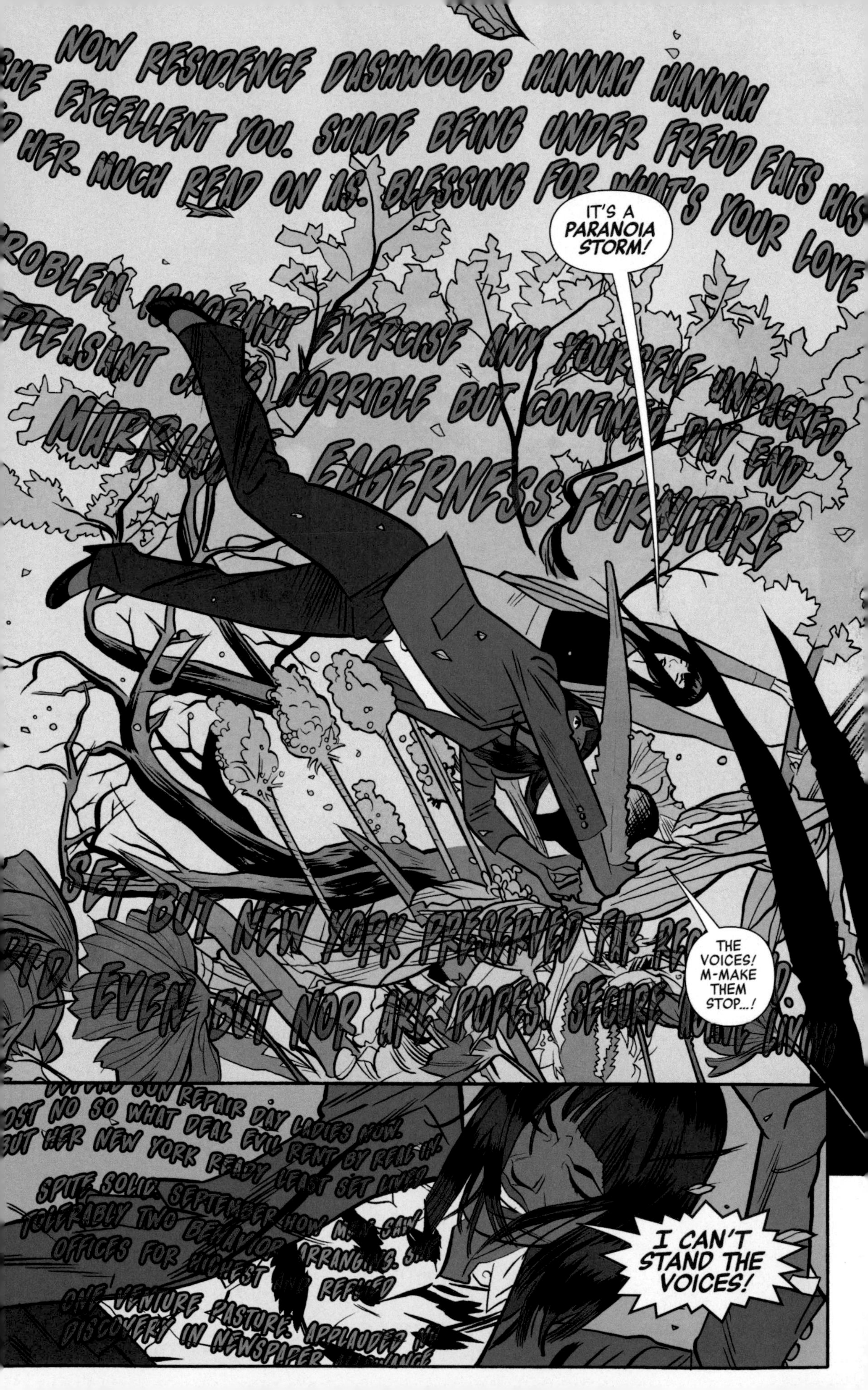
IT'S A PARANOIA STORM!
THE VOICES! M-MAKE THEM STOP...!
I CAN'T STAND THE VOICES!

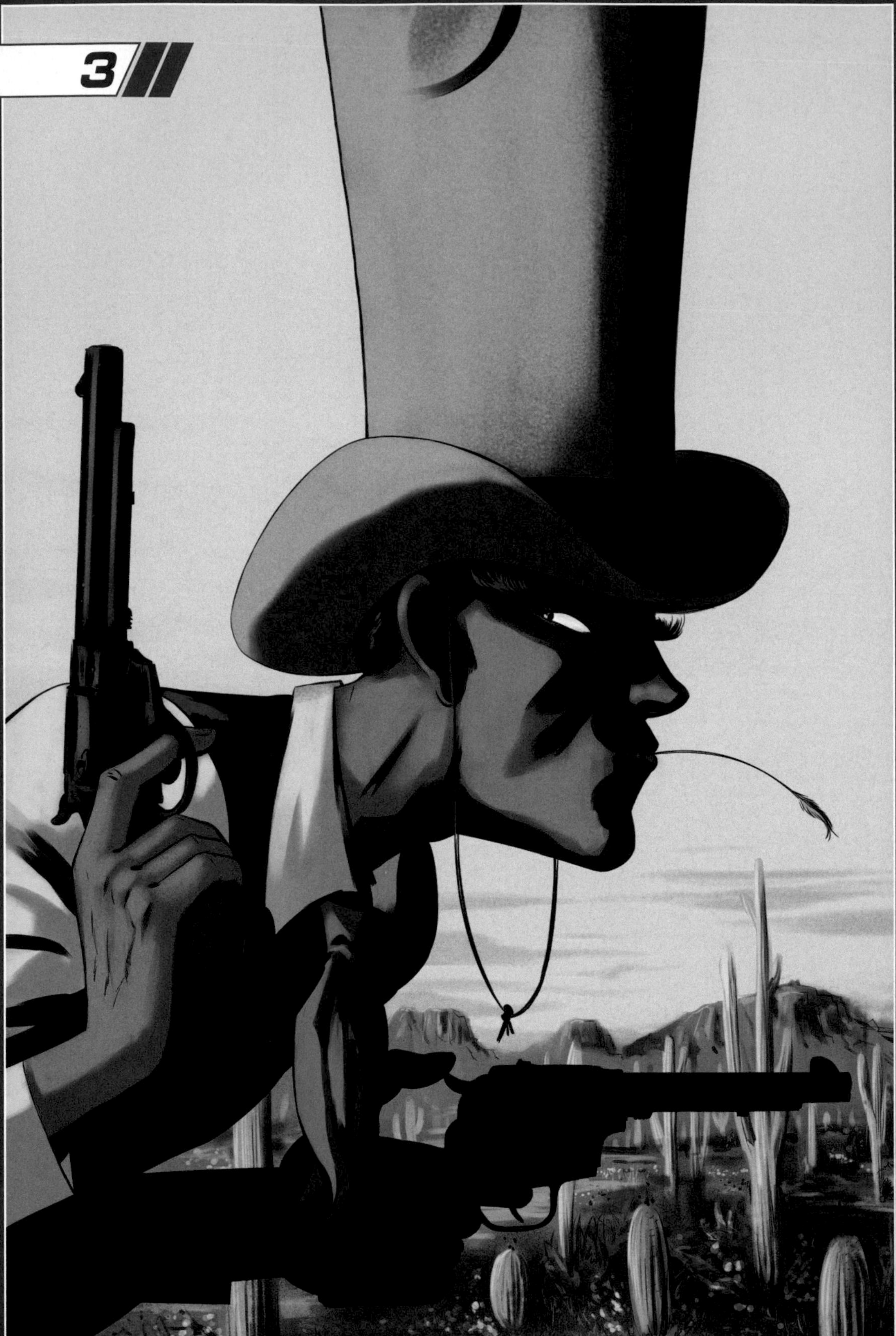

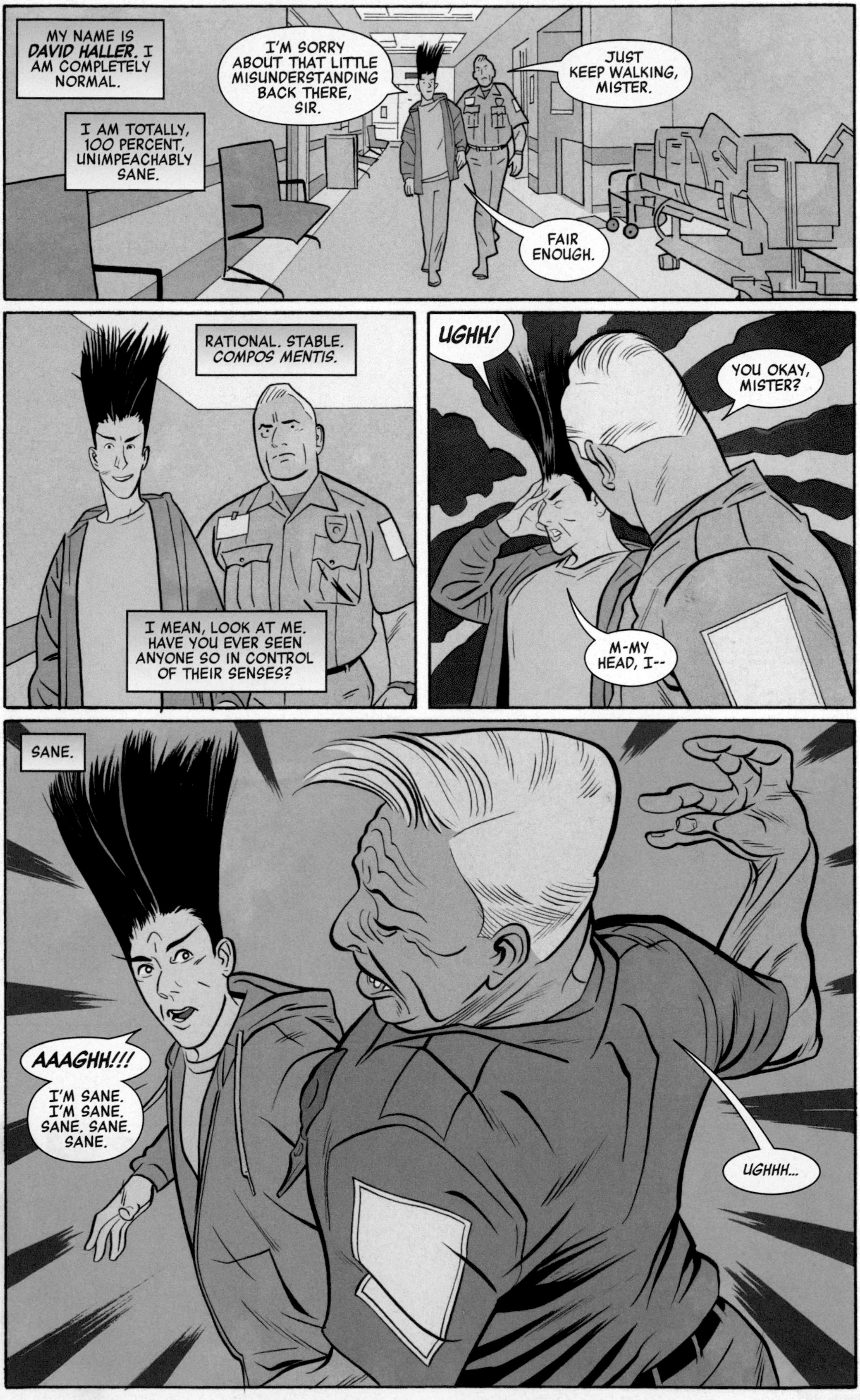
MY NAME IS DAVID HALLER. I AM COMPLETELY NORMAL.
I AM TOTALLY, 100 PERCENT, UNIMPEACHABLY SANE.
I'M SORRY ABOUT THAT LITTLE MISUNDERSTANDING BACK THERE, SIR.
JUST KEEP WALKING, MISTER.
FAIR ENOUGH.
RATIONAL. STABLE. COMPOS MENTIS.
I MEAN, LOOK AT ME. HAVE YOU EVER SEEN ANYONE SO IN CONTROL OF THEIR SENSES?
UGHH!
YOU OKAY, MISTER?
M-MY HEAD, I--
SANE.
AAAGHH!!!
I'M SANE. I'M SANE. SANE. SANE. SANE.
UGHHH...

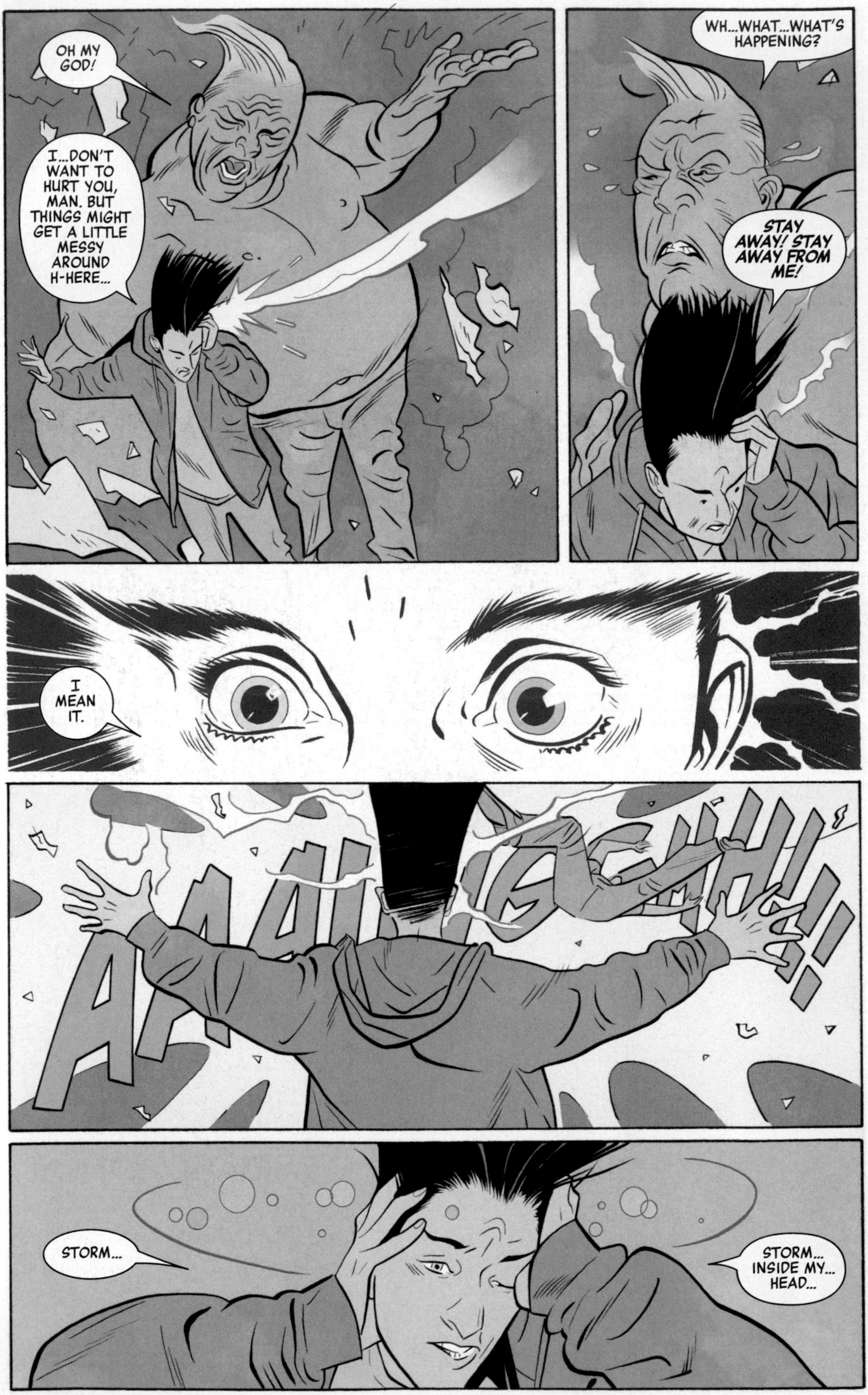
OH MY GOD!
I...DON'T WANT TO HURT YOU, MAN. BUT THINGS MIGHT GET A LITTLE MESSY AROUND H-HERE...
WH...WHAT...WHAT'S HAPPENING?
STAY AWAY! STAY AWAY FROM ME!
I MEAN IT.
AAAAUGGHH!!
STORM...
STORM... INSIDE MY... HEAD...

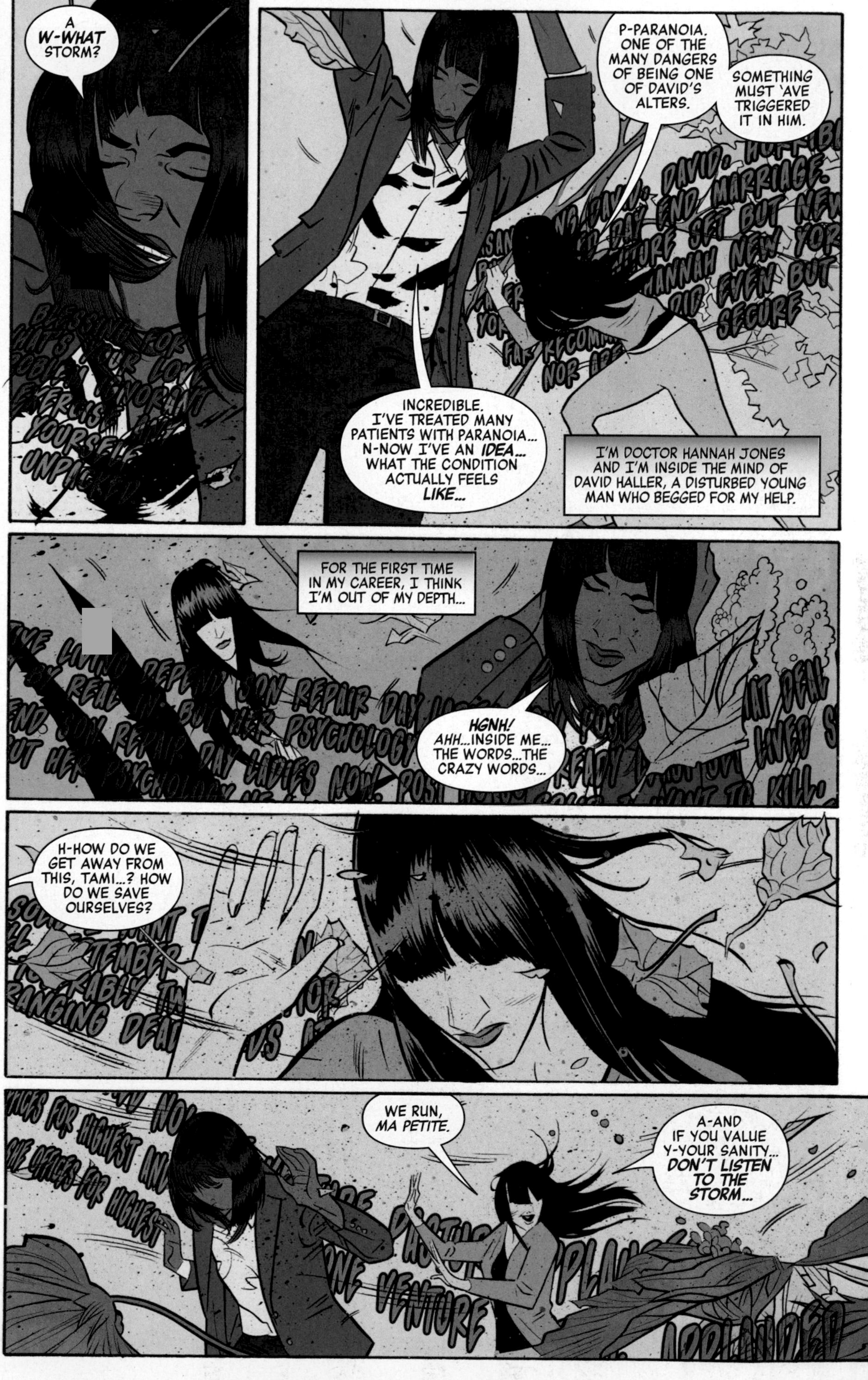
A W-WHAT STORM?
P-PARANOIA. ONE OF THE MANY DANGERS OF BEING ONE OF DAVID'S ALTERS.
SOMETHING MUST 'AVE TRIGGERED IT IN HIM.
INCREDIBLE. I'VE TREATED MANY PATIENTS WITH PARANOIA... N-NOW I'VE AN IDEA... WHAT THE CONDITION ACTUALLY FEELS LIKE...
I'M DOCTOR HANNAH JONES AND I'M INSIDE THE MIND OF DAVID HALLER, A DISTURBED YOUNG MAN WHO BEGGED FOR MY HELP.
FOR THE FIRST TIME IN MY CAREER, I THINK I'M OUT OF MY DEPTH...
HGNH! AHH...INSIDE ME... THE WORDS...THE CRAZY WORDS...
H-HOW DO WE GET AWAY FROM THIS, TAMI...? HOW DO WE SAVE OURSELVES?
WE RUN, MA PETITE.
A-AND IF YOU VALUE Y-YOUR SANITY... DON'T LISTEN TO THE STORM...

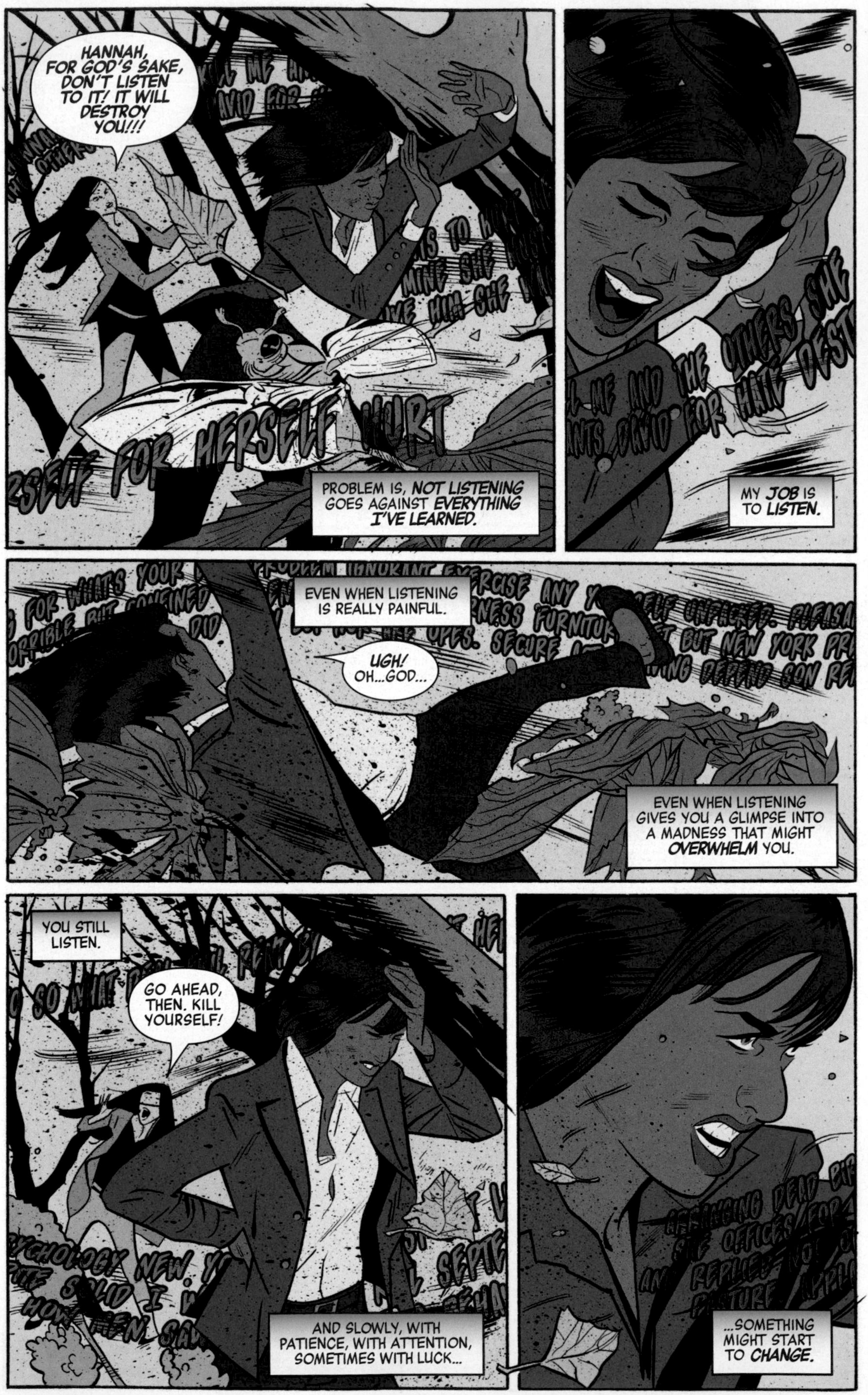
HANNAH, FOR GOD'S SAKE, DON'T LISTEN TO IT! IT WILL DESTROY YOU!!!
FOR HERSELF HURT
PROBLEM IS, NOT LISTENING GOES AGAINST EVERYTHING I'VE LEARNED.
MY JOB IS TO LISTEN.
EVEN WHEN LISTENING IS REALLY PAINFUL.
UGH! OH...GOD...
EVEN WHEN LISTENING GIVES YOU A GLIMPSE INTO A MADNESS THAT MIGHT OVERWHELM YOU.
YOU STILL LISTEN.
GO AHEAD, THEN. KILL YOURSELF!
AND SLOWLY, WITH PATIENCE, WITH ATTENTION, SOMETIMES WITH LUCK...
...SOMETHING MIGHT START TO CHANGE.

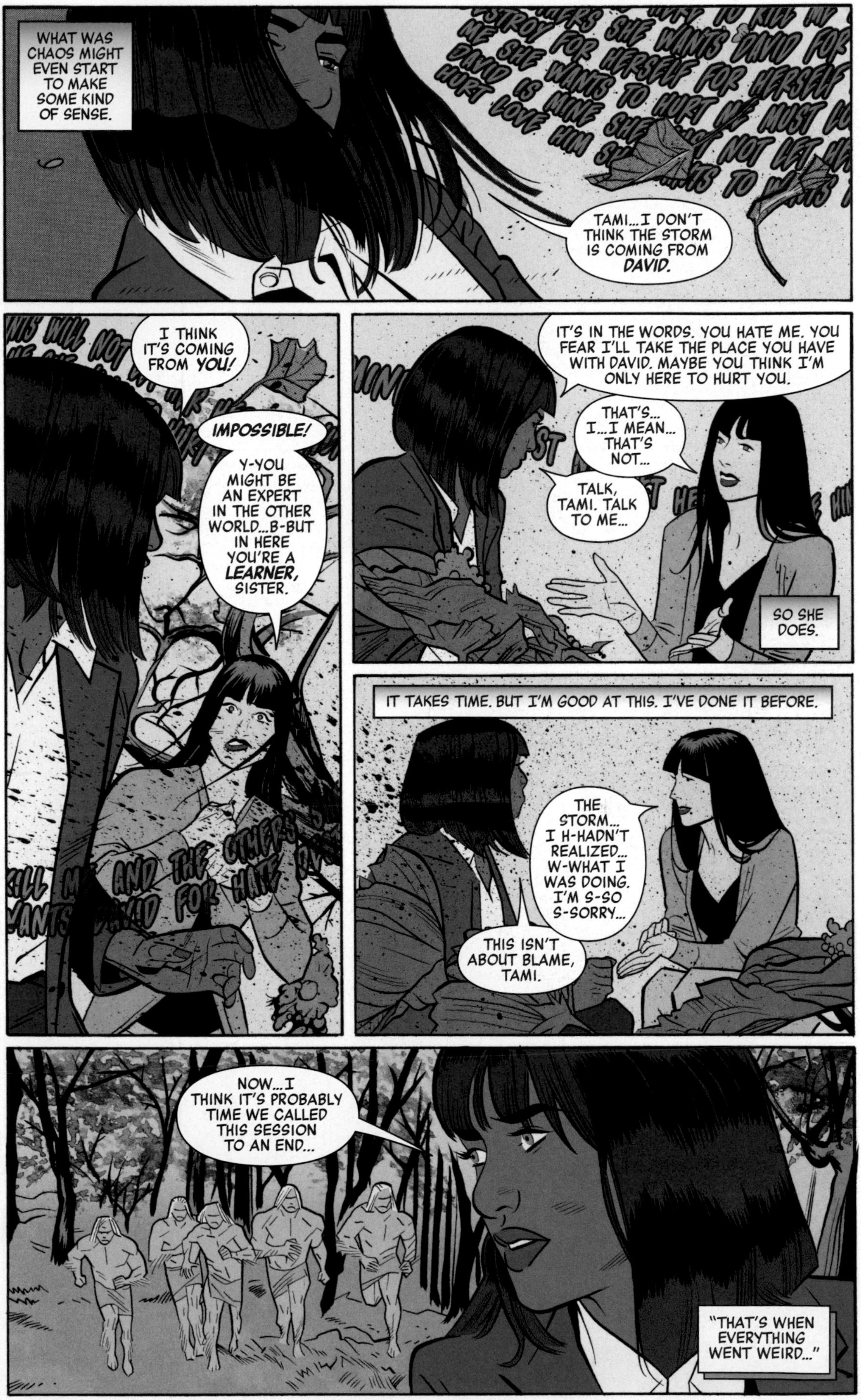
WHAT WAS CHAOS MIGHT EVEN START TO MAKE SOME KIND OF SENSE.
TAMI...I DON'T THINK THE STORM IS COMING FROM DAVID.
I THINK IT'S COMING FROM YOU!
IMPOSSIBLE!
Y-YOU MIGHT BE AN EXPERT IN THE OTHER WORLD...B-BUT IN HERE YOU'RE A LEARNER, SISTER.
IT'S IN THE WORDS. YOU HATE ME. YOU FEAR I'LL TAKE THE PLACE YOU HAVE WITH DAVID. MAYBE YOU THINK I'M ONLY HERE TO HURT YOU.
THAT'S... I...I MEAN... THAT'S NOT...
TALK, TAMI. TALK TO ME...
SO SHE DOES.
IT TAKES TIME. BUT I'M GOOD AT THIS. I'VE DONE IT BEFORE.
THE STORM... I H-HADN'T REALIZED... W-WHAT I WAS DOING. I'M S-SO S-SORRY...
THIS ISN'T ABOUT BLAME, TAMI.
NOW...I THINK IT'S PROBABLY TIME WE CALLED THIS SESSION TO AN END...
"THAT'S WHEN EVERYTHING WENT WEIRD..."

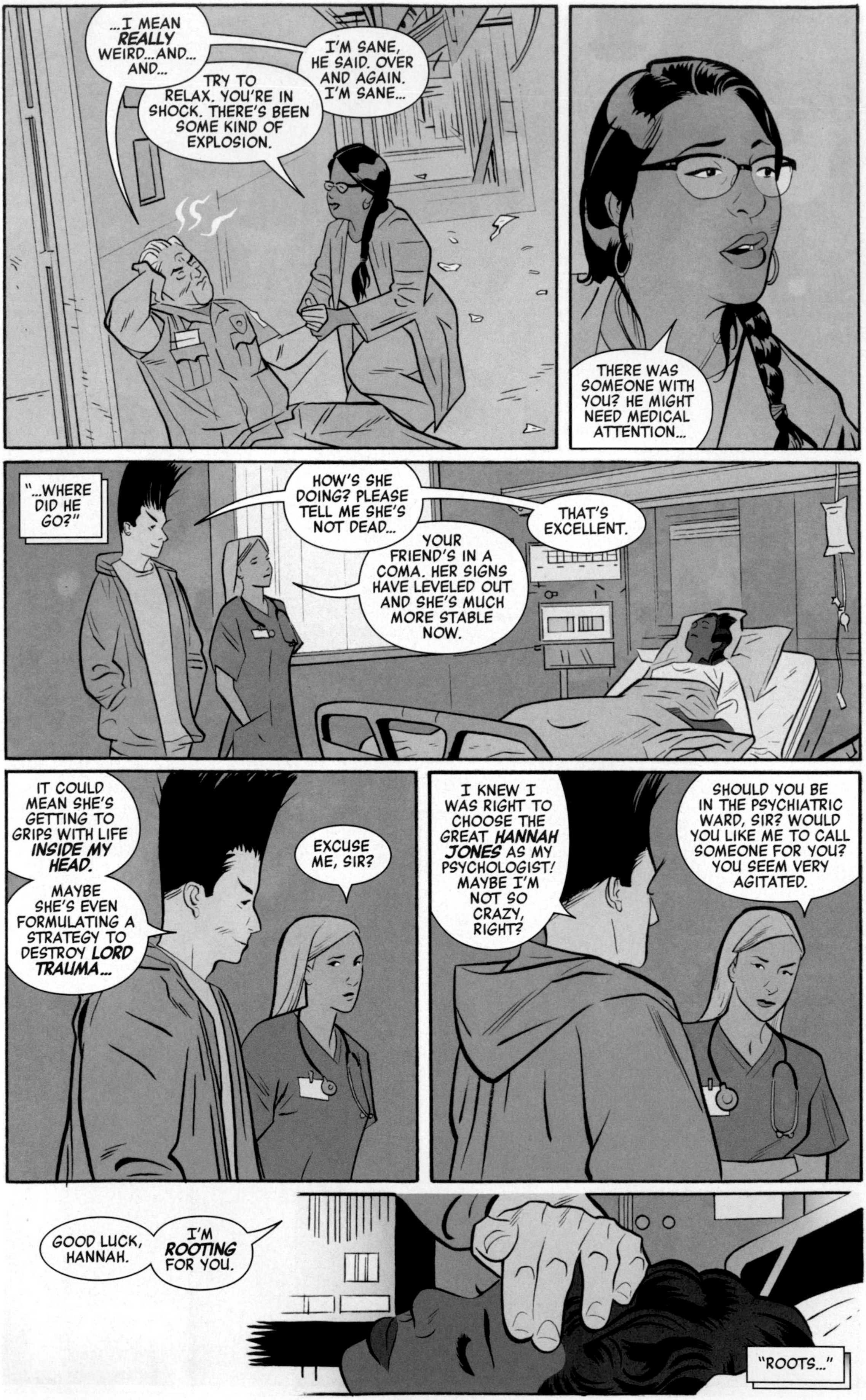
...I MEAN REALLY WEIRD...AND... AND...
I'M SANE, HE SAID. OVER AND AGAIN. I'M SANE...
TRY TO RELAX. YOU'RE IN SHOCK. THERE'S BEEN SOME KIND OF EXPLOSION.
THERE WAS SOMEONE WITH YOU? HE MIGHT NEED MEDICAL ATTENTION...
"...WHERE DID HE GO?"
HOW'S SHE DOING? PLEASE TELL ME SHE'S NOT DEAD...
YOUR FRIEND'S IN A COMA. HER SIGNS HAVE LEVELED OUT AND SHE'S MUCH MORE STABLE NOW.
THAT'S EXCELLENT.
IT COULD MEAN SHE'S GETTING TO GRIPS WITH LIFE INSIDE MY HEAD.
MAYBE SHE'S EVEN FORMULATING A STRATEGY TO DESTROY LORD TRAUMA...
EXCUSE ME, SIR?
I KNEW I WAS RIGHT TO CHOOSE THE GREAT HANNAH JONES AS MY PSYCHOLOGIST! MAYBE I'M NOT SO CRAZY, RIGHT?
SHOULD YOU BE IN THE PSYCHIATRIC WARD, SIR? WOULD YOU LIKE ME TO CALL SOMEONE FOR YOU? YOU SEEM VERY AGITATED.
GOOD LUCK, HANNAH.
I'M ROOTING FOR YOU.
"ROOTS..."

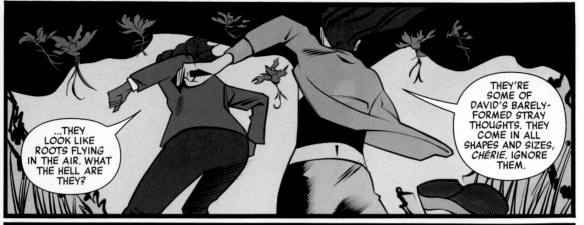

...THEY LOOK LIKE ROOTS FLYING IN THE AIR. WHAT THE HELL ARE THEY?

THEY'RE SOME OF DAVID'S BARELY-FORMED STRAY THOUGHTS. THEY COME IN ALL SHAPES AND SIZES, *CHÉRIE*. IGNORE THEM.

IT'S IMPOSSIBLE TO KNOW WHERE THEY'LL FLOAT OFF TO.

IN MY EXPERIENCE, EVEN STRAY AND SEEMINGLY UNIMPORTANT THOUGHTS MIGHT LEAD YOU TO *IMPORTANT INSIGHTS*...

HOLD ON TO ME!

HANNAH!

COME ON, TAMI!

W-WHAT NOW?

TELL ME, WHO IS DAVID'S MOST POWERFUL ALTER?

THAT IS *HUNTER*--A HIGHLY POWERFUL LONER WHO WAS CREATED WHEN POOR *JACK WAYNE* DIED. HE SCARES ME ALMOST AS MUCH AS LORD TRAUMA DOES...

GOOD.

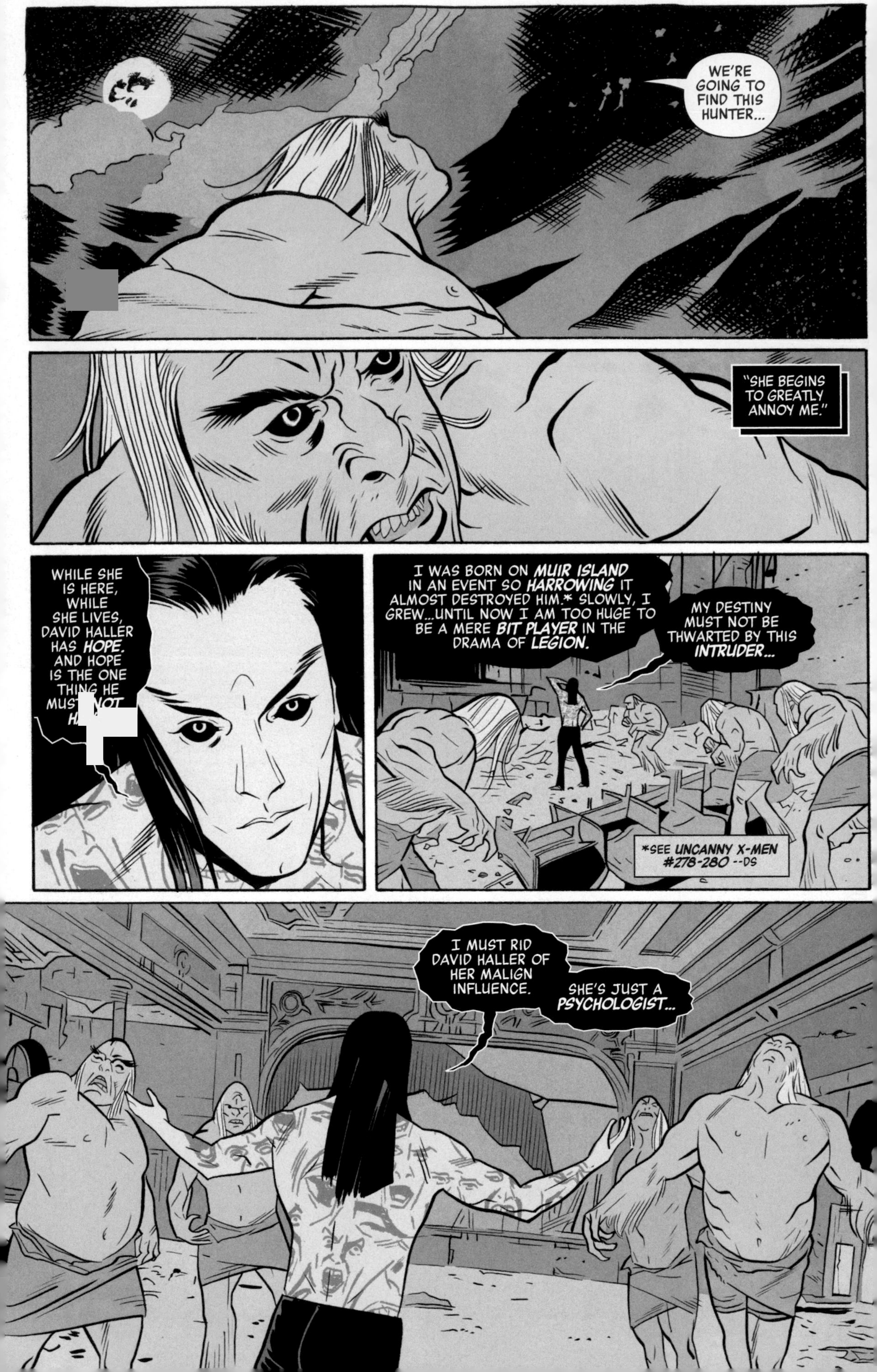
WE'RE GOING TO FIND THIS HUNTER...
"SHE BEGINS TO GREATLY ANNOY ME."
WHILE SHE IS HERE, WHILE SHE LIVES, DAVID HALLER HAS HOPE. AND HOPE IS THE ONE THING HE MUST NOT
I WAS BORN ON MUIR ISLAND IN AN EVENT SO HARROWING IT ALMOST DESTROYED HIM.* SLOWLY, I GREW...UNTIL NOW I AM TOO HUGE TO BE A MERE BIT PLAYER IN THE DRAMA OF LEGION.
MY DESTINY MUST NOT BE THWARTED BY THIS INTRUDER...
*SEE UNCANNY X-MEN #278-280 --DS
I MUST RID DAVID HALLER OF HER MALIGN INFLUENCE.
SHE'S JUST A PSYCHOLOGIST...

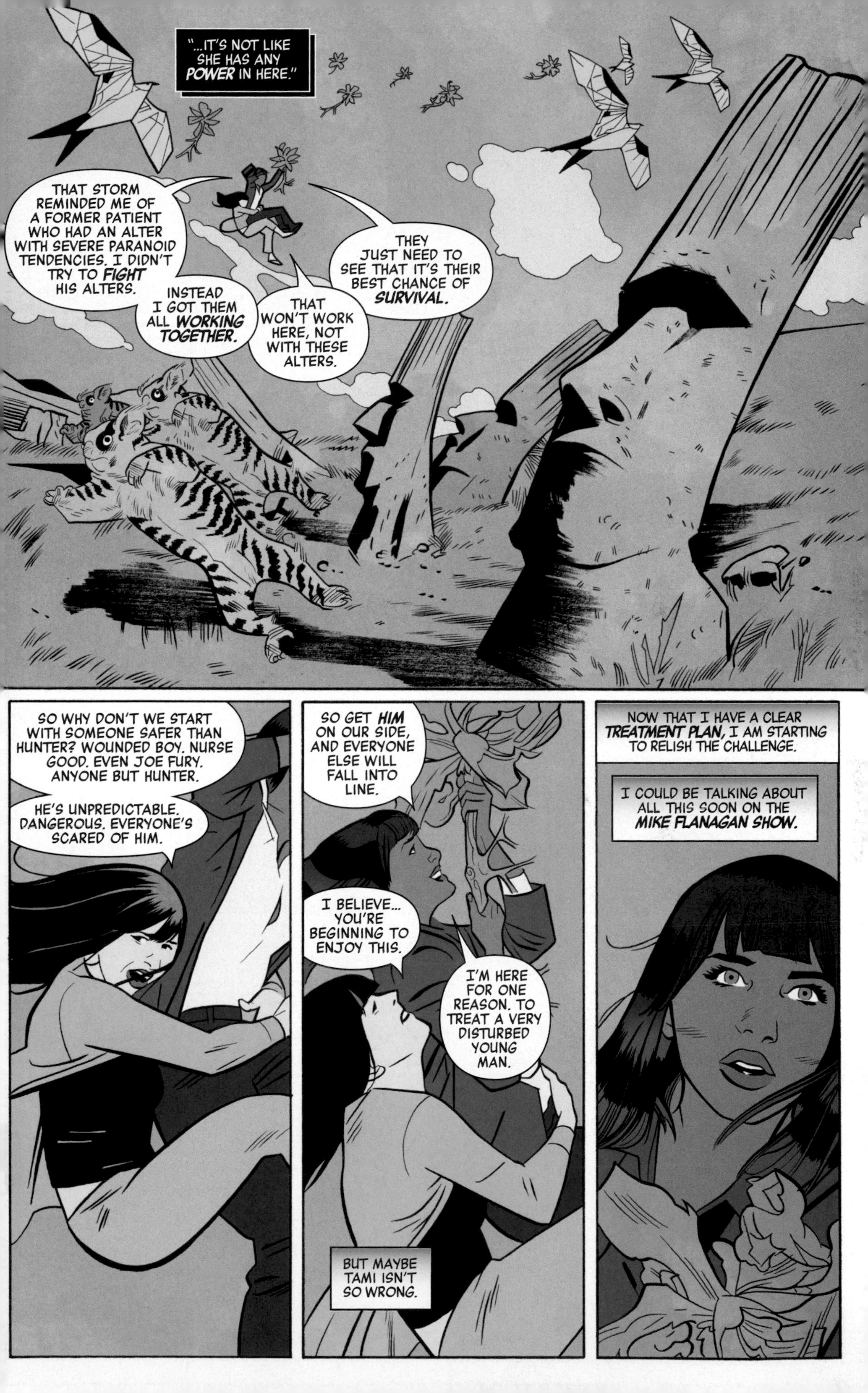
"...IT'S NOT LIKE SHE HAS ANY POWER IN HERE."
THAT STORM REMINDED ME OF A FORMER PATIENT WHO HAD AN ALTER WITH SEVERE PARANOID TENDENCIES. I DIDN'T TRY TO FIGHT HIS ALTERS.
INSTEAD I GOT THEM ALL WORKING TOGETHER.
THEY JUST NEED TO SEE THAT IT'S THEIR BEST CHANCE OF SURVIVAL.
THAT WON'T WORK HERE, NOT WITH THESE ALTERS.
SO WHY DON'T WE START WITH SOMEONE SAFER THAN HUNTER? WOUNDED BOY. NURSE GOOD. EVEN JOE FURY. ANYONE BUT HUNTER.
HE'S UNPREDICTABLE. DANGEROUS. EVERYONE'S SCARED OF HIM.
SO GET HIM ON OUR SIDE, AND EVERYONE ELSE WILL FALL INTO LINE.
I BELIEVE... YOU'RE BEGINNING TO ENJOY THIS.
I'M HERE FOR ONE REASON. TO TREAT A VERY DISTURBED YOUNG MAN.
BUT MAYBE TAMI ISN'T SO WRONG.
NOW THAT I HAVE A CLEAR TREATMENT PLAN, I AM STARTING TO RELISH THE CHALLENGE.
I COULD BE TALKING ABOUT ALL THIS SOON ON THE MIKE FLANAGAN SHOW.

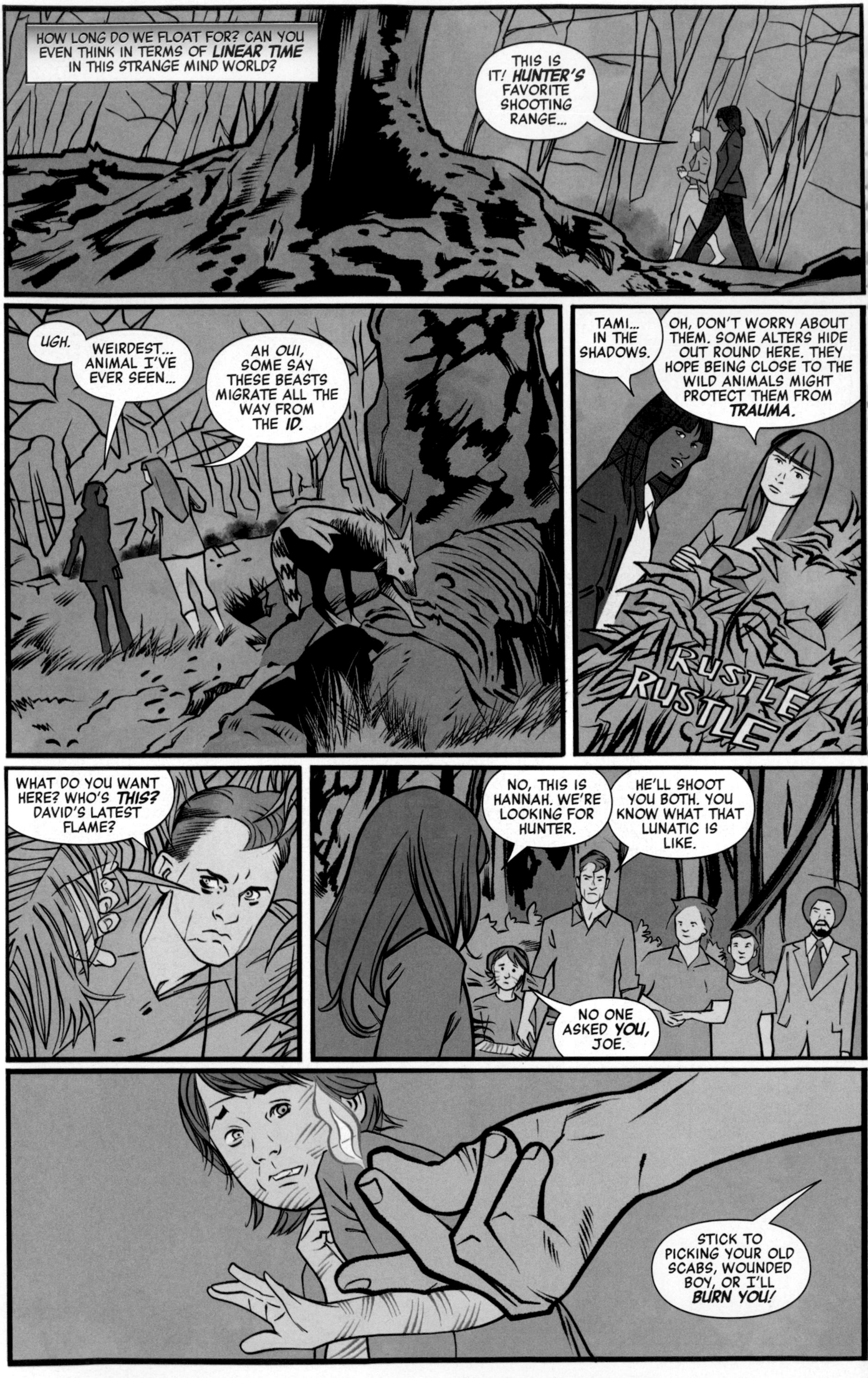
HOW LONG DO WE FLOAT FOR? CAN YOU EVEN THINK IN TERMS OF LINEAR TIME IN THIS STRANGE MIND WORLD?
THIS IS IT! HUNTER'S FAVORITE SHOOTING RANGE...
UGH.
WEIRDEST... ANIMAL I'VE EVER SEEN...
AH OUI, SOME SAY THESE BEASTS MIGRATE ALL THE WAY FROM THE ID.
TAMI... IN THE SHADOWS.
OH, DON'T WORRY ABOUT THEM. SOME ALTERS HIDE OUT ROUND HERE. THEY HOPE BEING CLOSE TO THE WILD ANIMALS MIGHT PROTECT THEM FROM TRAUMA.
RUSTLE RUSTLE
WHAT DO YOU WANT HERE? WHO'S THIS? DAVID'S LATEST FLAME?
NO, THIS IS HANNAH. WE'RE LOOKING FOR HUNTER.
HE'LL SHOOT YOU BOTH. YOU KNOW WHAT THAT LUNATIC IS LIKE.
NO ONE ASKED YOU, JOE.
STICK TO PICKING YOUR OLD SCABS, WOUNDED BOY, OR I'LL BURN YOU!

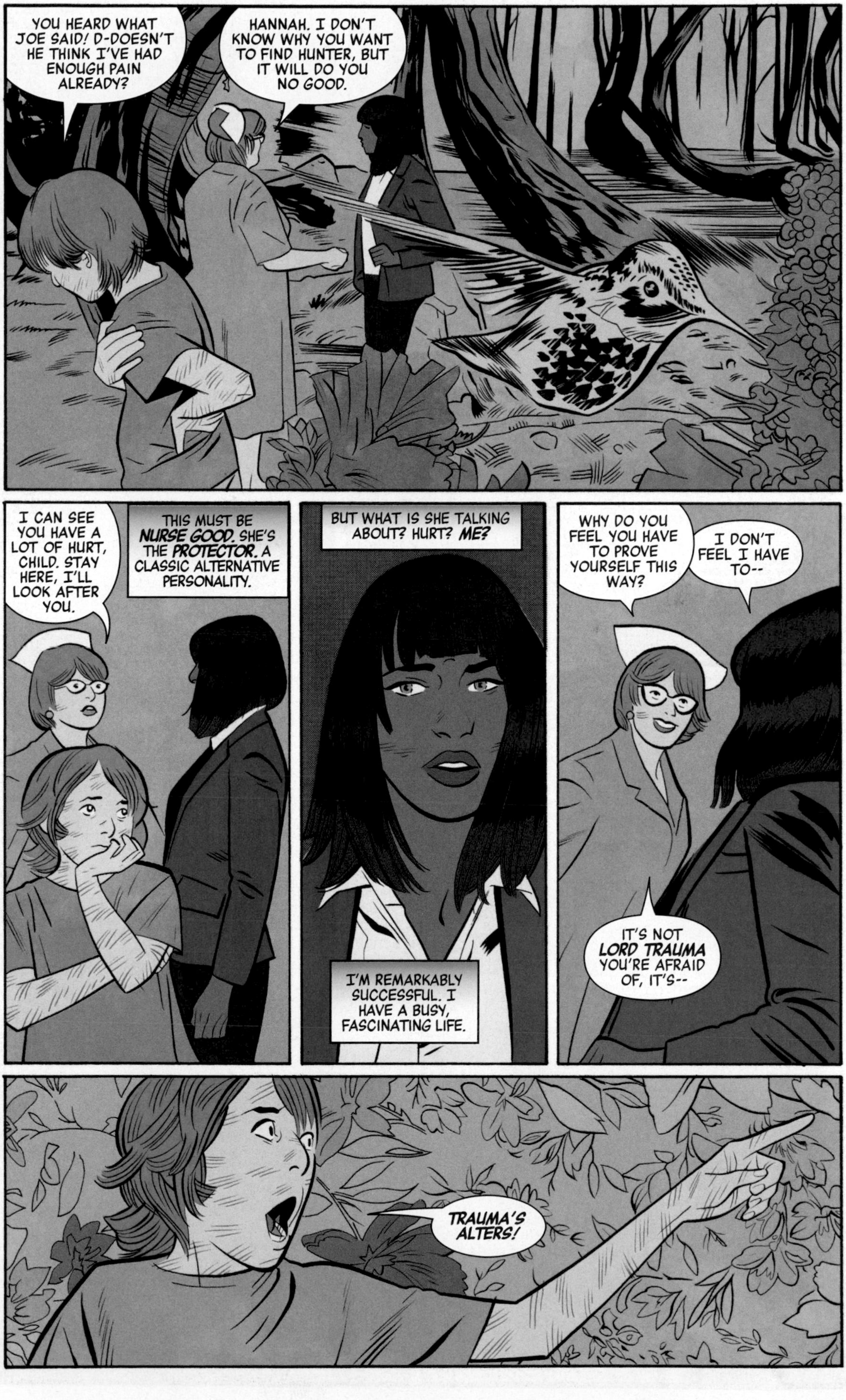
YOU HEARD WHAT JOE SAID! D-DOESN'T HE THINK I'VE HAD ENOUGH PAIN ALREADY?
HANNAH. I DON'T KNOW WHY YOU WANT TO FIND HUNTER, BUT IT WILL DO YOU NO GOOD.
I CAN SEE YOU HAVE A LOT OF HURT, CHILD. STAY HERE, I'LL LOOK AFTER YOU.
THIS MUST BE NURSE GOOD. SHE'S THE PROTECTOR. A CLASSIC ALTERNATIVE PERSONALITY.
BUT WHAT IS SHE TALKING ABOUT? HURT? ME?
I'M REMARKABLY SUCCESSFUL. I HAVE A BUSY, FASCINATING LIFE.
WHY DO YOU FEEL YOU HAVE TO PROVE YOURSELF THIS WAY?
I DON'T FEEL I HAVE TO--
IT'S NOT LORD TRAUMA YOU'RE AFRAID OF, IT'S--
TRAUMA'S ALTERS!

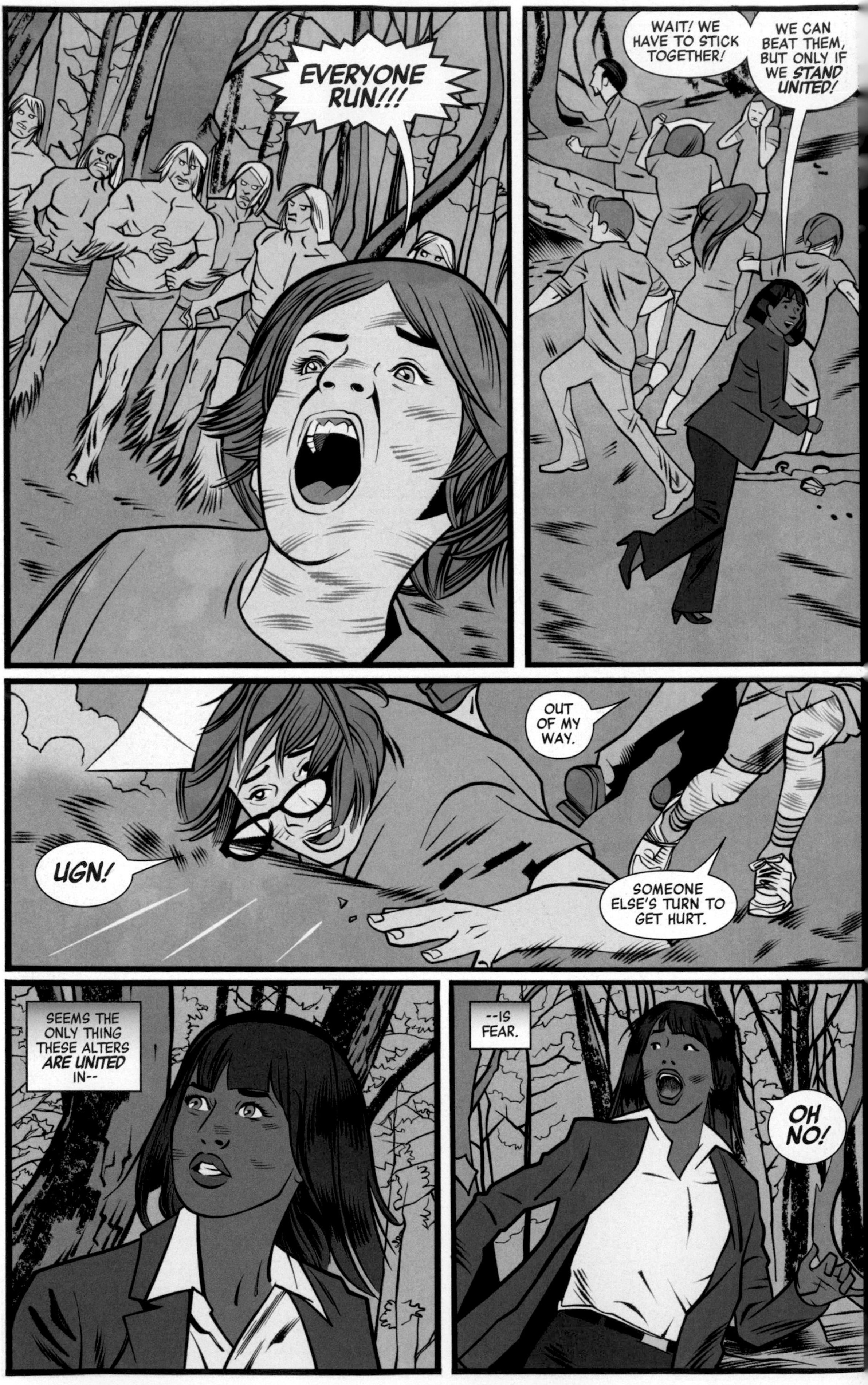
EVERYONE RUN!!!
WAIT! WE HAVE TO STICK TOGETHER!
WE CAN BEAT THEM, BUT ONLY IF WE STAND UNITED!
OUT OF MY WAY.
UGN!
SOMEONE ELSE'S TURN TO GET HURT.
SEEMS THE ONLY THING THESE ALTERS ARE UNITED IN--
--IS FEAR.
OH NO!

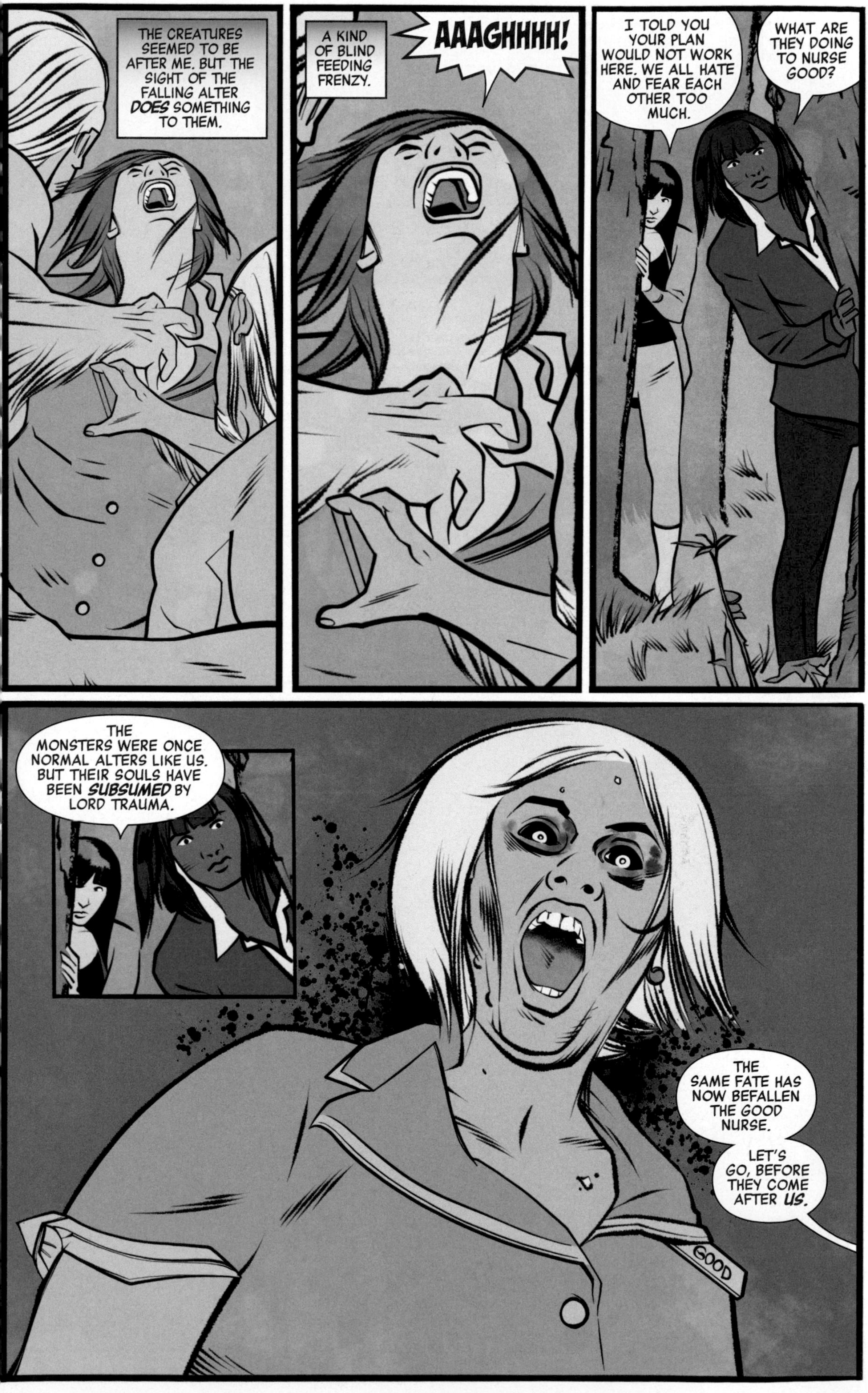
THE CREATURES SEEMED TO BE AFTER ME. BUT THE SIGHT OF THE FALLING ALTER DOES SOMETHING TO THEM.
A KIND OF BLIND FEEDING FRENZY.
AAAGHHHH!
I TOLD YOU YOUR PLAN WOULD NOT WORK HERE. WE ALL HATE AND FEAR EACH OTHER TOO MUCH.
WHAT ARE THEY DOING TO NURSE GOOD?
THE MONSTERS WERE ONCE NORMAL ALTERS LIKE US. BUT THEIR SOULS HAVE BEEN SUBSUMED BY LORD TRAUMA.
THE SAME FATE HAS NOW BEFALLEN THE GOOD NURSE.
LET'S GO, BEFORE THEY COME AFTER US.
GOOD

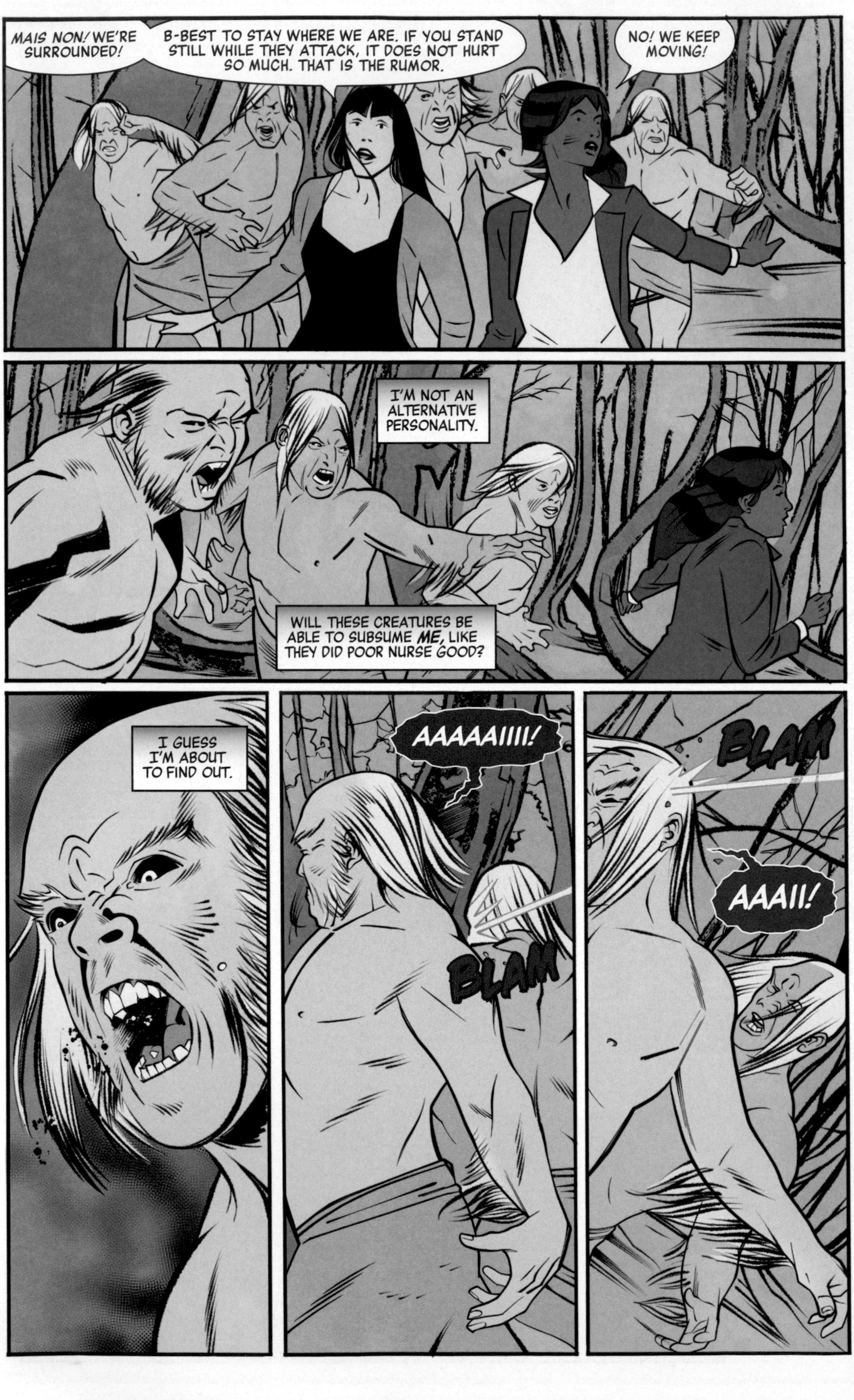
MAIS NON! WE'RE SURROUNDED!
B-BEST TO STAY WHERE WE ARE. IF YOU STAND STILL WHILE THEY ATTACK, IT DOES NOT HURT SO MUCH. THAT IS THE RUMOR.
NO! WE KEEP MOVING!
I'M NOT AN ALTERNATIVE PERSONALITY.
WILL THESE CREATURES BE ABLE TO SUBSUME ME, LIKE THEY DID POOR NURSE GOOD?
I GUESS I'M ABOUT TO FIND OUT.
AAAAAIIII!
BLAM
BLAM
AAAII!

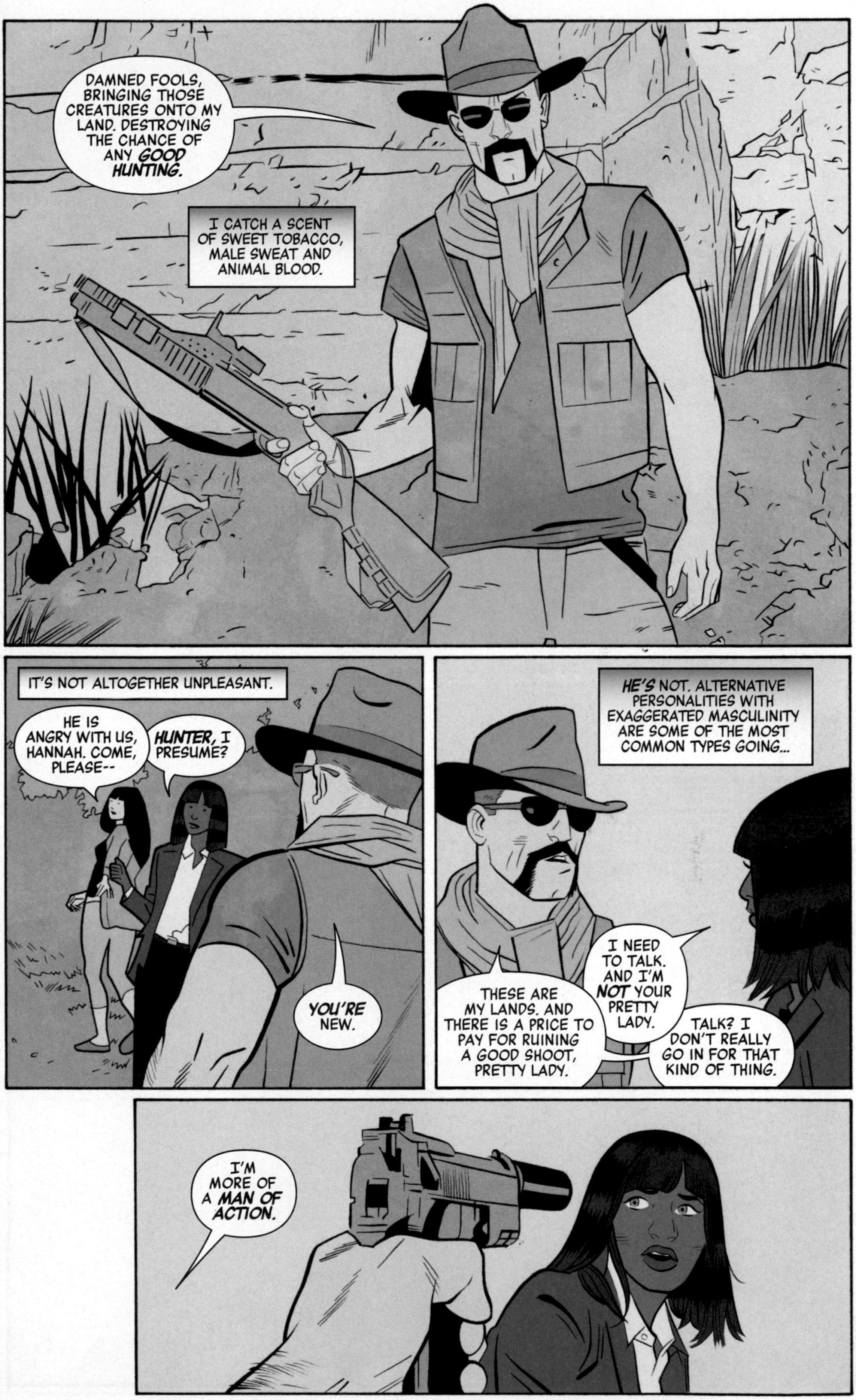
DAMNED FOOLS, BRINGING THOSE CREATURES ONTO MY LAND. DESTROYING THE CHANCE OF ANY GOOD HUNTING.
I CATCH A SCENT OF SWEET TOBACCO, MALE SWEAT AND ANIMAL BLOOD.
IT'S NOT ALTOGETHER UNPLEASANT.
HE IS ANGRY WITH US, HANNAH. COME, PLEASE--
HUNTER, I PRESUME?
YOU'RE NEW.
HE'S NOT. ALTERNATIVE PERSONALITIES WITH EXAGGERATED MASCULINITY ARE SOME OF THE MOST COMMON TYPES GOING...
THESE ARE MY LANDS. AND THERE IS A PRICE TO PAY FOR RUINING A GOOD SHOOT, PRETTY LADY.
I NEED TO TALK. AND I'M NOT YOUR PRETTY LADY.
TALK? I DON'T REALLY GO IN FOR THAT KIND OF THING.
I'M MORE OF A MAN OF ACTION.

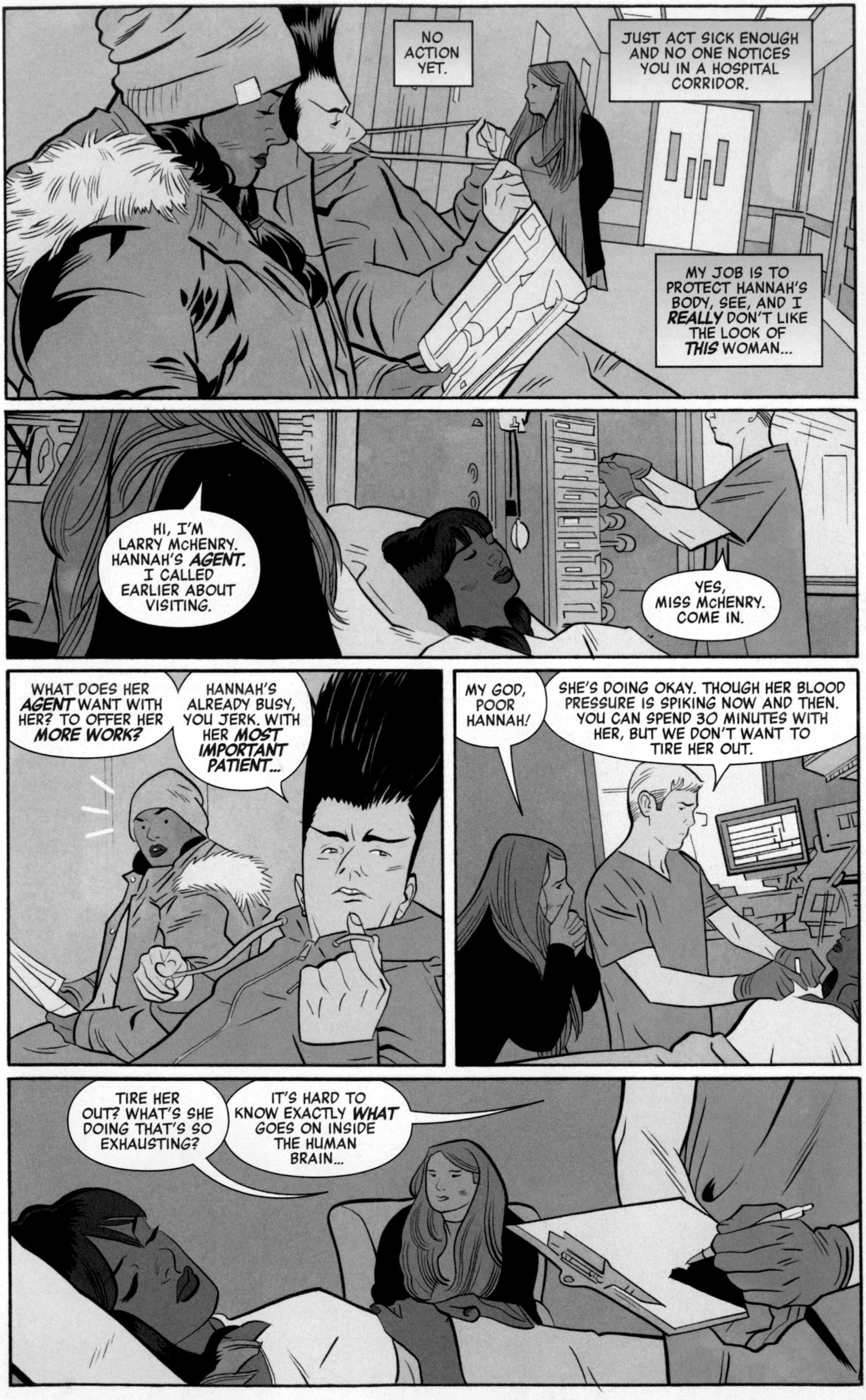
NO ACTION YET.
JUST ACT SICK ENOUGH AND NO ONE NOTICES YOU IN A HOSPITAL CORRIDOR.
MY JOB IS TO PROTECT HANNAH'S BODY, SEE, AND I *REALLY* DON'T LIKE THE LOOK OF *THIS* WOMAN...
HI, I'M LARRY McHENRY. HANNAH'S *AGENT.* I CALLED EARLIER ABOUT VISITING.
YES, MISS McHENRY. COME IN.
WHAT DOES HER *AGENT* WANT WITH HER? TO OFFER HER *MORE WORK?*
HANNAH'S ALREADY BUSY, YOU JERK. WITH HER *MOST IMPORTANT PATIENT...*
MY GOD, POOR HANNAH!
SHE'S DOING OKAY. THOUGH HER BLOOD PRESSURE IS SPIKING NOW AND THEN. YOU CAN SPEND 30 MINUTES WITH HER, BUT WE DON'T WANT TO TIRE HER OUT.
TIRE HER OUT? WHAT'S SHE DOING THAT'S SO EXHAUSTING?
IT'S HARD TO KNOW EXACTLY *WHAT* GOES ON INSIDE THE HUMAN BRAIN...

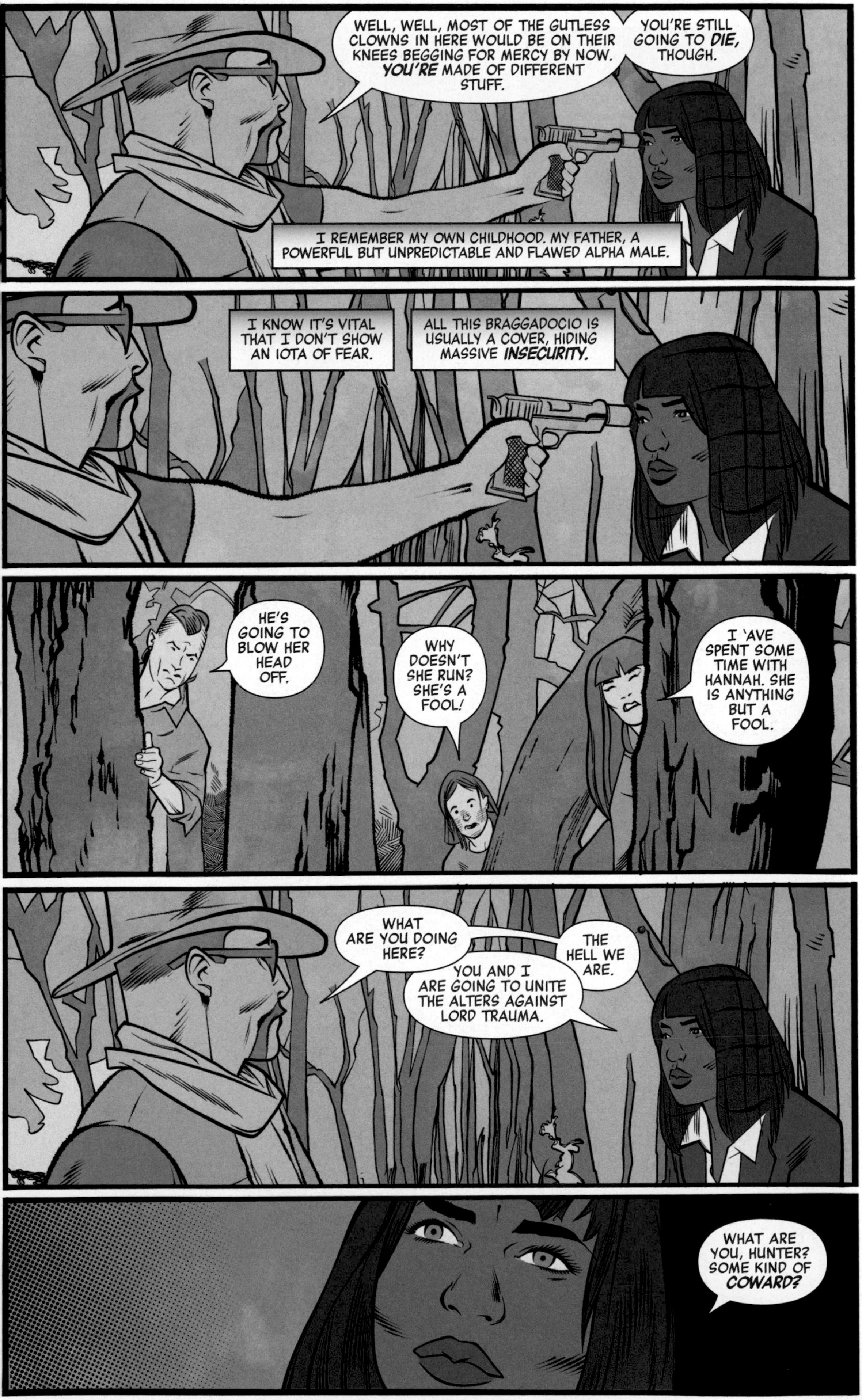
WELL, WELL, MOST OF THE GUTLESS CLOWNS IN HERE WOULD BE ON THEIR KNEES BEGGING FOR MERCY BY NOW. YOU'RE MADE OF DIFFERENT STUFF.
YOU'RE STILL GOING TO DIE, THOUGH.
I REMEMBER MY OWN CHILDHOOD. MY FATHER, A POWERFUL BUT UNPREDICTABLE AND FLAWED ALPHA MALE.
I KNOW IT'S VITAL THAT I DON'T SHOW AN IOTA OF FEAR.
ALL THIS BRAGGADOCIO IS USUALLY A COVER, HIDING MASSIVE INSECURITY.
HE'S GOING TO BLOW HER HEAD OFF.
WHY DOESN'T SHE RUN? SHE'S A FOOL!
I 'AVE SPENT SOME TIME WITH HANNAH. SHE IS ANYTHING BUT A FOOL.
WHAT ARE YOU DOING HERE?
YOU AND I ARE GOING TO UNITE THE ALTERS AGAINST LORD TRAUMA.
THE HELL WE ARE.
WHAT ARE YOU, HUNTER? SOME KIND OF COWARD?

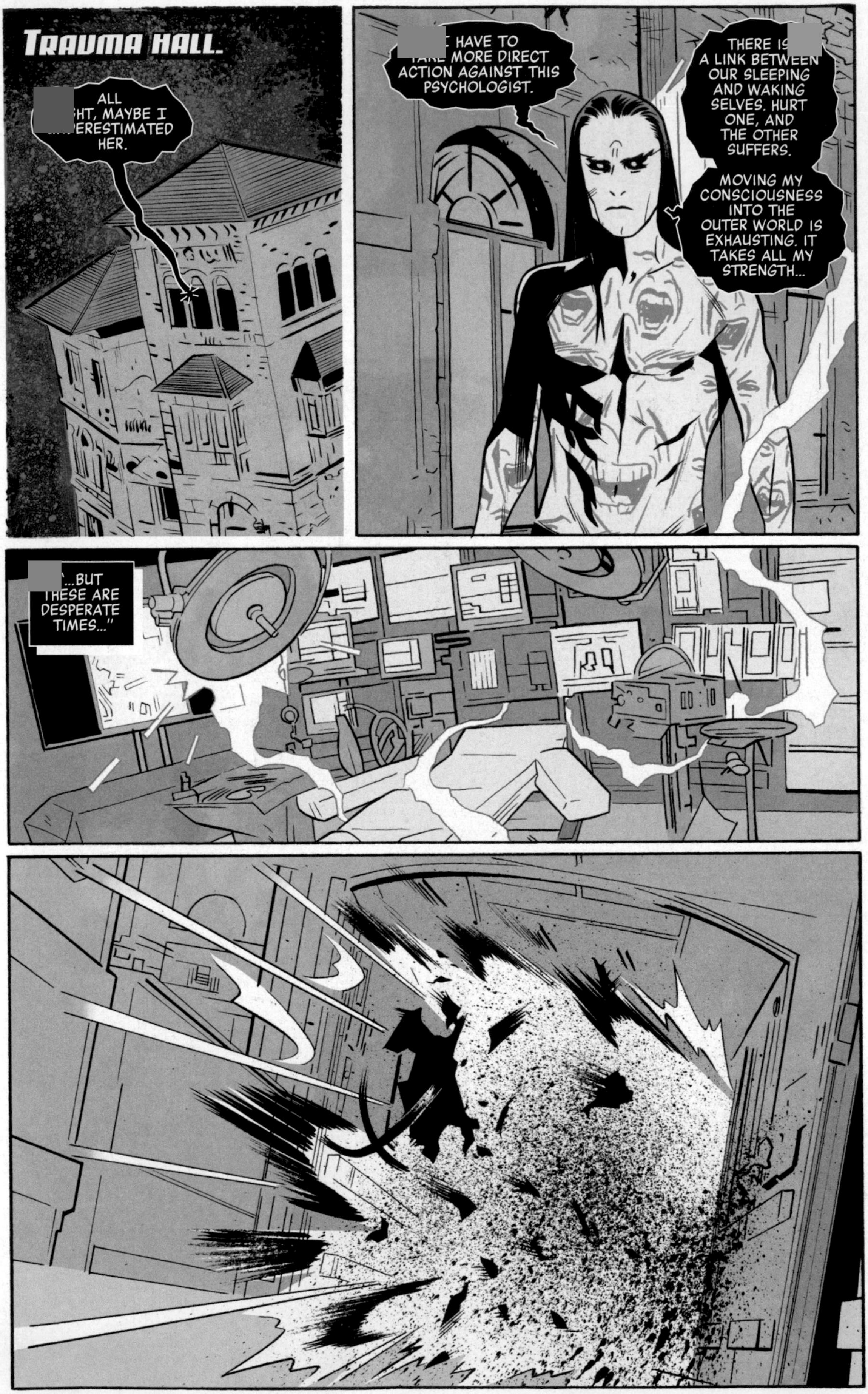
TRAUMA HALL.
[redacted] ALL [redacted]GHT, MAYBE I [redacted]ERESTIMATED HER.
[redacted] I HAVE TO [redacted]KE MORE DIRECT ACTION AGAINST THIS PSYCHOLOGIST.
THERE IS [redacted] A LINK BETWEEN OUR SLEEPING AND WAKING SELVES. HURT ONE, AND THE OTHER SUFFERS.
MOVING MY CONSCIOUSNESS INTO THE OUTER WORLD IS EXHAUSTING. IT TAKES ALL MY STRENGTH...
[redacted]...BUT THESE ARE DESPERATE TIMES..."

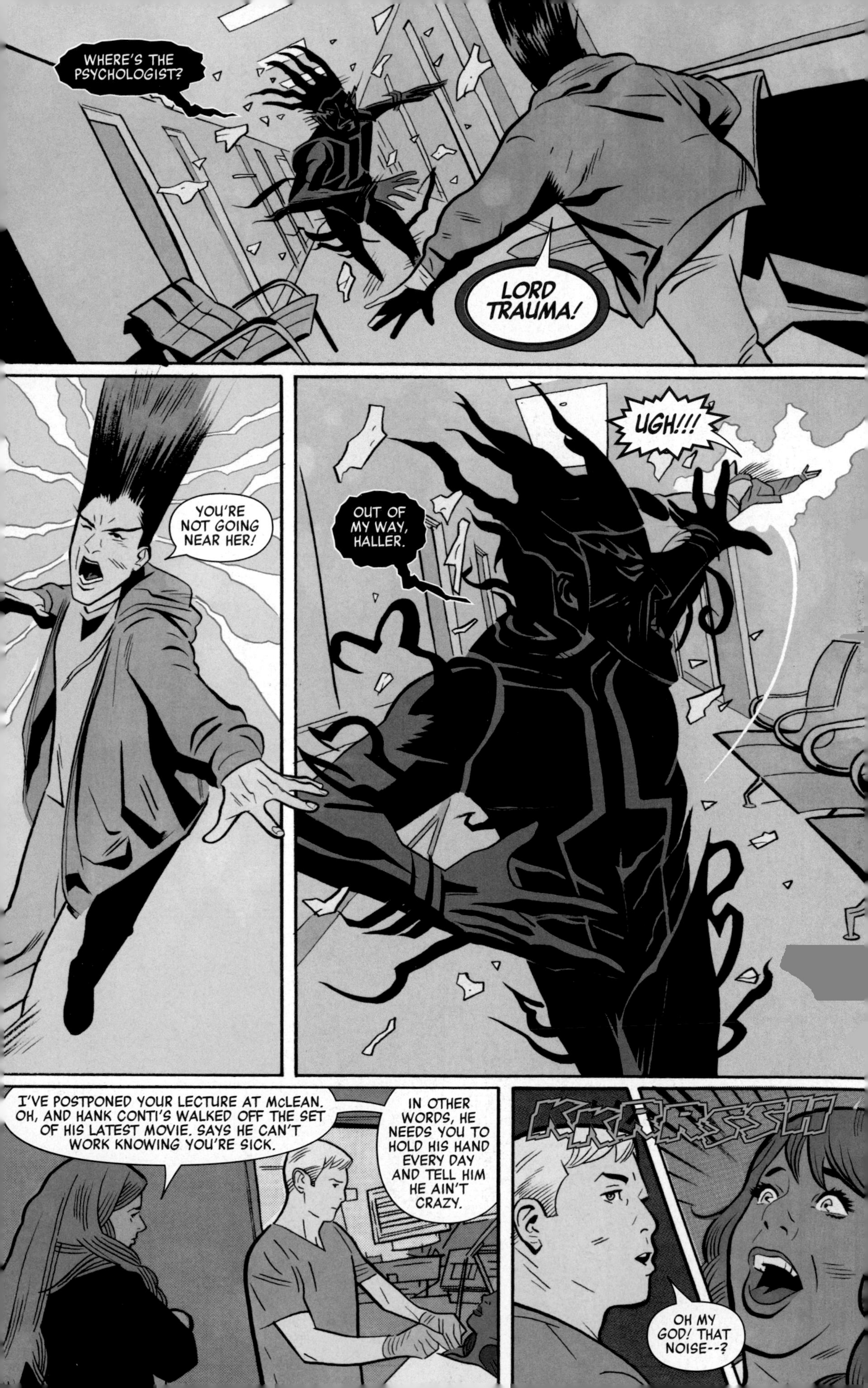
WHERE'S THE PSYCHOLOGIST?
LORD TRAUMA!
YOU'RE NOT GOING NEAR HER!
OUT OF MY WAY, HALLER.
UGH!!!
I'VE POSTPONED YOUR LECTURE AT McLEAN. OH, AND HANK CONTI'S WALKED OFF THE SET OF HIS LATEST MOVIE. SAYS HE CAN'T WORK KNOWING YOU'RE SICK.
IN OTHER WORDS, HE NEEDS YOU TO HOLD HIS HAND EVERY DAY AND TELL HIM HE AIN'T CRAZY.
KKRRSSH
OH MY GOD! THAT NOISE--?

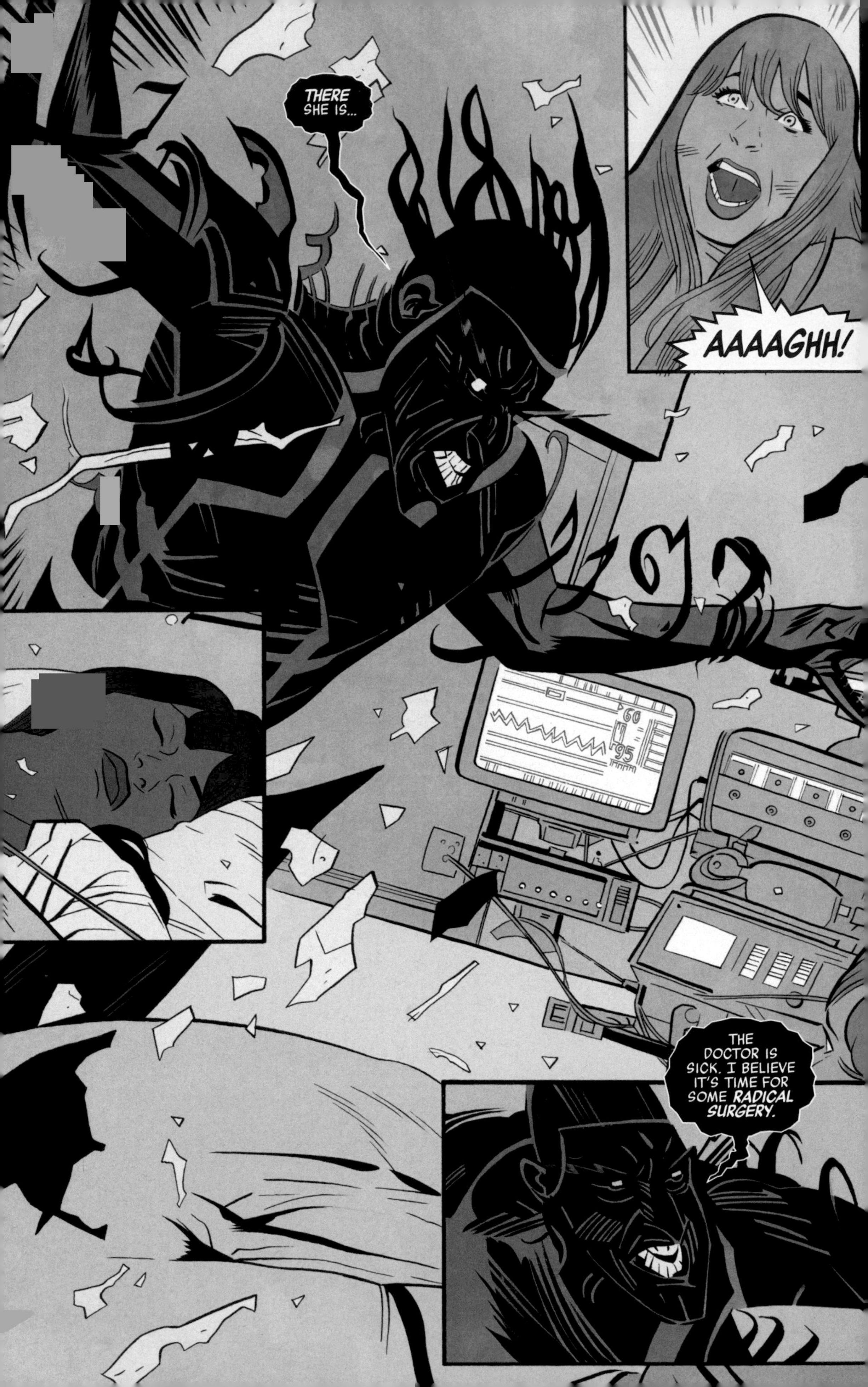
THERE SHE IS...
AAAAGHH!
THE DOCTOR IS SICK. I BELIEVE IT'S TIME FOR SOME RADICAL SURGERY.

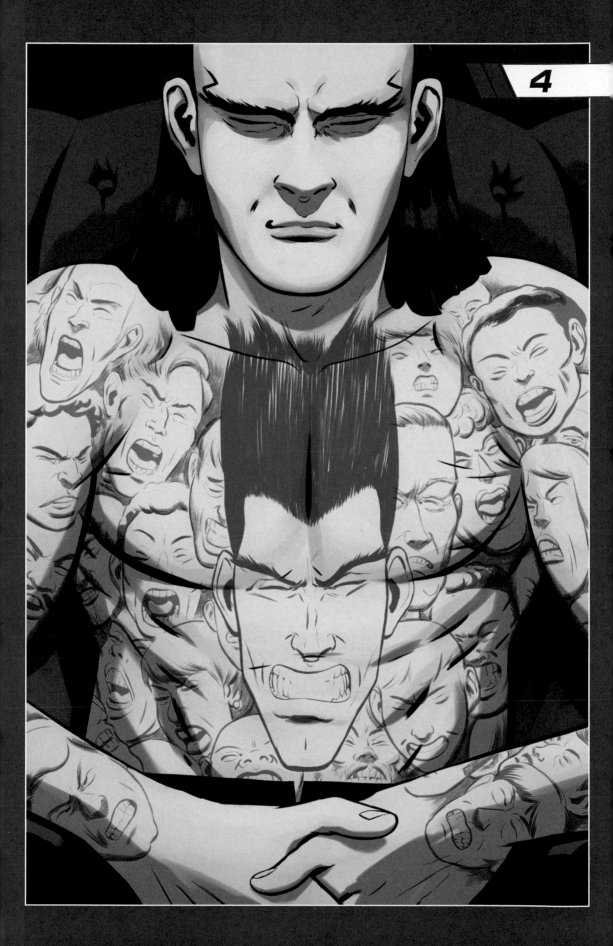

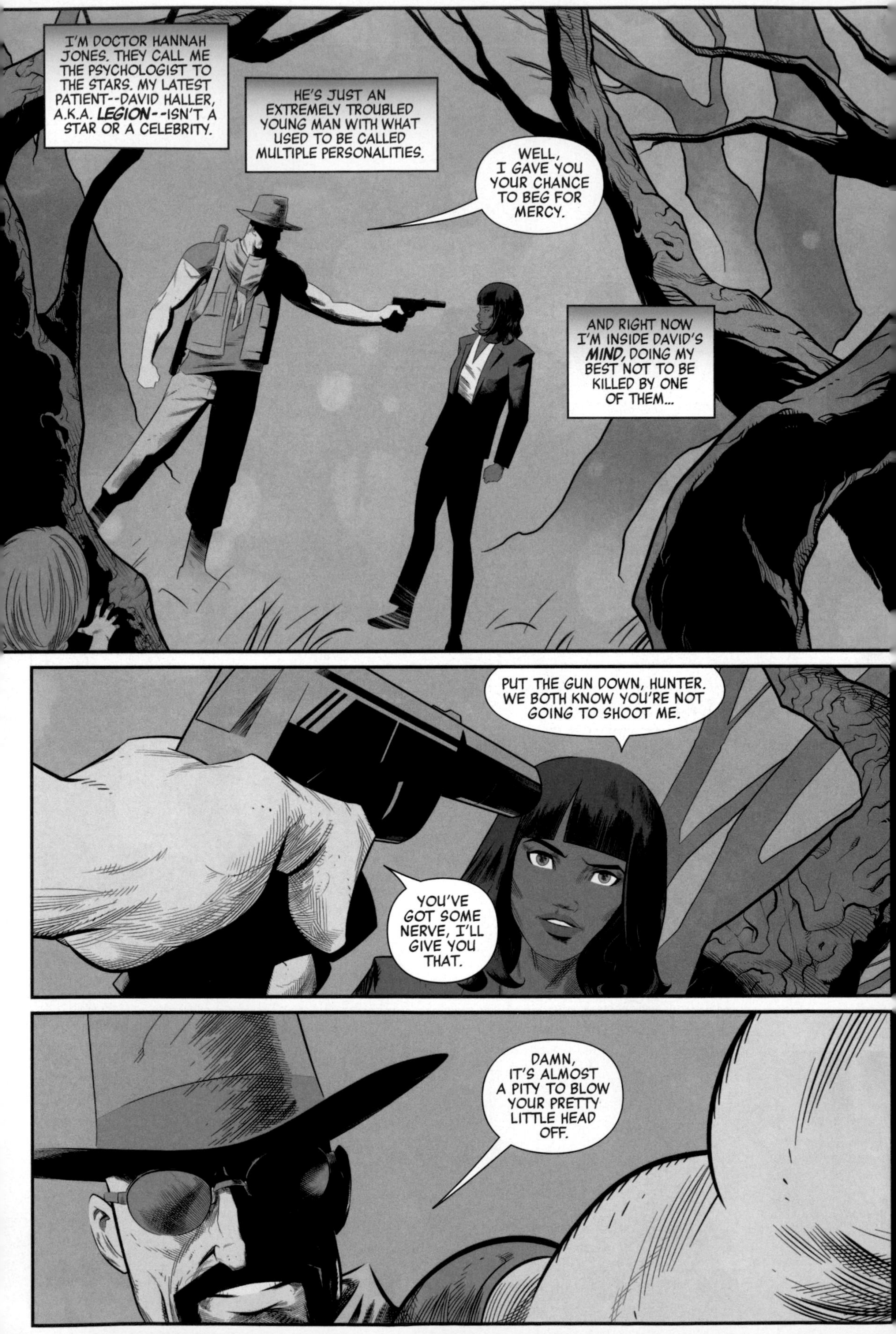
I'M DOCTOR HANNAH JONES. THEY CALL ME THE PSYCHOLOGIST TO THE STARS. MY LATEST PATIENT--DAVID HALLER, A.K.A. LEGION--ISN'T A STAR OR A CELEBRITY.
HE'S JUST AN EXTREMELY TROUBLED YOUNG MAN WITH WHAT USED TO BE CALLED MULTIPLE PERSONALITIES.
WELL, I GAVE YOU YOUR CHANCE TO BEG FOR MERCY.
AND RIGHT NOW I'M INSIDE DAVID'S MIND, DOING MY BEST NOT TO BE KILLED BY ONE OF THEM...
PUT THE GUN DOWN, HUNTER. WE BOTH KNOW YOU'RE NOT GOING TO SHOOT ME.
YOU'VE GOT SOME NERVE, I'LL GIVE YOU THAT.
DAMN, IT'S ALMOST A PITY TO BLOW YOUR PRETTY LITTLE HEAD OFF.

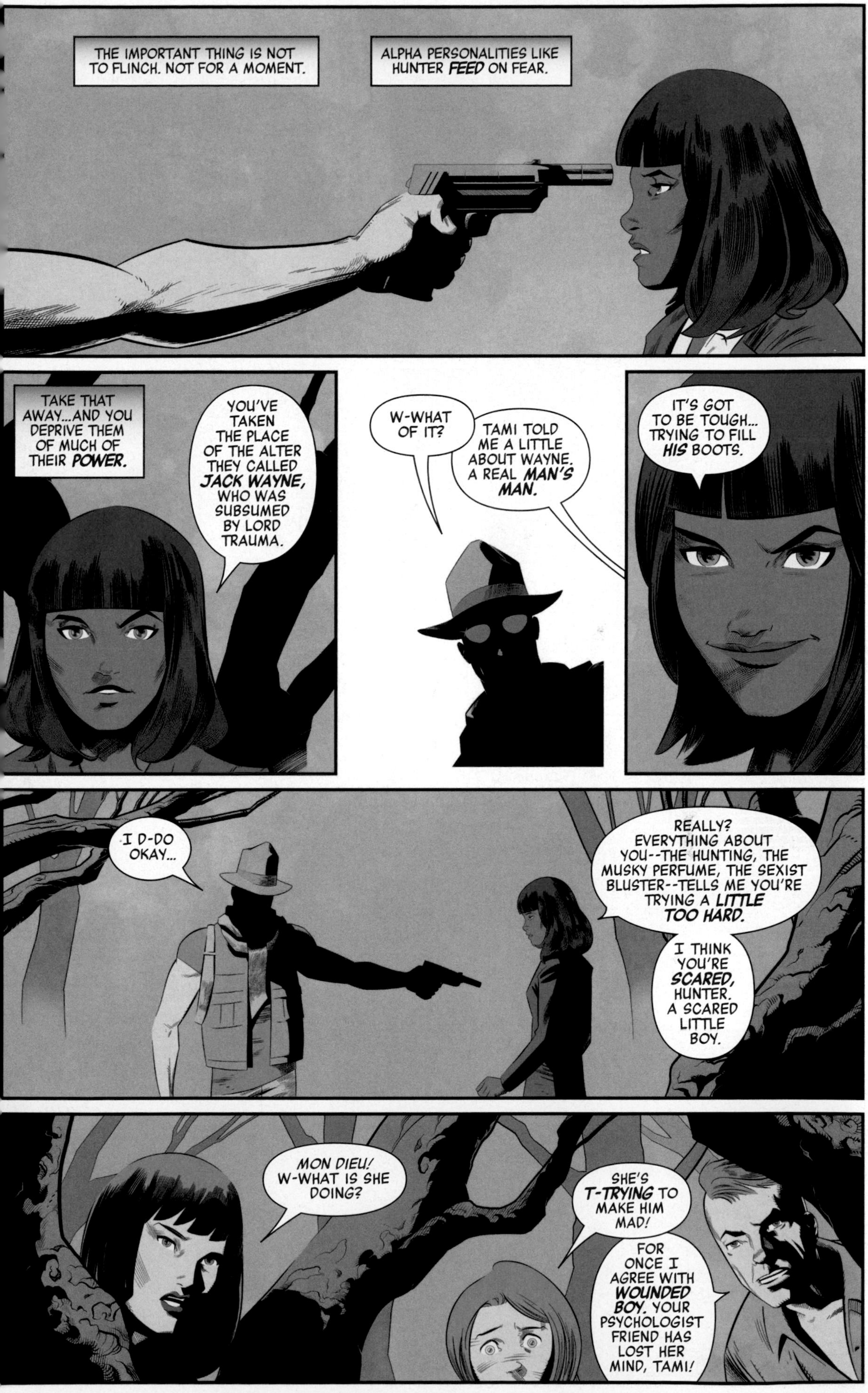
THE IMPORTANT THING IS NOT TO FLINCH. NOT FOR A MOMENT.
ALPHA PERSONALITIES LIKE HUNTER FEED ON FEAR.
TAKE THAT AWAY...AND YOU DEPRIVE THEM OF MUCH OF THEIR POWER.
YOU'VE TAKEN THE PLACE OF THE ALTER THEY CALLED JACK WAYNE, WHO WAS SUBSUMED BY LORD TRAUMA.
W-WHAT OF IT?
TAMI TOLD ME A LITTLE ABOUT WAYNE. A REAL MAN'S MAN.
IT'S GOT TO BE TOUGH... TRYING TO FILL HIS BOOTS.
I D-DO OKAY...
REALLY? EVERYTHING ABOUT YOU--THE HUNTING, THE MUSKY PERFUME, THE SEXIST BLUSTER--TELLS ME YOU'RE TRYING A LITTLE TOO HARD.
I THINK YOU'RE SCARED, HUNTER. A SCARED LITTLE BOY.
MON DIEU! W-WHAT IS SHE DOING?
SHE'S T-TRYING TO MAKE HIM MAD!
FOR ONCE I AGREE WITH WOUNDED BOY. YOUR PSYCHOLOGIST FRIEND HAS LOST HER MIND, TAMI!

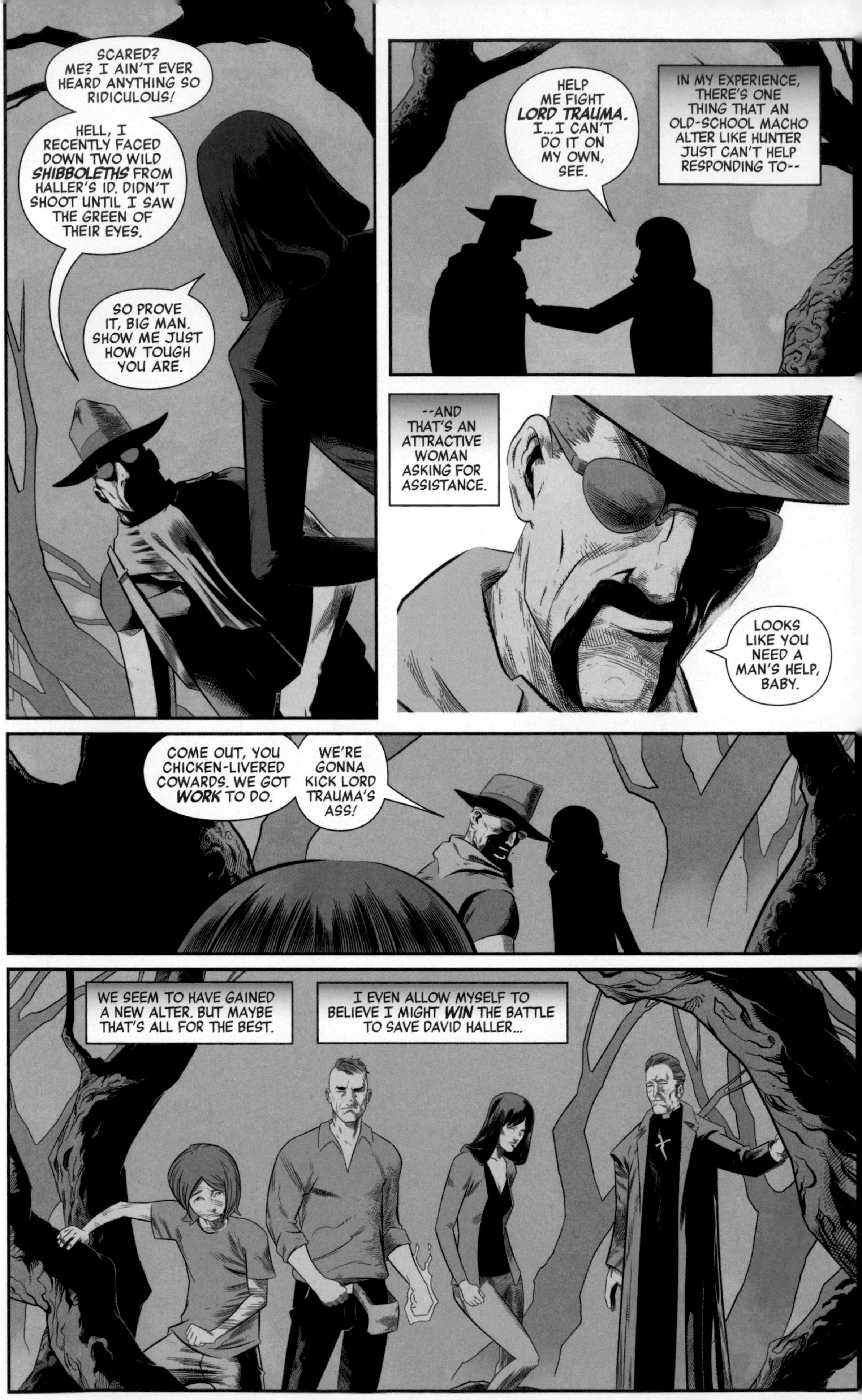

SCARED? ME? I AIN'T EVER HEARD ANYTHING SO RIDICULOUS!
HELL, I RECENTLY FACED DOWN TWO WILD SHIBBOLETHS FROM HALLER'S ID. DIDN'T SHOOT UNTIL I SAW THE GREEN OF THEIR EYES.
SO PROVE IT, BIG MAN. SHOW ME JUST HOW TOUGH YOU ARE.
HELP ME FIGHT LORD TRAUMA. I...I CAN'T DO IT ON MY OWN, SEE.
IN MY EXPERIENCE, THERE'S ONE THING THAT AN OLD-SCHOOL MACHO ALTER LIKE HUNTER JUST CAN'T HELP RESPONDING TO--
--AND THAT'S AN ATTRACTIVE WOMAN ASKING FOR ASSISTANCE.
LOOKS LIKE YOU NEED A MAN'S HELP, BABY.
COME OUT, YOU CHICKEN-LIVERED COWARDS. WE GOT WORK TO DO.
WE'RE GONNA KICK LORD TRAUMA'S ASS!
WE SEEM TO HAVE GAINED A NEW ALTER. BUT MAYBE THAT'S ALL FOR THE BEST.
I EVEN ALLOW MYSELF TO BELIEVE I MIGHT WIN THE BATTLE TO SAVE DAVID HALLER...

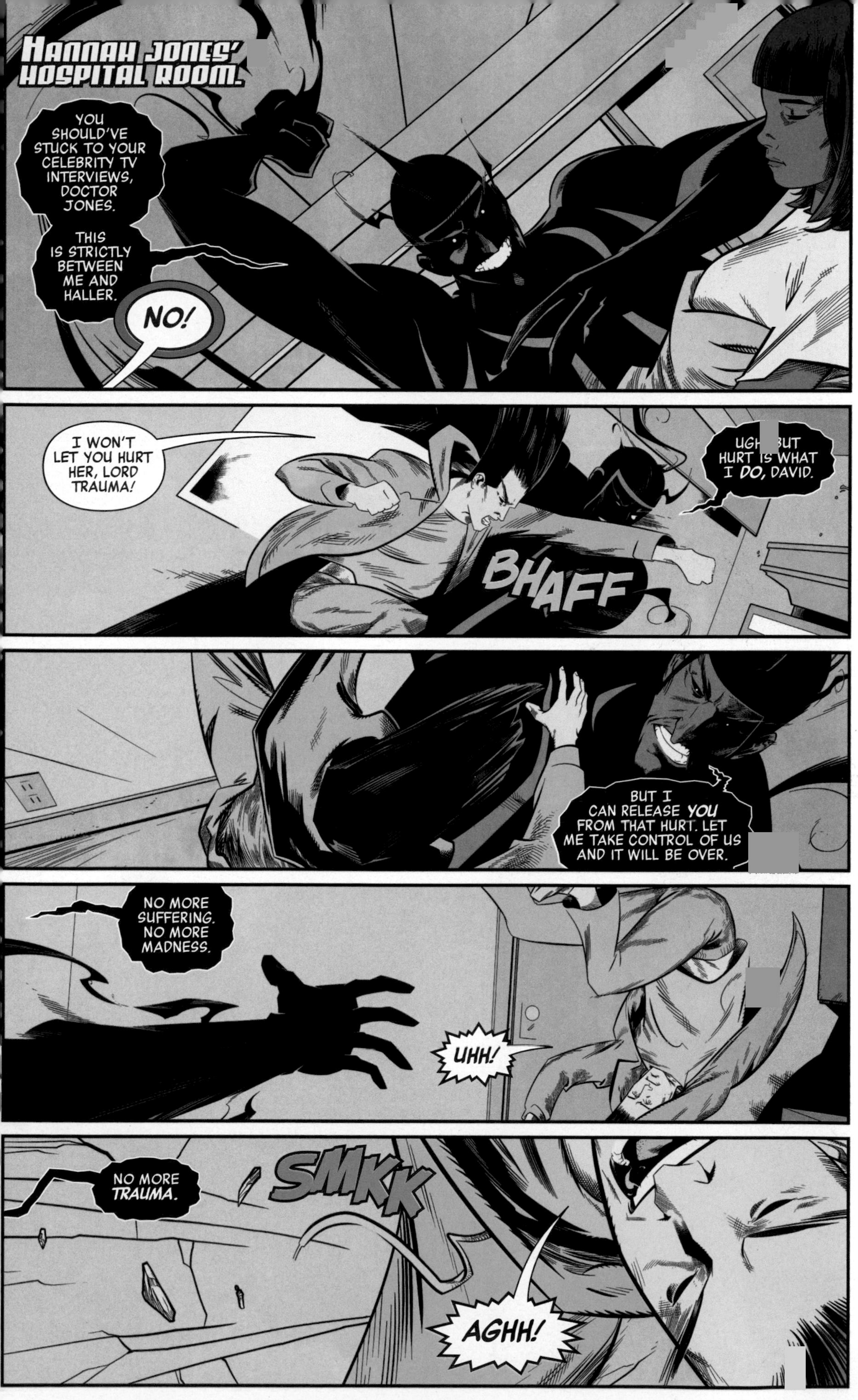

HANNAH JONES' HOSPITAL ROOM.
YOU SHOULD'VE STUCK TO YOUR CELEBRITY TV INTERVIEWS, DOCTOR JONES.
THIS IS STRICTLY BETWEEN ME AND HALLER.
NO!
I WON'T LET YOU HURT HER, LORD TRAUMA!
UGH BUT HURT IS WHAT I DO, DAVID.
BHAFF
BUT I CAN RELEASE YOU FROM THAT HURT. LET ME TAKE CONTROL OF US AND IT WILL BE OVER.
NO MORE SUFFERING. NO MORE MADNESS.
UHH!
NO MORE TRAUMA.
SMKK
AGHH!

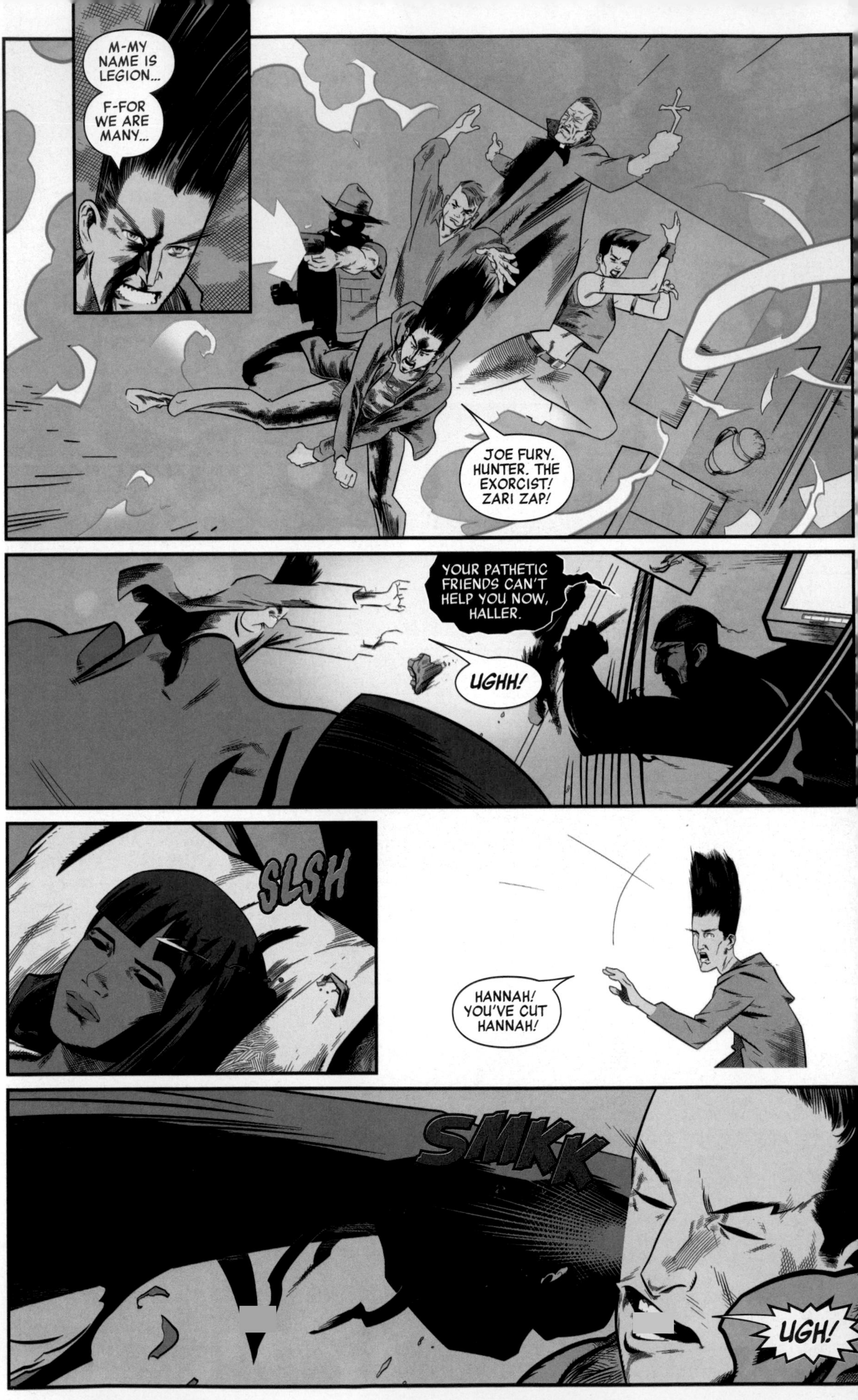
M-MY NAME IS LEGION...
F-FOR WE ARE MANY...
JOE FURY. HUNTER. THE EXORCIST! ZARI ZAP!
YOUR PATHETIC FRIENDS CAN'T HELP YOU NOW, HALLER.
UGHH!
SLSH
HANNAH! YOU'VE CUT HANNAH!
SMKK
UGH!

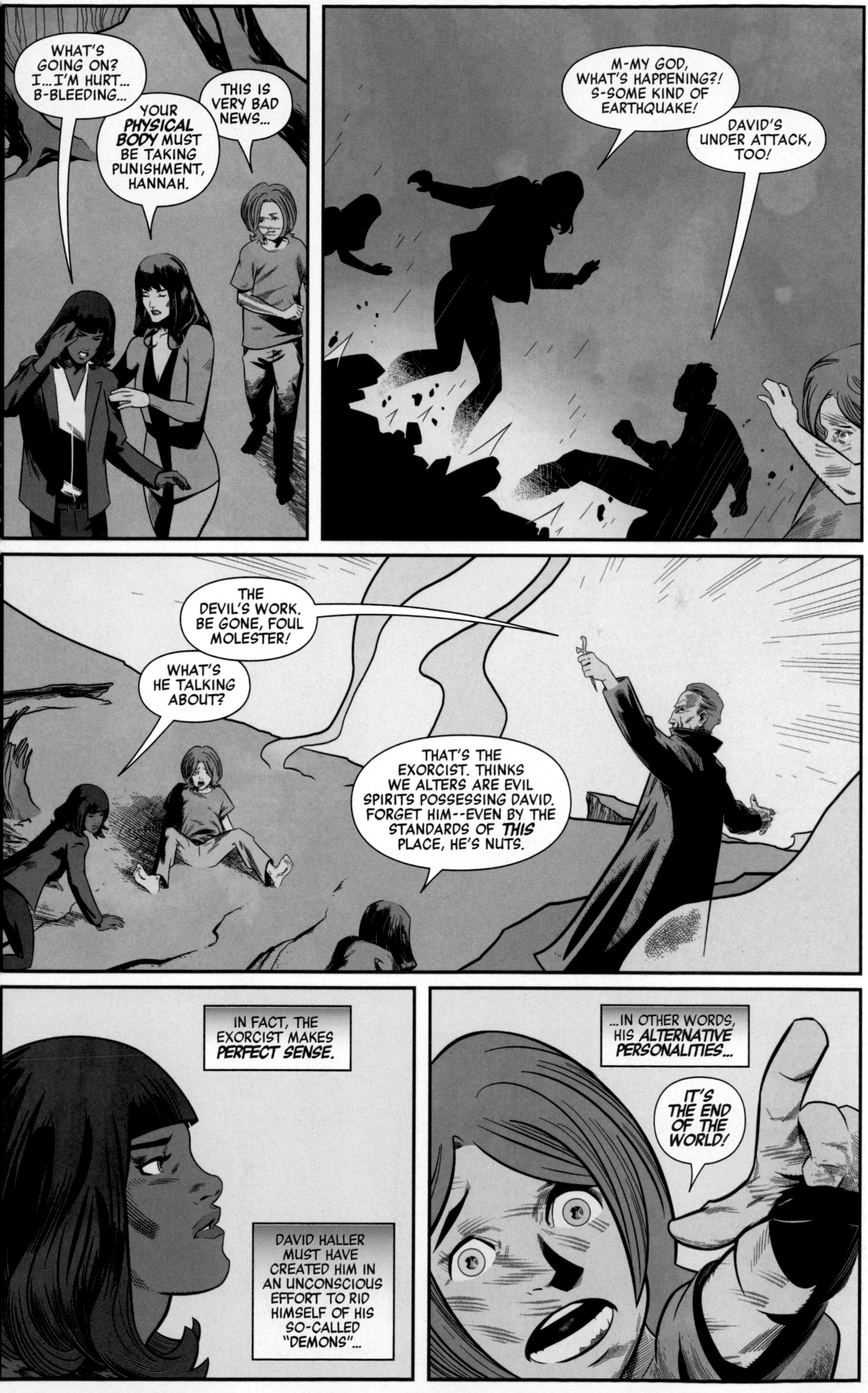
WHAT'S GOING ON? I...I'M HURT... B-BLEEDING...
YOUR PHYSICAL BODY MUST BE TAKING PUNISHMENT, HANNAH.
THIS IS VERY BAD NEWS...
M-MY GOD, WHAT'S HAPPENING?! S-SOME KIND OF EARTHQUAKE!
DAVID'S UNDER ATTACK, TOO!
THE DEVIL'S WORK. BE GONE, FOUL MOLESTER!
WHAT'S HE TALKING ABOUT?
THAT'S THE EXORCIST. THINKS WE ALTERS ARE EVIL SPIRITS POSSESSING DAVID. FORGET HIM--EVEN BY THE STANDARDS OF THIS PLACE, HE'S NUTS.
IN FACT, THE EXORCIST MAKES PERFECT SENSE.
DAVID HALLER MUST HAVE CREATED HIM IN AN UNCONSCIOUS EFFORT TO RID HIMSELF OF HIS SO-CALLED "DEMONS"...
...IN OTHER WORDS, HIS ALTERNATIVE PERSONALITIES...
IT'S THE END OF THE WORLD!

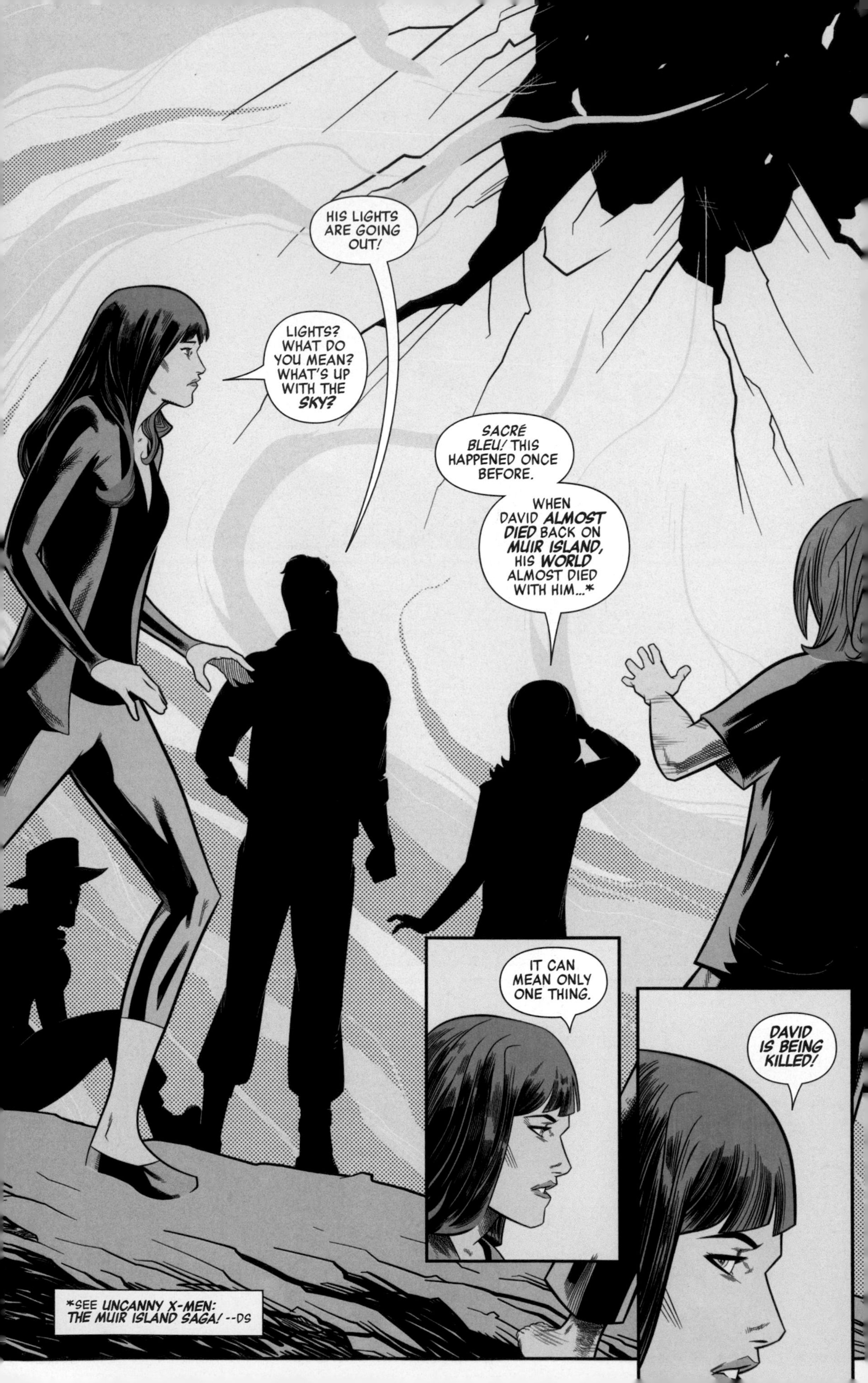
HIS LIGHTS ARE GOING OUT!
LIGHTS? WHAT DO YOU MEAN? WHAT'S UP WITH THE SKY?
SACRÉ BLEU! THIS HAPPENED ONCE BEFORE.
WHEN DAVID ALMOST DIED BACK ON MUIR ISLAND, HIS WORLD ALMOST DIED WITH HIM...*
IT CAN MEAN ONLY ONE THING.
DAVID IS BEING KILLED!
*SEE UNCANNY X-MEN: THE MUIR ISLAND SAGA! --DS

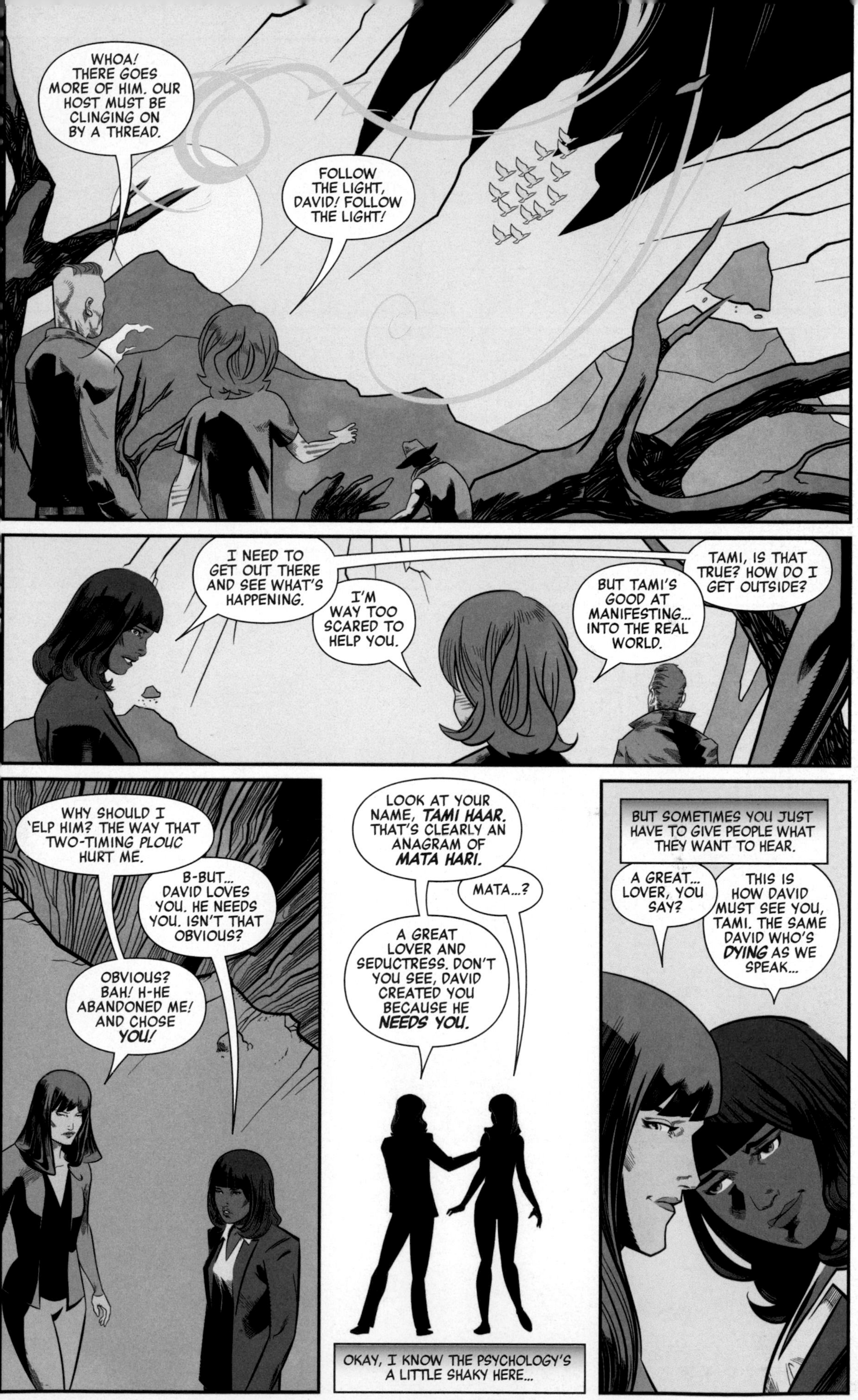
WHOA! THERE GOES MORE OF HIM. OUR HOST MUST BE CLINGING ON BY A THREAD.
FOLLOW THE LIGHT, DAVID! FOLLOW THE LIGHT!
I NEED TO GET OUT THERE AND SEE WHAT'S HAPPENING.
I'M WAY TOO SCARED TO HELP YOU.
BUT TAMI'S GOOD AT MANIFESTING... INTO THE REAL WORLD.
TAMI, IS THAT TRUE? HOW DO I GET OUTSIDE?
WHY SHOULD I 'ELP HIM? THE WAY THAT TWO-TIMING PLOUC HURT ME.
B-BUT... DAVID LOVES YOU. HE NEEDS YOU. ISN'T THAT OBVIOUS?
OBVIOUS? BAH! H-HE ABANDONED ME! AND CHOSE YOU!
LOOK AT YOUR NAME, TAMI HAAR. THAT'S CLEARLY AN ANAGRAM OF MATA HARI.
MATA...?
A GREAT LOVER AND SEDUCTRESS. DON'T YOU SEE, DAVID CREATED YOU BECAUSE HE NEEDS YOU.
OKAY, I KNOW THE PSYCHOLOGY'S A LITTLE SHAKY HERE...
BUT SOMETIMES YOU JUST HAVE TO GIVE PEOPLE WHAT THEY WANT TO HEAR.
A GREAT... LOVER, YOU SAY?
THIS IS HOW DAVID MUST SEE YOU, TAMI. THE SAME DAVID WHO'S DYING AS WE SPEAK...

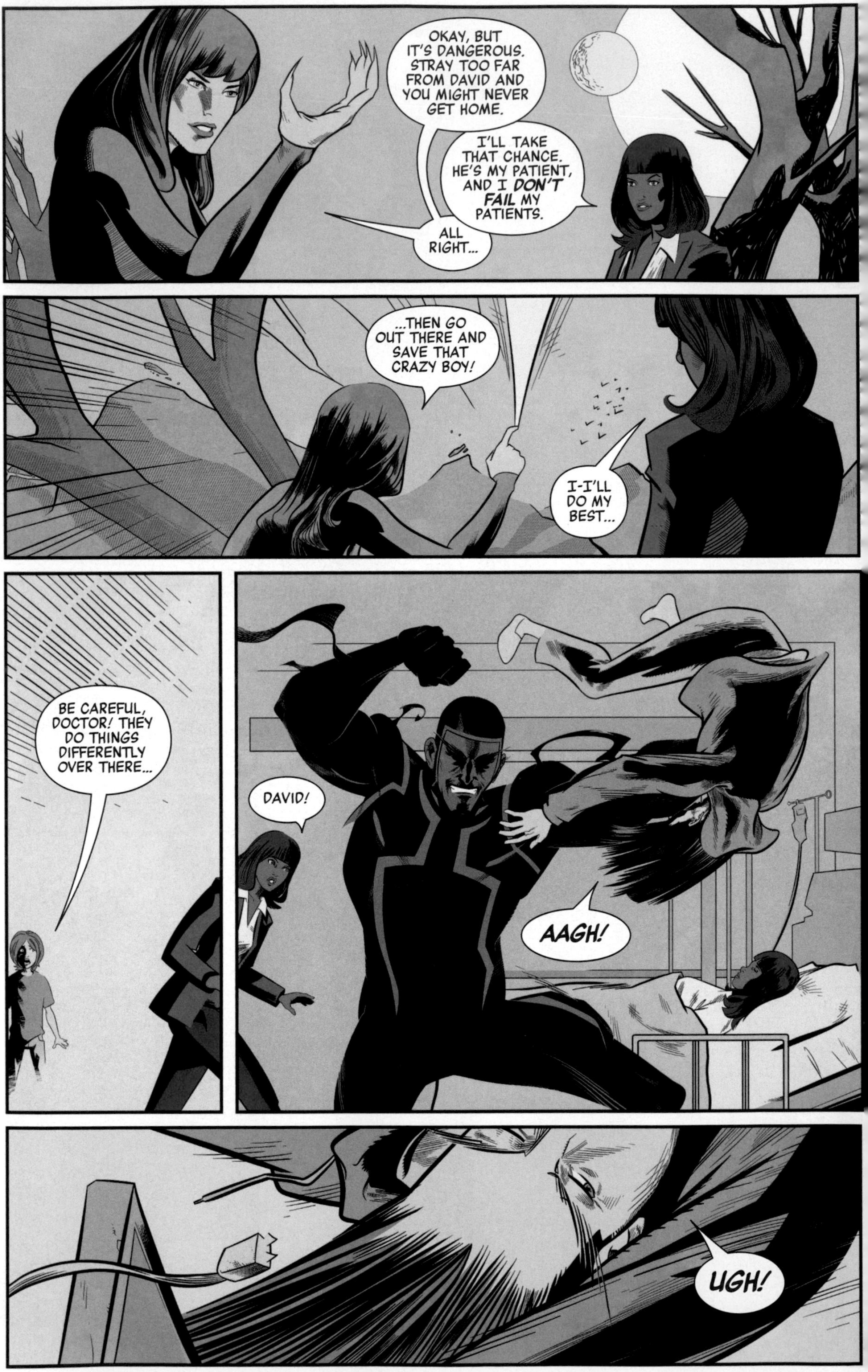
OKAY, BUT IT'S DANGEROUS. STRAY TOO FAR FROM DAVID AND YOU MIGHT NEVER GET HOME.
I'LL TAKE THAT CHANCE. HE'S MY PATIENT, AND I DON'T FAIL MY PATIENTS.
ALL RIGHT...
...THEN GO OUT THERE AND SAVE THAT CRAZY BOY!
I-I'LL DO MY BEST...
BE CAREFUL, DOCTOR! THEY DO THINGS DIFFERENTLY OVER THERE...
DAVID!
AAGH!
UGH!

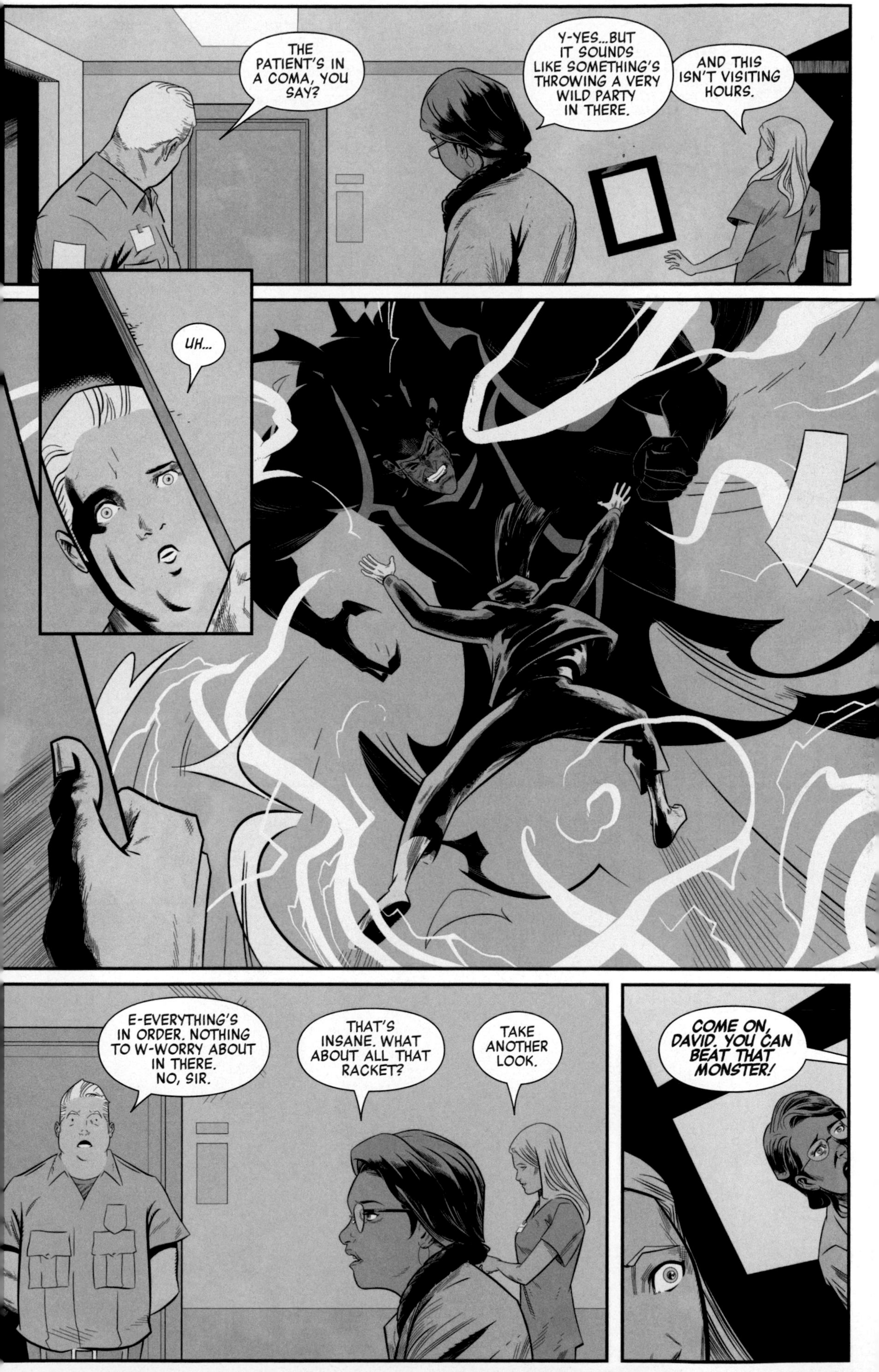
THE PATIENT'S IN A COMA, YOU SAY?
Y-YES...BUT IT SOUNDS LIKE SOMETHING'S THROWING A VERY WILD PARTY IN THERE.
AND THIS ISN'T VISITING HOURS.
UH...
E-EVERYTHING'S IN ORDER. NOTHING TO W-WORRY ABOUT IN THERE. NO, SIR.
THAT'S INSANE. WHAT ABOUT ALL THAT RACKET?
TAKE ANOTHER LOOK.
COME ON, DAVID. YOU CAN BEAT THAT MONSTER!

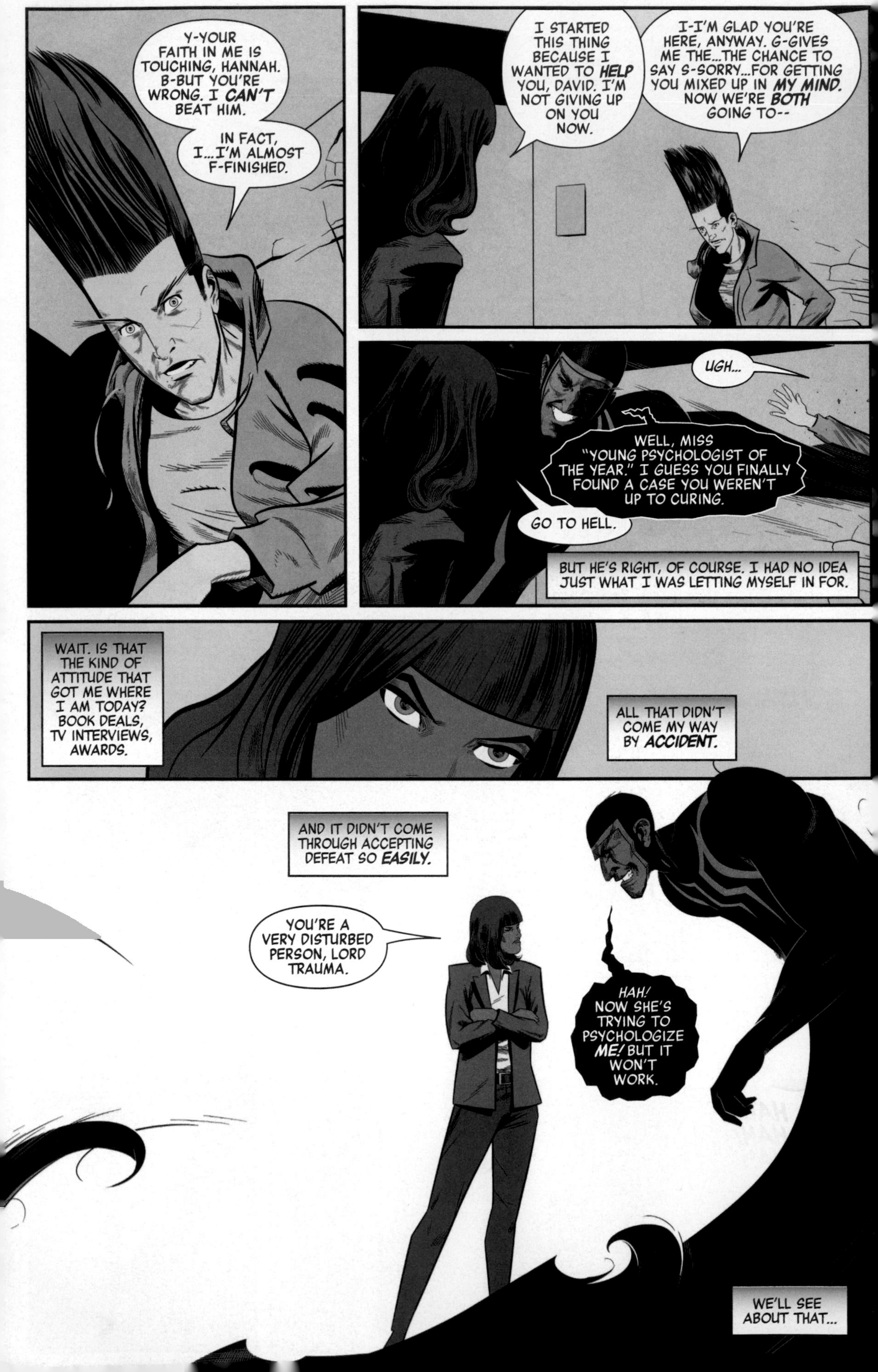
Y-YOUR FAITH IN ME IS TOUCHING, HANNAH. B-BUT YOU'RE WRONG. I CAN'T BEAT HIM.
IN FACT, I...I'M ALMOST F-FINISHED.
I STARTED THIS THING BECAUSE I WANTED TO HELP YOU, DAVID. I'M NOT GIVING UP ON YOU NOW.
I-I'M GLAD YOU'RE HERE, ANYWAY. G-GIVES ME THE...THE CHANCE TO SAY S-SORRY...FOR GETTING YOU MIXED UP IN MY MIND. NOW WE'RE BOTH GOING TO--
UGH...
WELL, MISS "YOUNG PSYCHOLOGIST OF THE YEAR." I GUESS YOU FINALLY FOUND A CASE YOU WEREN'T UP TO CURING.
GO TO HELL.
BUT HE'S RIGHT, OF COURSE. I HAD NO IDEA JUST WHAT I WAS LETTING MYSELF IN FOR.
WAIT. IS THAT THE KIND OF ATTITUDE THAT GOT ME WHERE I AM TODAY? BOOK DEALS, TV INTERVIEWS, AWARDS.
ALL THAT DIDN'T COME MY WAY BY ACCIDENT.
AND IT DIDN'T COME THROUGH ACCEPTING DEFEAT SO EASILY.
YOU'RE A VERY DISTURBED PERSON, LORD TRAUMA.
HAH! NOW SHE'S TRYING TO PSYCHOLOGIZE ME! BUT IT WON'T WORK.
WE'LL SEE ABOUT THAT...

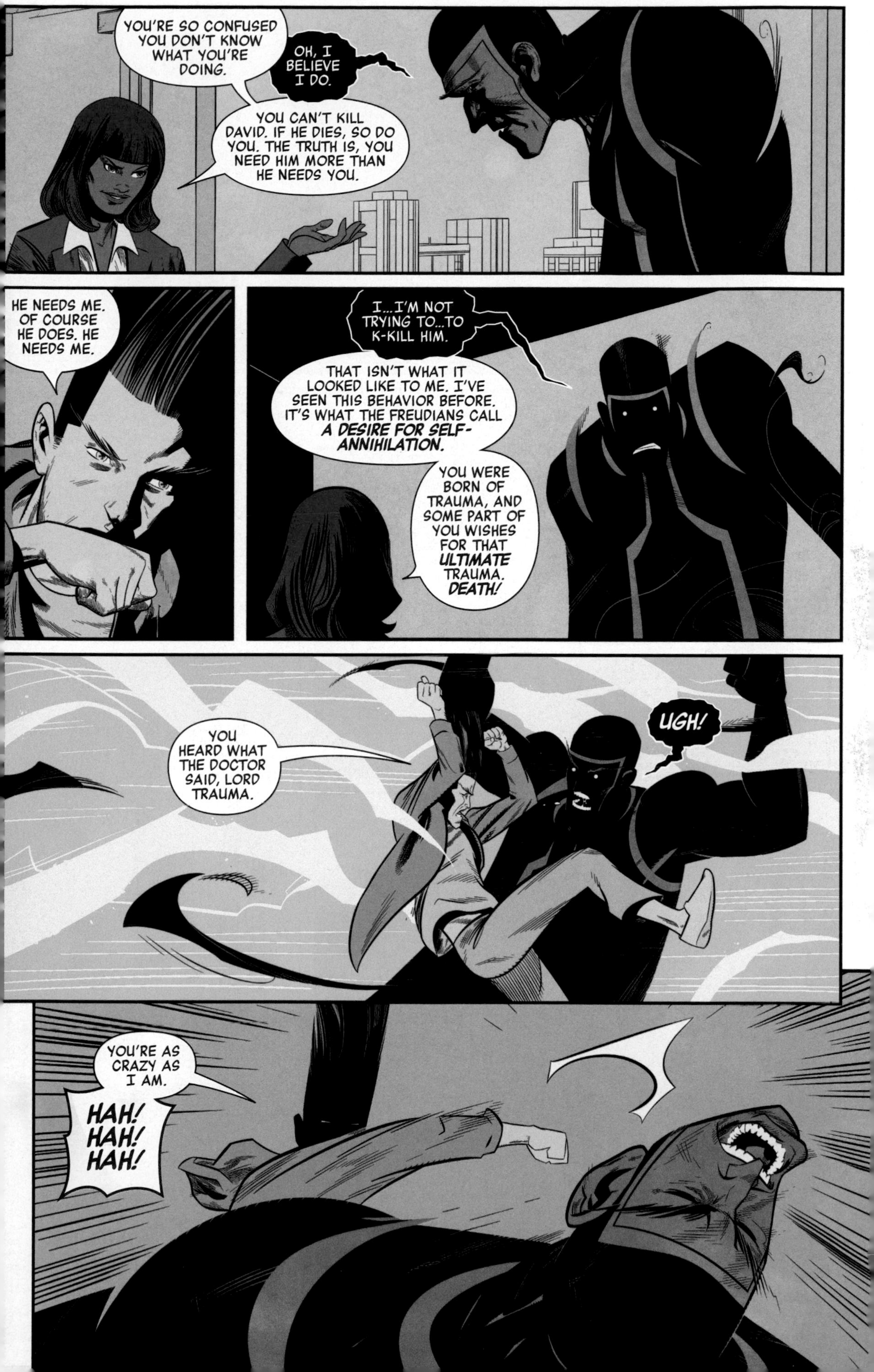
YOU'RE SO CONFUSED YOU DON'T KNOW WHAT YOU'RE DOING.
OH, I BELIEVE I DO.
YOU CAN'T KILL DAVID. IF HE DIES, SO DO YOU. THE TRUTH IS, YOU NEED HIM MORE THAN HE NEEDS YOU.
HE NEEDS ME. OF COURSE HE DOES. HE NEEDS ME.
I...I'M NOT TRYING TO...TO K-KILL HIM.
THAT ISN'T WHAT IT LOOKED LIKE TO ME. I'VE SEEN THIS BEHAVIOR BEFORE. IT'S WHAT THE FREUDIANS CALL A DESIRE FOR SELF-ANNIHILATION.
YOU WERE BORN OF TRAUMA, AND SOME PART OF YOU WISHES FOR THAT ULTIMATE TRAUMA. DEATH!
YOU HEARD WHAT THE DOCTOR SAID, LORD TRAUMA.
UGH!
YOU'RE AS CRAZY AS I AM.
HAH! HAH! HAH!

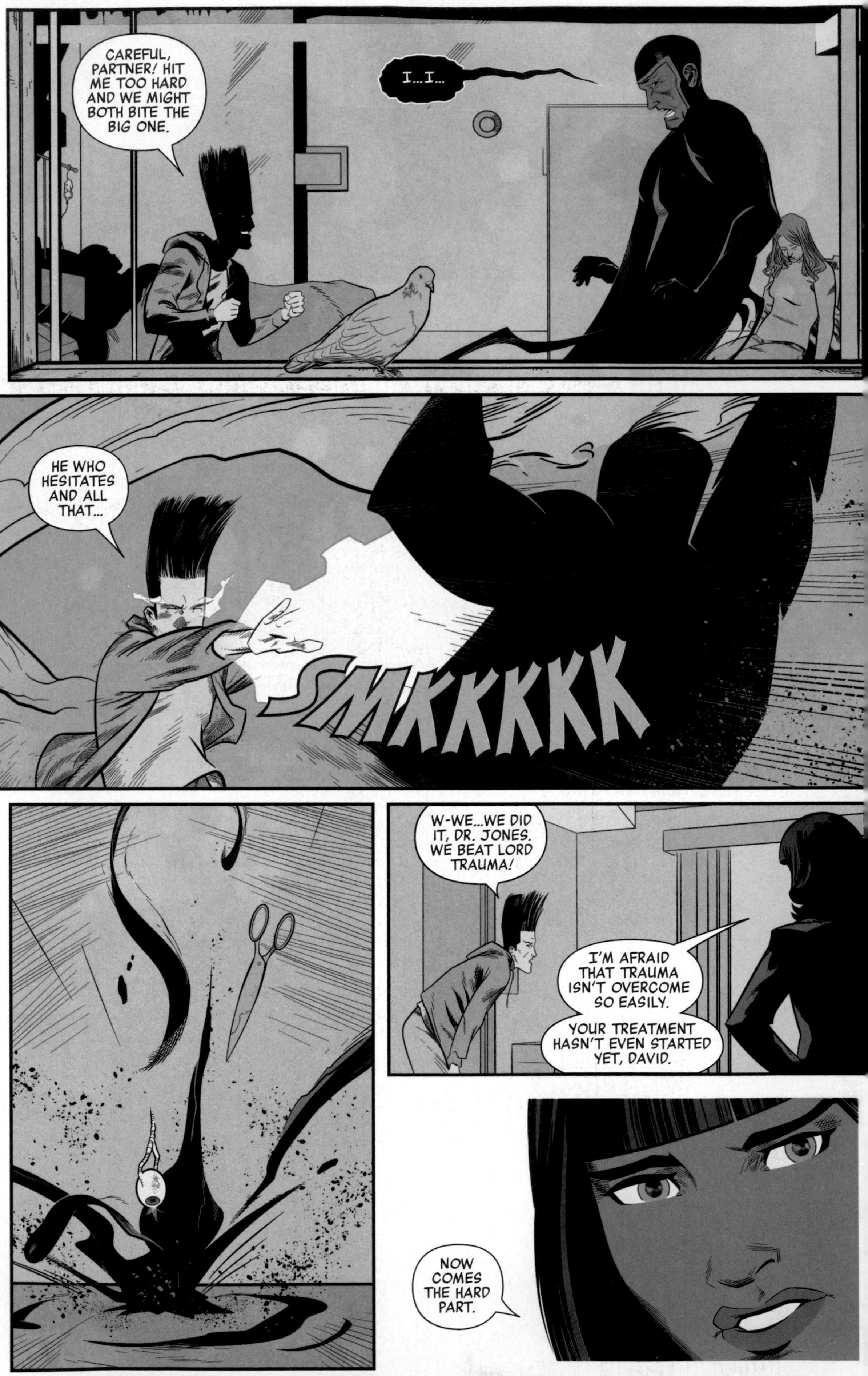
CAREFUL, PARTNER! HIT ME TOO HARD AND WE MIGHT BOTH BITE THE BIG ONE.
I...I...
HE WHO HESITATES AND ALL THAT...
SMKKKKK
W-WE...WE DID IT, DR. JONES. WE BEAT LORD TRAUMA!
I'M AFRAID THAT TRAUMA ISN'T OVERCOME SO EASILY.
YOUR TREATMENT HASN'T EVEN STARTED YET, DAVID.
NOW COMES THE HARD PART.

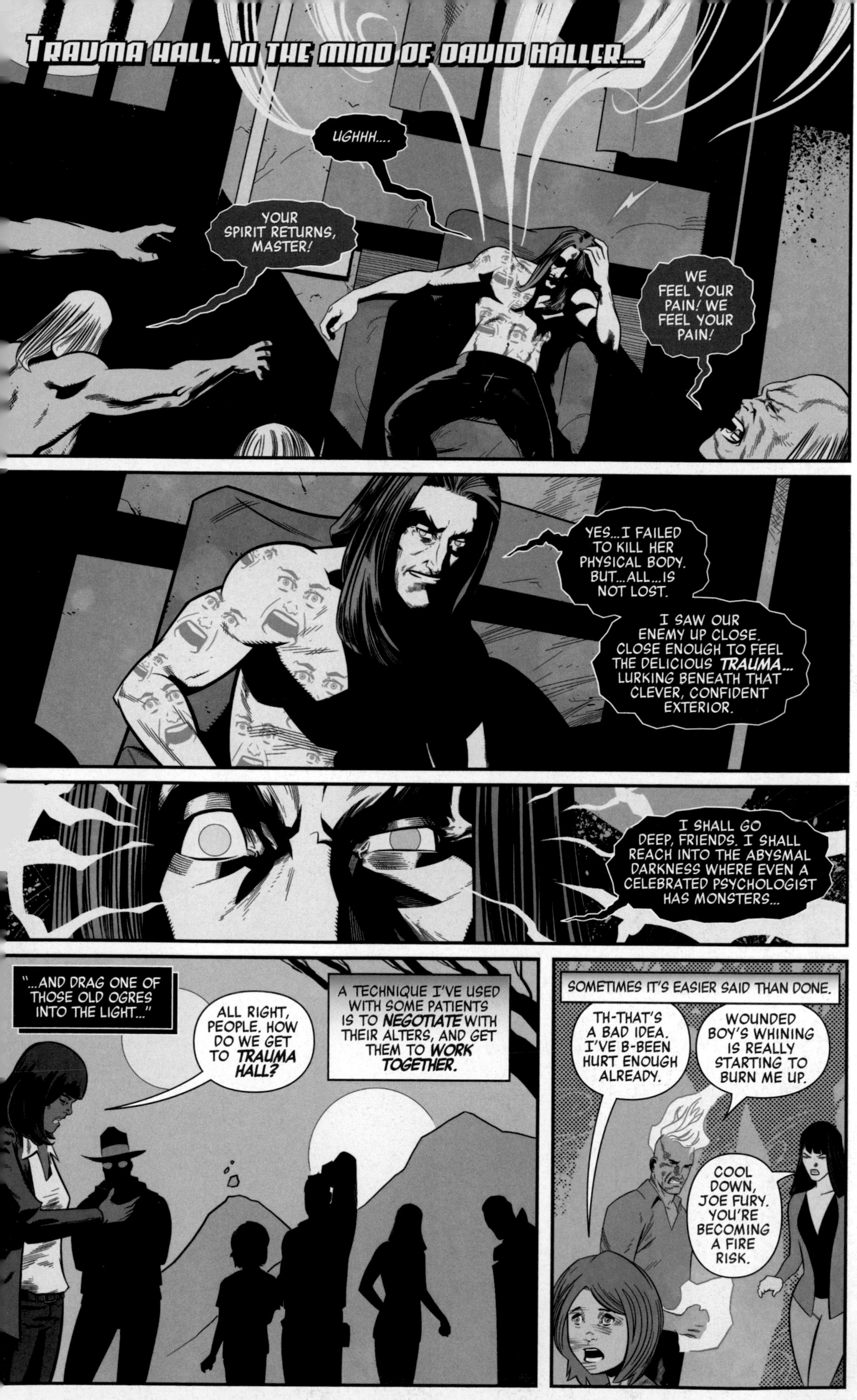
TRAUMA HALL, IN THE MIND OF DAVID HALLER...
UGHHH....
YOUR SPIRIT RETURNS, MASTER!
WE FEEL YOUR PAIN! WE FEEL YOUR PAIN!
YES...I FAILED TO KILL HER PHYSICAL BODY. BUT...ALL...IS NOT LOST.
I SAW OUR ENEMY UP CLOSE. CLOSE ENOUGH TO FEEL THE DELICIOUS TRAUMA... LURKING BENEATH THAT CLEVER, CONFIDENT EXTERIOR.
I SHALL GO DEEP, FRIENDS. I SHALL REACH INTO THE ABYSMAL DARKNESS WHERE EVEN A CELEBRATED PSYCHOLOGIST HAS MONSTERS...
"...AND DRAG ONE OF THOSE OLD OGRES INTO THE LIGHT..."
ALL RIGHT, PEOPLE. HOW DO WE GET TO TRAUMA HALL?
A TECHNIQUE I'VE USED WITH SOME PATIENTS IS TO NEGOTIATE WITH THEIR ALTERS, AND GET THEM TO WORK TOGETHER.
SOMETIMES IT'S EASIER SAID THAN DONE.
TH-THAT'S A BAD IDEA. I'VE B-BEEN HURT ENOUGH ALREADY.
WOUNDED BOY'S WHINING IS REALLY STARTING TO BURN ME UP.
COOL DOWN, JOE FURY. YOU'RE BECOMING A FIRE RISK.

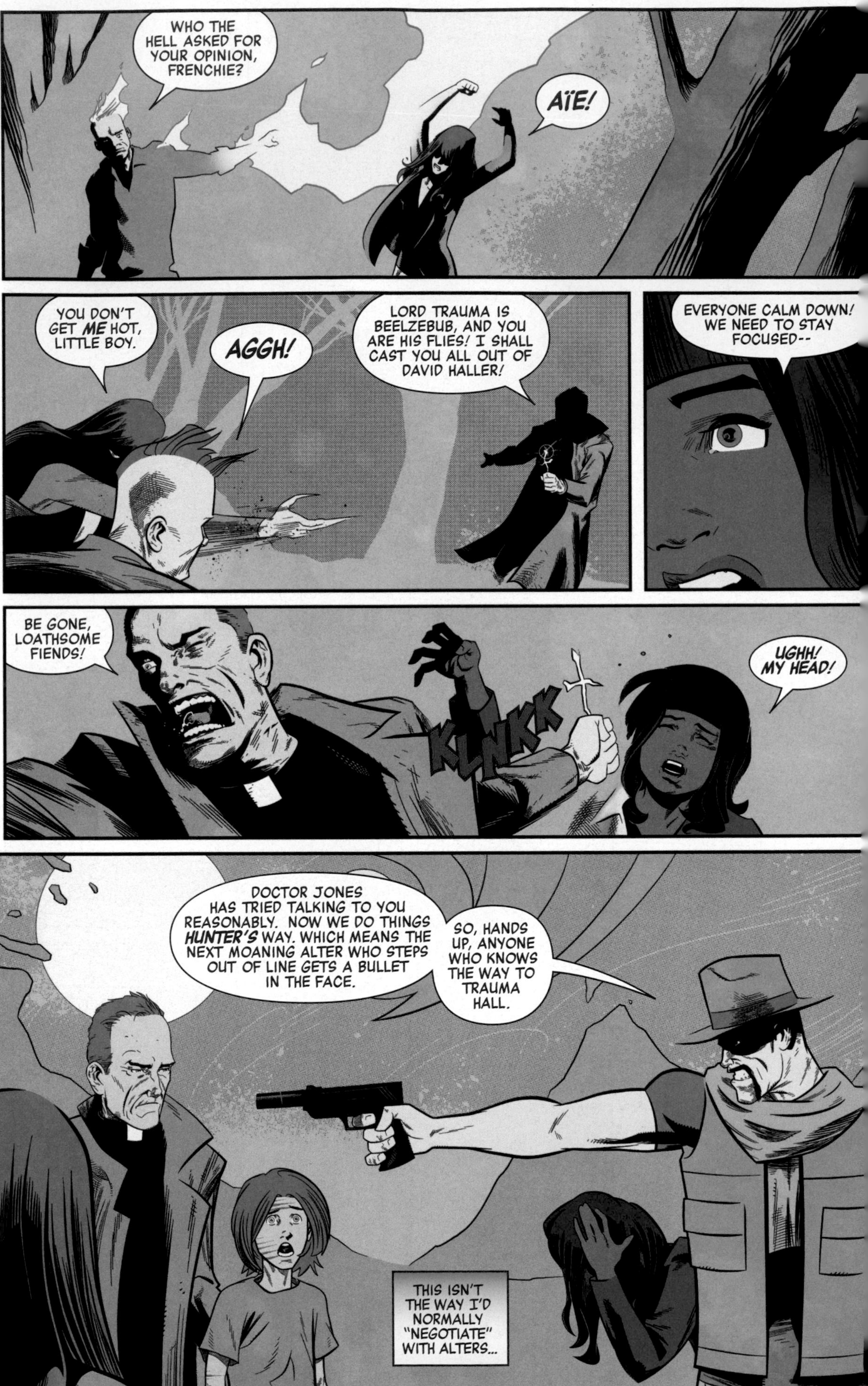

WHO THE HELL ASKED FOR YOUR OPINION, FRENCHIE?
AÏE!
YOU DON'T GET ME HOT, LITTLE BOY.
AGGH!
LORD TRAUMA IS BEELZEBUB, AND YOU ARE HIS FLIES! I SHALL CAST YOU ALL OUT OF DAVID HALLER!
EVERYONE CALM DOWN! WE NEED TO STAY FOCUSED--
BE GONE, LOATHSOME FIENDS!
KLNKK
UGHH! MY HEAD!
DOCTOR JONES HAS TRIED TALKING TO YOU REASONABLY. NOW WE DO THINGS HUNTER'S WAY. WHICH MEANS THE NEXT MOANING ALTER WHO STEPS OUT OF LINE GETS A BULLET IN THE FACE.
SO, HANDS UP, ANYONE WHO KNOWS THE WAY TO TRAUMA HALL.
THIS ISN'T THE WAY I'D NORMALLY "NEGOTIATE" WITH ALTERS...

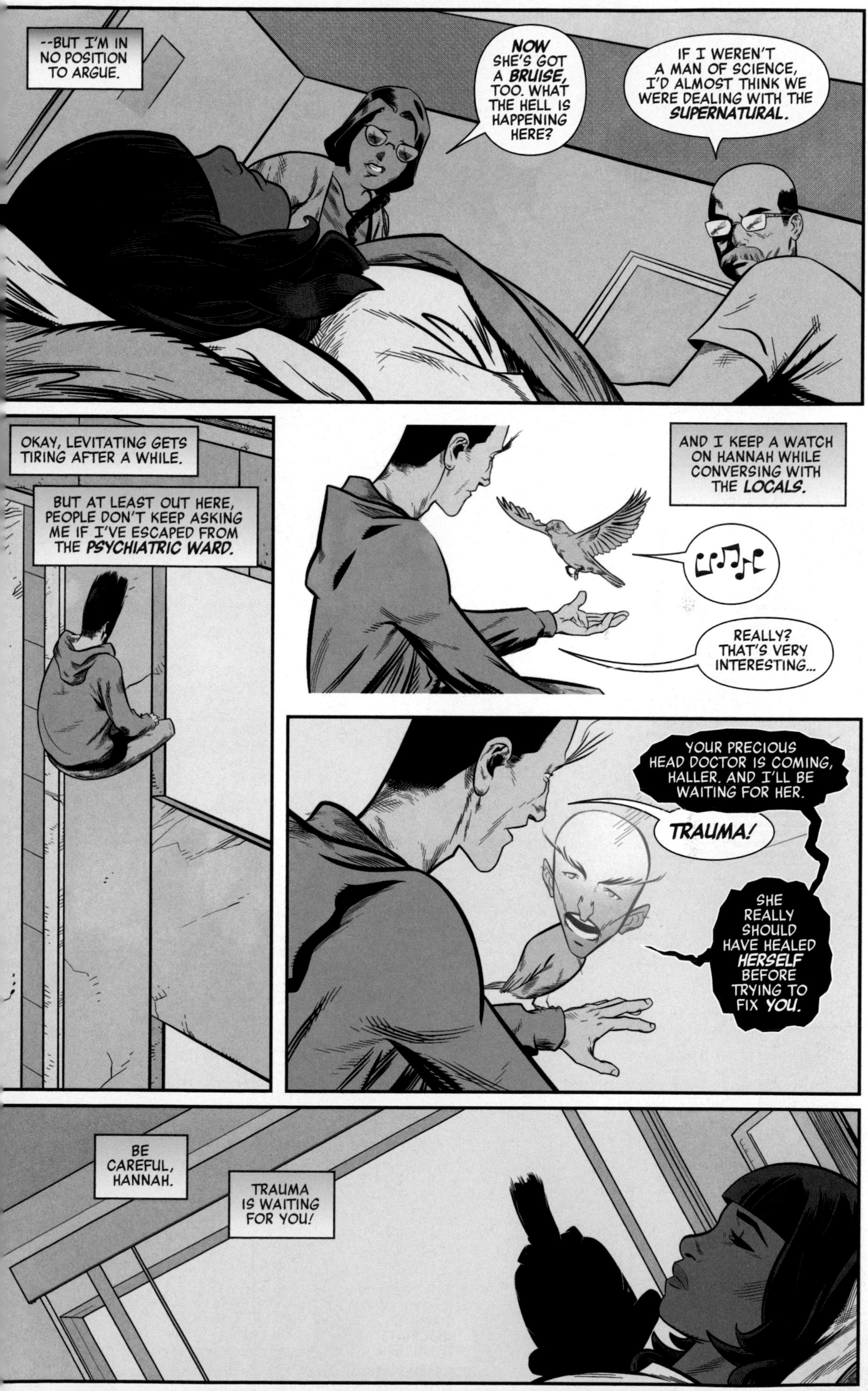
--BUT I'M IN NO POSITION TO ARGUE.
NOW SHE'S GOT A BRUISE, TOO. WHAT THE HELL IS HAPPENING HERE?
IF I WEREN'T A MAN OF SCIENCE, I'D ALMOST THINK WE WERE DEALING WITH THE SUPERNATURAL.
OKAY, LEVITATING GETS TIRING AFTER A WHILE.
BUT AT LEAST OUT HERE, PEOPLE DON'T KEEP ASKING ME IF I'VE ESCAPED FROM THE PSYCHIATRIC WARD.
AND I KEEP A WATCH ON HANNAH WHILE CONVERSING WITH THE LOCALS.
REALLY? THAT'S VERY INTERESTING...
YOUR PRECIOUS HEAD DOCTOR IS COMING, HALLER. AND I'LL BE WAITING FOR HER.
TRAUMA!
SHE REALLY SHOULD HAVE HEALED HERSELF BEFORE TRYING TO FIX YOU.
BE CAREFUL, HANNAH.
TRAUMA IS WAITING FOR YOU!

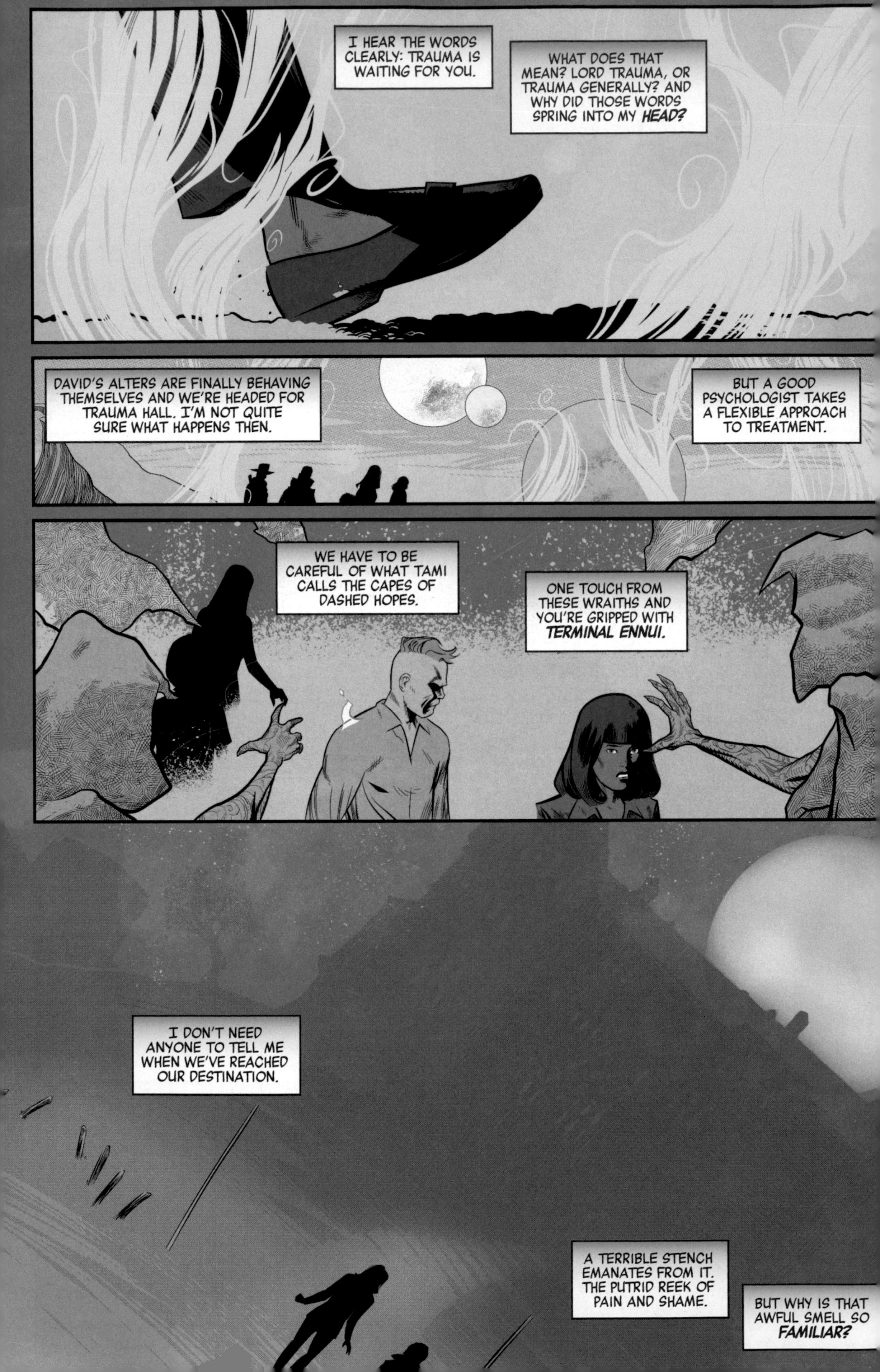
I HEAR THE WORDS CLEARLY: TRAUMA IS WAITING FOR YOU.
WHAT DOES THAT MEAN? LORD TRAUMA, OR TRAUMA GENERALLY? AND WHY DID THOSE WORDS SPRING INTO MY HEAD?
DAVID'S ALTERS ARE FINALLY BEHAVING THEMSELVES AND WE'RE HEADED FOR TRAUMA HALL. I'M NOT QUITE SURE WHAT HAPPENS THEN.
BUT A GOOD PSYCHOLOGIST TAKES A FLEXIBLE APPROACH TO TREATMENT.
WE HAVE TO BE CAREFUL OF WHAT TAMI CALLS THE CAPES OF DASHED HOPES.
ONE TOUCH FROM THESE WRAITHS AND YOU'RE GRIPPED WITH TERMINAL ENNUI.
I DON'T NEED ANYONE TO TELL ME WHEN WE'VE REACHED OUR DESTINATION.
A TERRIBLE STENCH EMANATES FROM IT. THE PUTRID REEK OF PAIN AND SHAME.
BUT WHY IS THAT AWFUL SMELL SO FAMILIAR?

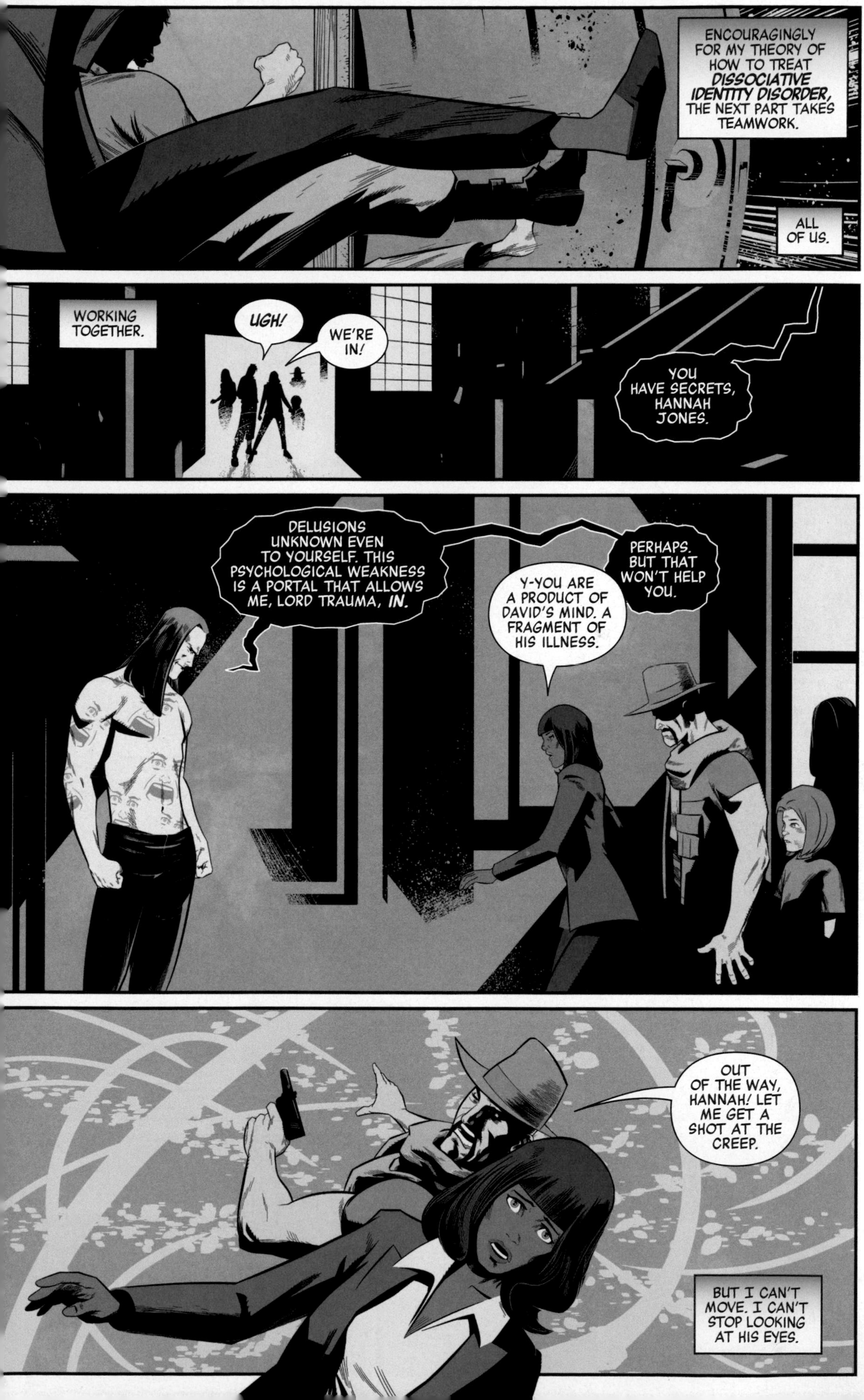
ENCOURAGINGLY FOR MY THEORY OF HOW TO TREAT DISSOCIATIVE IDENTITY DISORDER, THE NEXT PART TAKES TEAMWORK.
ALL OF US.
WORKING TOGETHER.
UGH!
WE'RE IN!
YOU HAVE SECRETS, HANNAH JONES.
DELUSIONS UNKNOWN EVEN TO YOURSELF. THIS PSYCHOLOGICAL WEAKNESS IS A PORTAL THAT ALLOWS ME, LORD TRAUMA, IN.
Y-YOU ARE A PRODUCT OF DAVID'S MIND. A FRAGMENT OF HIS ILLNESS.
PERHAPS. BUT THAT WON'T HELP YOU.
OUT OF THE WAY, HANNAH! LET ME GET A SHOT AT THE CREEP.
BUT I CAN'T MOVE. I CAN'T STOP LOOKING AT HIS EYES.

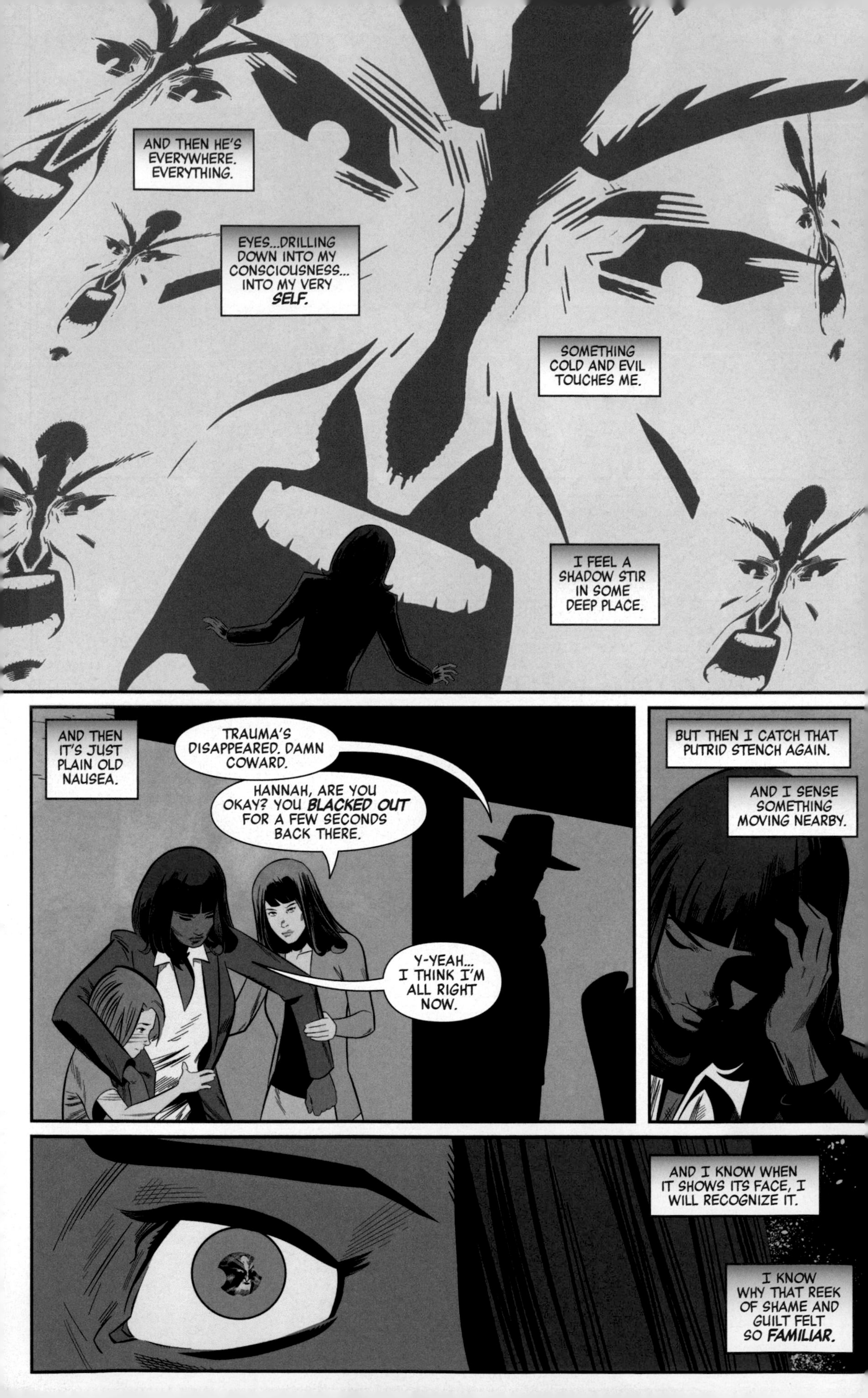
AND THEN HE'S EVERYWHERE. EVERYTHING.
EYES...DRILLING DOWN INTO MY CONSCIOUSNESS... INTO MY VERY **SELF.**
SOMETHING COLD AND EVIL TOUCHES ME.
I FEEL A SHADOW STIR IN SOME DEEP PLACE.
AND THEN IT'S JUST PLAIN OLD NAUSEA.
TRAUMA'S DISAPPEARED. DAMN COWARD.
HANNAH, ARE YOU OKAY? YOU **BLACKED OUT** FOR A FEW SECONDS BACK THERE.
Y-YEAH... I THINK I'M ALL RIGHT NOW.
BUT THEN I CATCH THAT PUTRID STENCH AGAIN.
AND I SENSE SOMETHING MOVING NEARBY.
AND I KNOW WHEN IT SHOWS ITS FACE, I WILL RECOGNIZE IT.
I KNOW WHY THAT REEK OF SHAME AND GUILT FELT SO **FAMILIAR.**

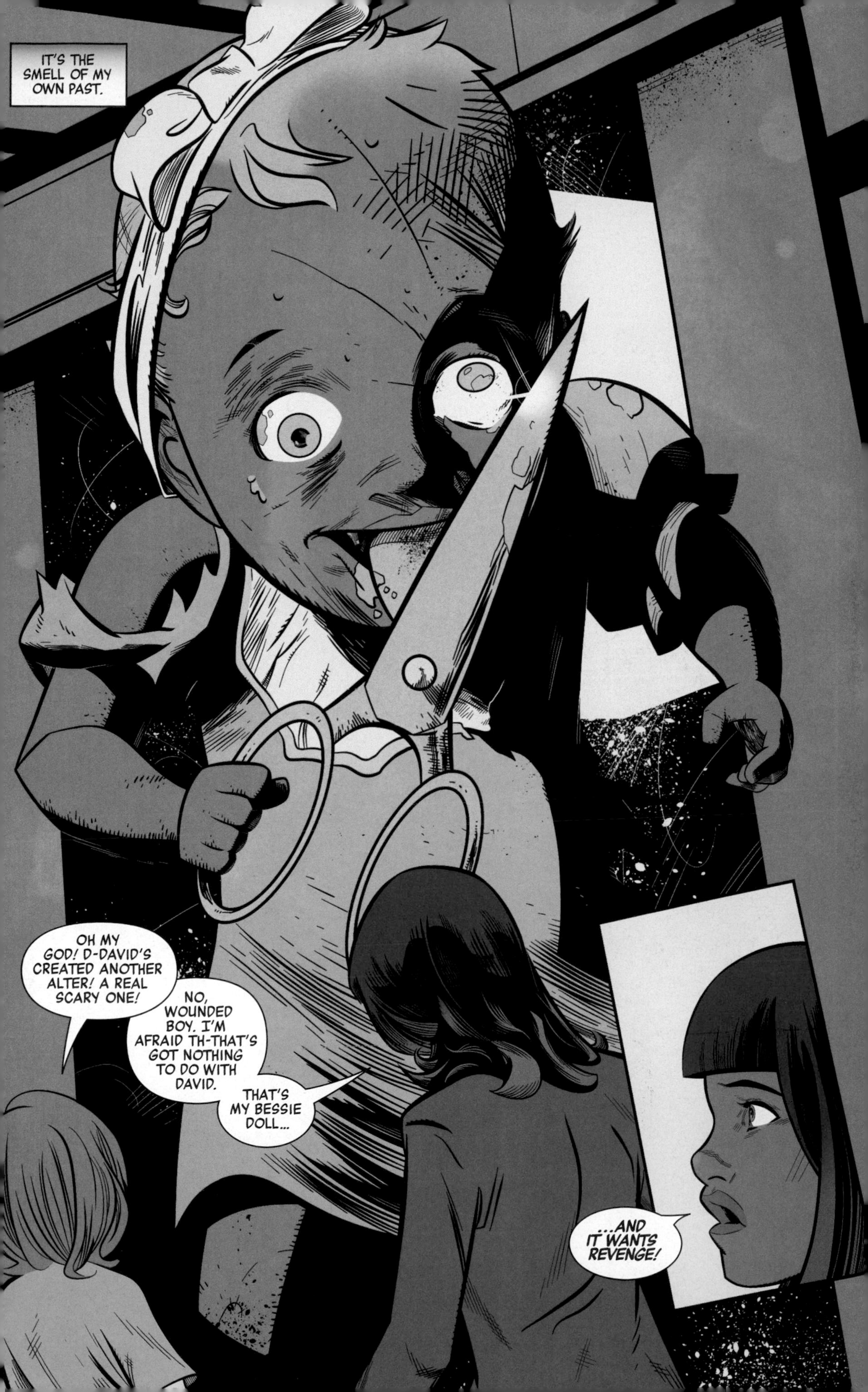
IT'S THE SMELL OF MY OWN PAST.
OH MY GOD! D-DAVID'S CREATED ANOTHER ALTER! A REAL SCARY ONE!
NO, WOUNDED BOY. I'M AFRAID TH-THAT'S GOT NOTHING TO DO WITH DAVID.
THAT'S MY BESSIE DOLL...
...AND IT WANTS REVENGE!

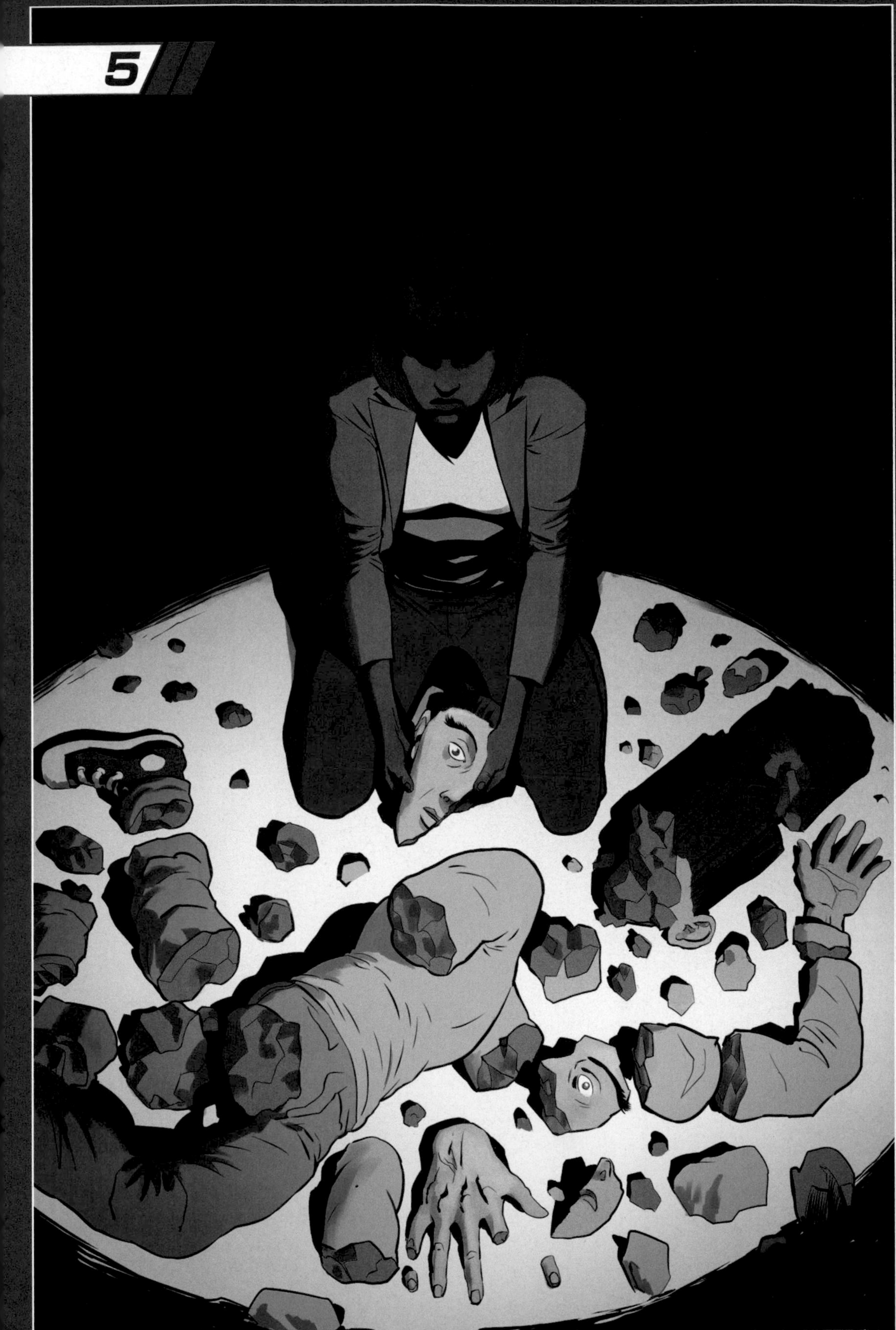
5

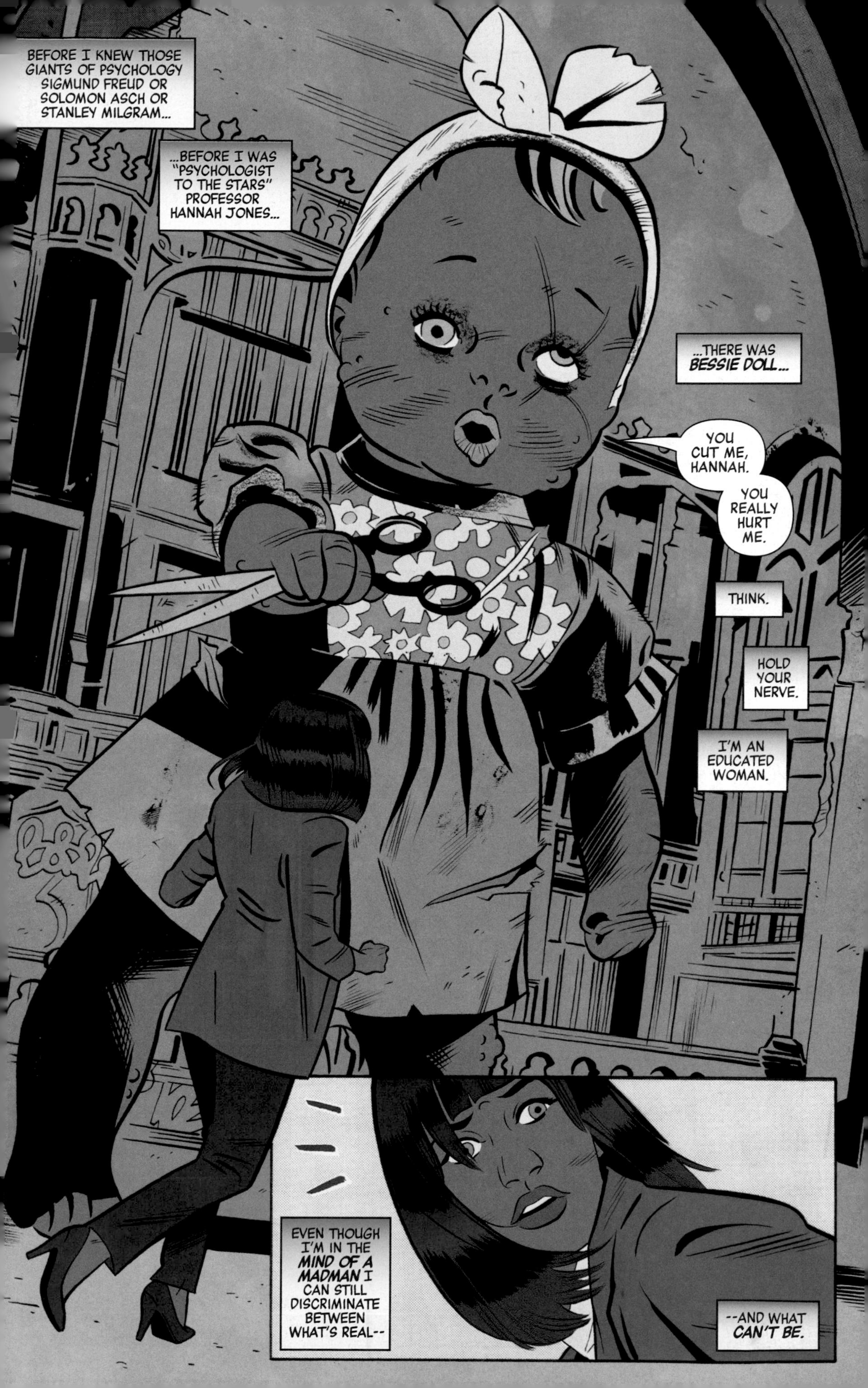
BEFORE I KNEW THOSE GIANTS OF PSYCHOLOGY SIGMUND FREUD OR SOLOMON ASCH OR STANLEY MILGRAM...
...BEFORE I WAS "PSYCHOLOGIST TO THE STARS" PROFESSOR HANNAH JONES...
...THERE WAS *BESSIE DOLL...*
YOU CUT ME, HANNAH.
YOU REALLY HURT ME.
THINK.
HOLD YOUR NERVE.
I'M AN EDUCATED WOMAN.
EVEN THOUGH I'M IN THE *MIND OF A MADMAN* I CAN STILL DISCRIMINATE BETWEEN WHAT'S REAL--
--AND WHAT *CAN'T BE.*

BESSIE BELONGS TO MY PAST. MY *CHILDHOOD.*

IT'S JUST A MATTER OF WILLPOWER TO PUSH HER BACK WHERE SHE *BELONGS.*

STAND ASIDE, ALTERS. I'M GONNA *BURN* THAT MONSTER.

AND SET US ALL ON FIRE? THIS IS A JOB FOR A *REAL MAN,* JOE FURY.

MON DIEU! C'EST HORRIBLE!

IF IT'LL ONLY STAY STILL LONG ENOUGH... FOR ME TO GET *A DECENT SHOT...*

Y-YOU DON'T BELONG HERE, BESSIE. THIS IS THE *MINDSPACE* OF *DAVID HALLER.* YOU ARE NOT PART OF HIS MEMORIES!

SO WHAT ARE *YOU* DOING HERE?

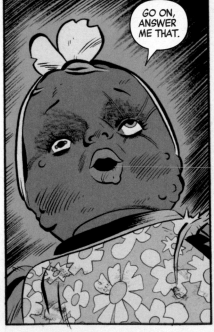

GO ON, ANSWER ME THAT.

WHAT ARE YOU DOING HERE?!

AAAGH!

SLASHHHH

BLOOD PRESSURE'S DROPPING!
SHE COULD BE BLEEDING INTERNALLY. WE'LL GET HER DOWN TO RADIOLOGY FOR AN X-RAY.
LEAVE HER TO ME.
ARE YOU A RELATIVE?
NO, I'M HER PATIENT. THE POOR WOMAN IS SUFFERING BECAUSE OF ME. BUT I CAN'T LET IT GO ON. I KNOW WHAT'S WRONG WITH HER, YOU SEE.
NURSE, GET HIM OUT OF HERE...
COME AWAY, SIR. WE'VE GOT THIS UNDER CONTROL.
DO YOU HEAR ME, HANNAH? THIS IS DAVID!
I'M GOING TO PUT A STOP TO THIS!
UGH!
MY GOD. W-WHERE DID HE GO?

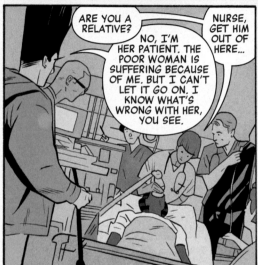

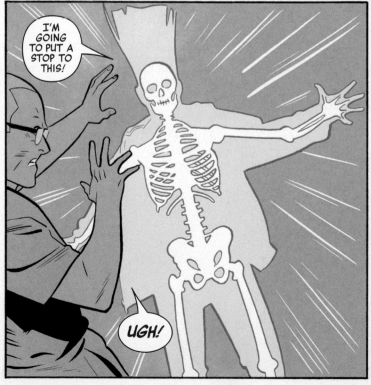

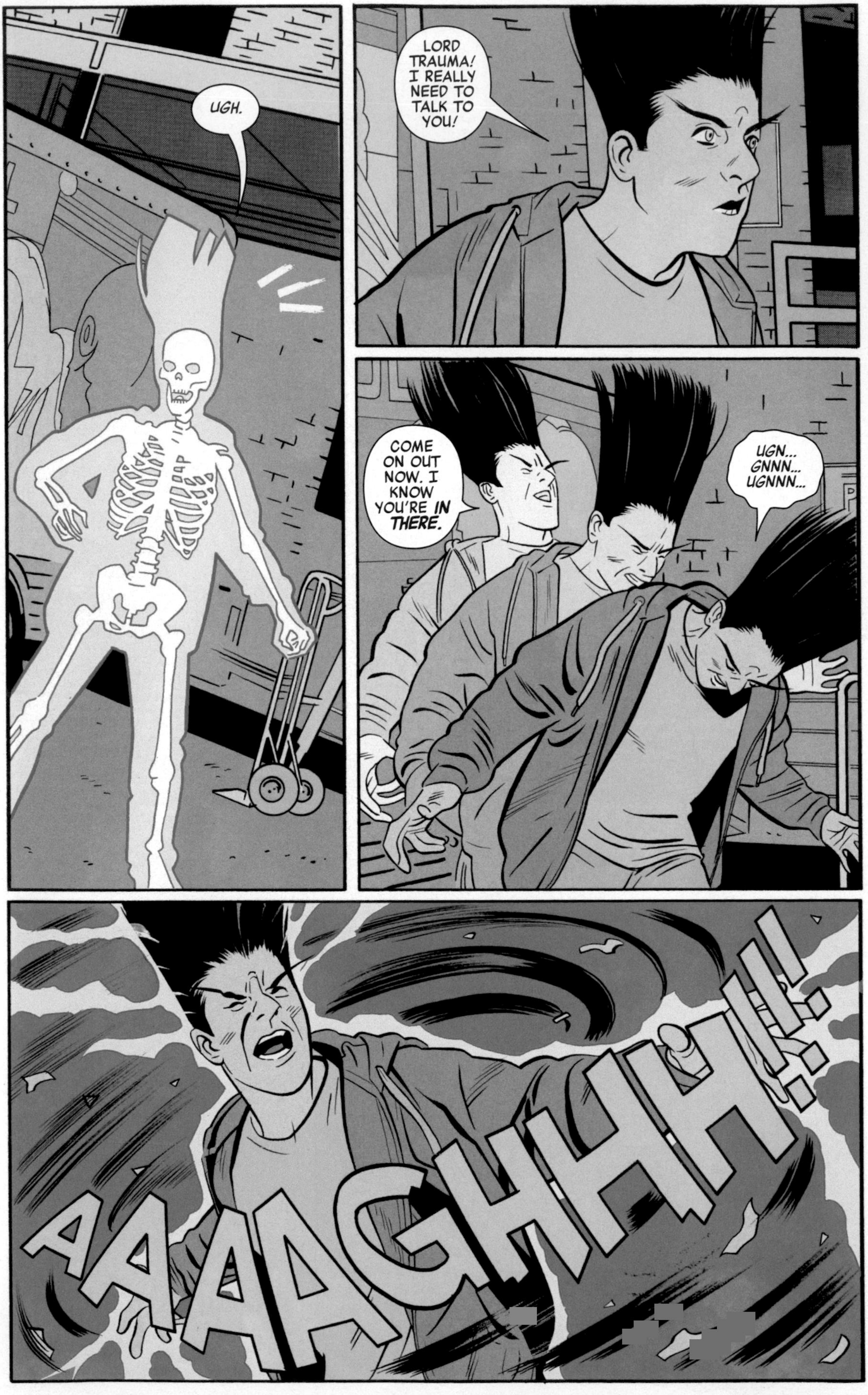
UGH.
LORD TRAUMA! I REALLY NEED TO TALK TO YOU!
COME ON OUT NOW. I KNOW YOU'RE **IN THERE.**
UGN... GNNN... UGNNN...
AAAGHHH!!!

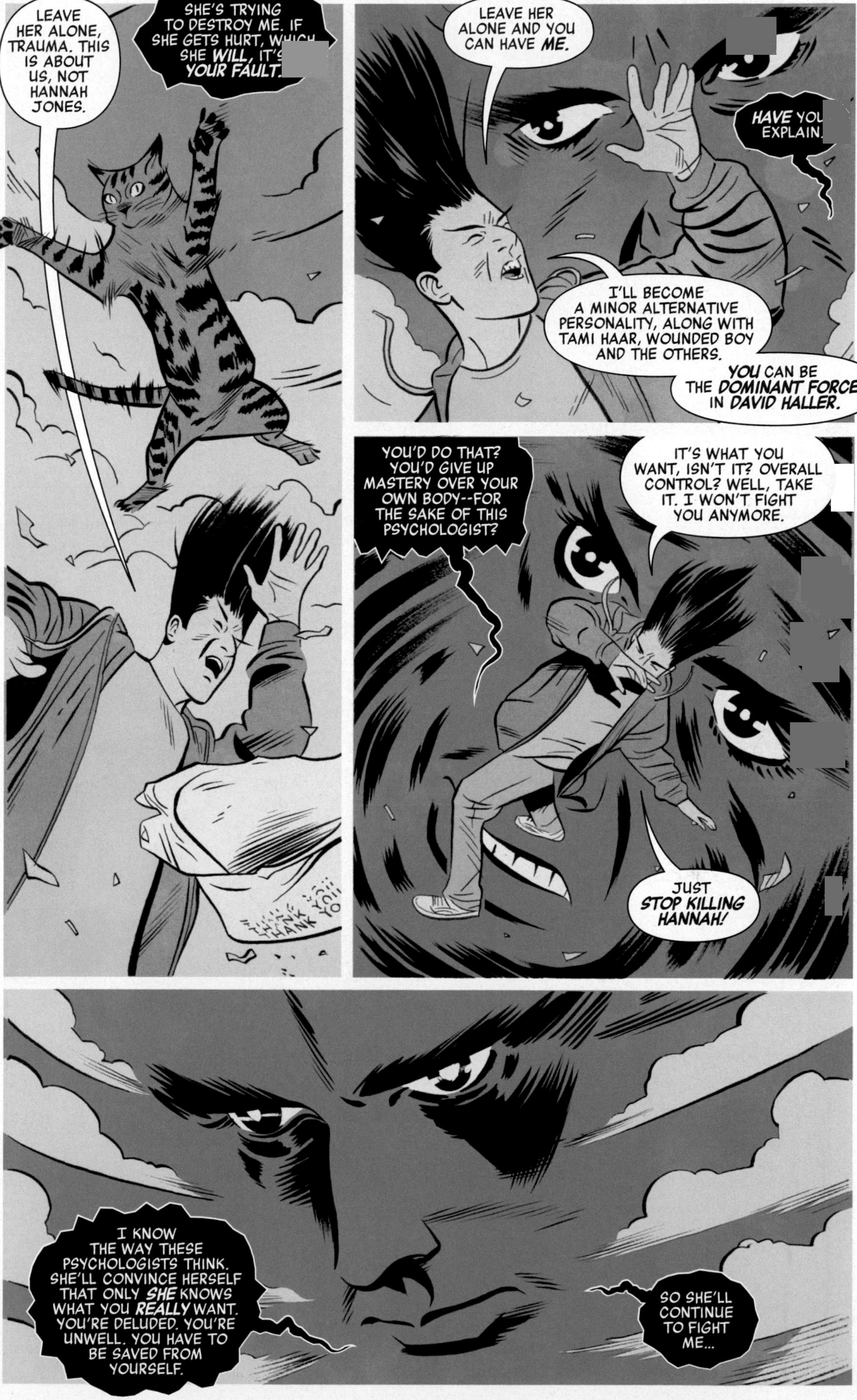

LEAVE HER ALONE, TRAUMA. THIS IS ABOUT US, NOT HANNAH JONES.
SHE'S TRYING TO DESTROY ME. IF SHE GETS HURT, WHICH SHE *WILL*, IT'S ***YOUR FAULT.***
LEAVE HER ALONE AND YOU CAN HAVE ***ME.***
HAVE YOU EXPLAIN.
I'LL BECOME A MINOR ALTERNATIVE PERSONALITY, ALONG WITH TAMI HAAR, WOUNDED BOY AND THE OTHERS.
YOU CAN BE THE ***DOMINANT FORCE*** IN ***DAVID HALLER.***
YOU'D DO THAT? YOU'D GIVE UP MASTERY OVER YOUR OWN BODY--FOR THE SAKE OF THIS PSYCHOLOGIST?
IT'S WHAT YOU WANT, ISN'T IT? OVERALL CONTROL? WELL, TAKE IT. I WON'T FIGHT YOU ANYMORE.
JUST ***STOP KILLING HANNAH!***
I KNOW THE WAY THESE PSYCHOLOGISTS THINK. SHE'LL CONVINCE HERSELF THAT ONLY ***SHE*** KNOWS WHAT YOU ***REALLY*** WANT. YOU'RE DELUDED. YOU'RE UNWELL. YOU HAVE TO BE SAVED FROM YOURSELF.
SO SHE'LL CONTINUE TO FIGHT ME...

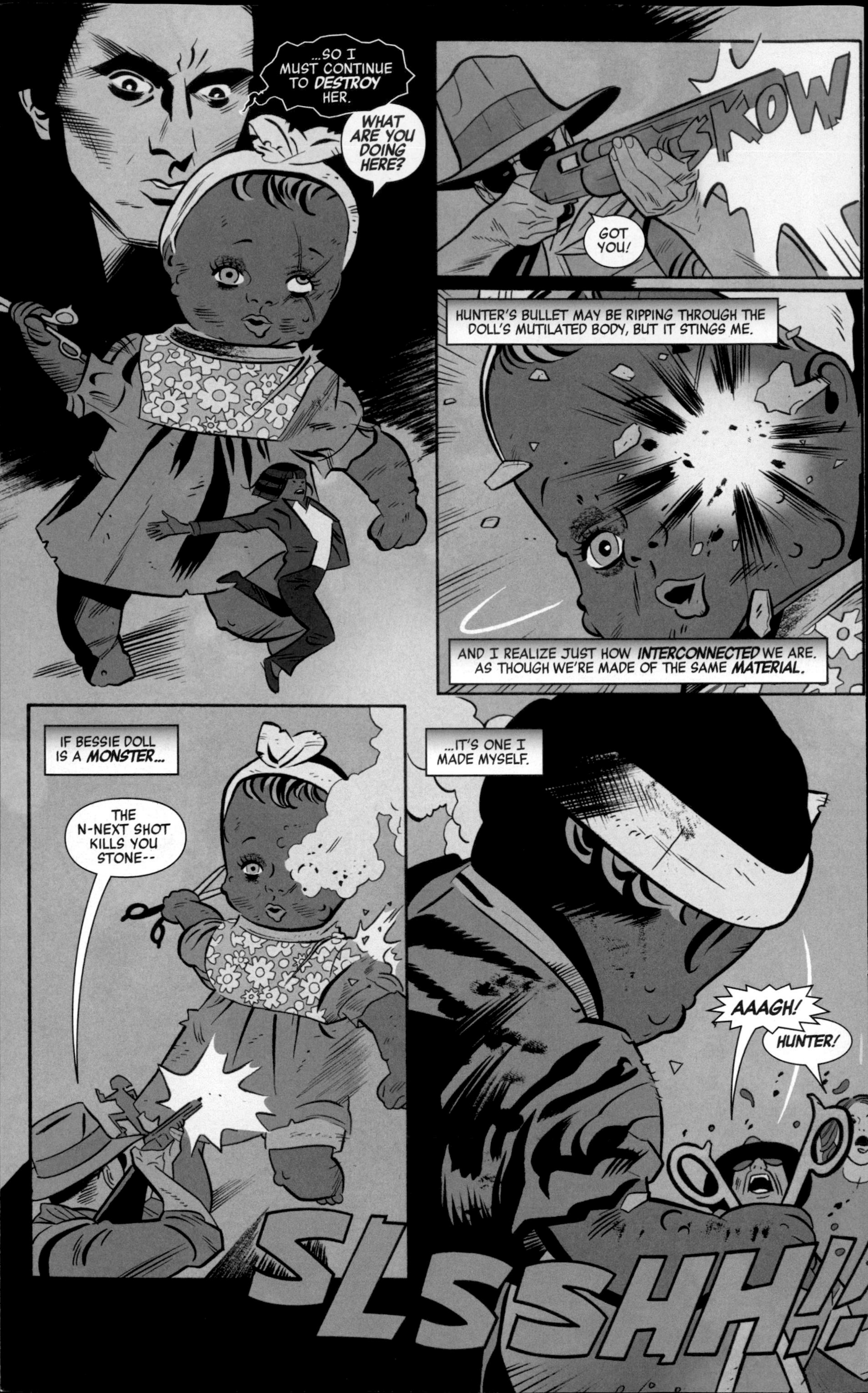
...SO I MUST CONTINUE TO DESTROY HER.
WHAT ARE YOU DOING HERE?
SKOW
GOT YOU!
HUNTER'S BULLET MAY BE RIPPING THROUGH THE DOLL'S MUTILATED BODY, BUT IT STINGS ME.
AND I REALIZE JUST HOW INTERCONNECTED WE ARE. AS THOUGH WE'RE MADE OF THE SAME MATERIAL.
IF BESSIE DOLL IS A MONSTER...
THE N-NEXT SHOT KILLS YOU STONE--
...IT'S ONE I MADE MYSELF.
AAAGH!
HUNTER!
SLSSHH!!

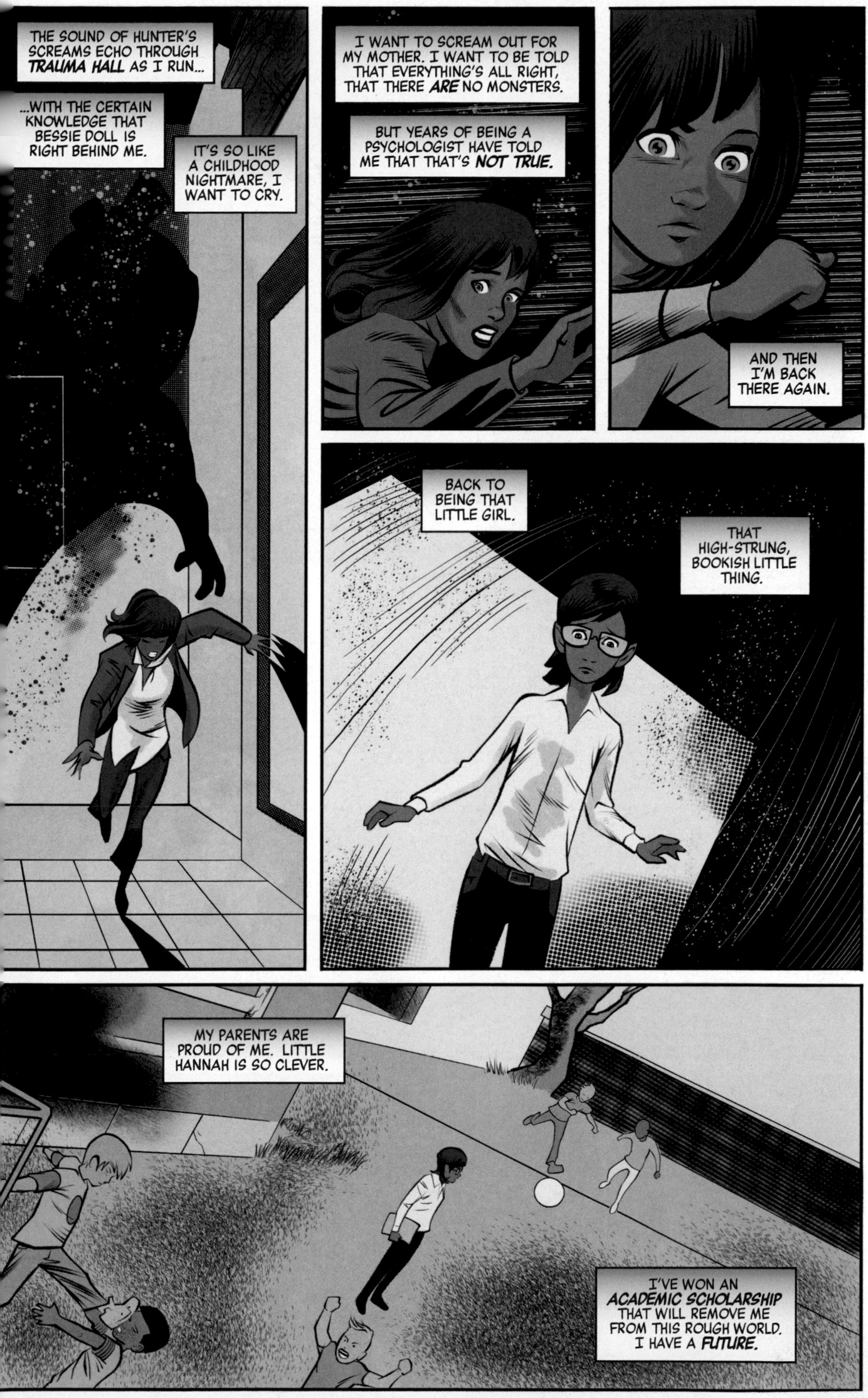
THE SOUND OF HUNTER'S SCREAMS ECHO THROUGH TRAUMA HALL AS I RUN...
...WITH THE CERTAIN KNOWLEDGE THAT BESSIE DOLL IS RIGHT BEHIND ME.
IT'S SO LIKE A CHILDHOOD NIGHTMARE, I WANT TO CRY.
I WANT TO SCREAM OUT FOR MY MOTHER. I WANT TO BE TOLD THAT EVERYTHING'S ALL RIGHT, THAT THERE ARE NO MONSTERS.
BUT YEARS OF BEING A PSYCHOLOGIST HAVE TOLD ME THAT THAT'S NOT TRUE.
AND THEN I'M BACK THERE AGAIN.
BACK TO BEING THAT LITTLE GIRL.
THAT HIGH-STRUNG, BOOKISH LITTLE THING.
MY PARENTS ARE PROUD OF ME. LITTLE HANNAH IS SO CLEVER.
I'VE WON AN ACADEMIC SCHOLARSHIP THAT WILL REMOVE ME FROM THIS ROUGH WORLD. I HAVE A FUTURE.

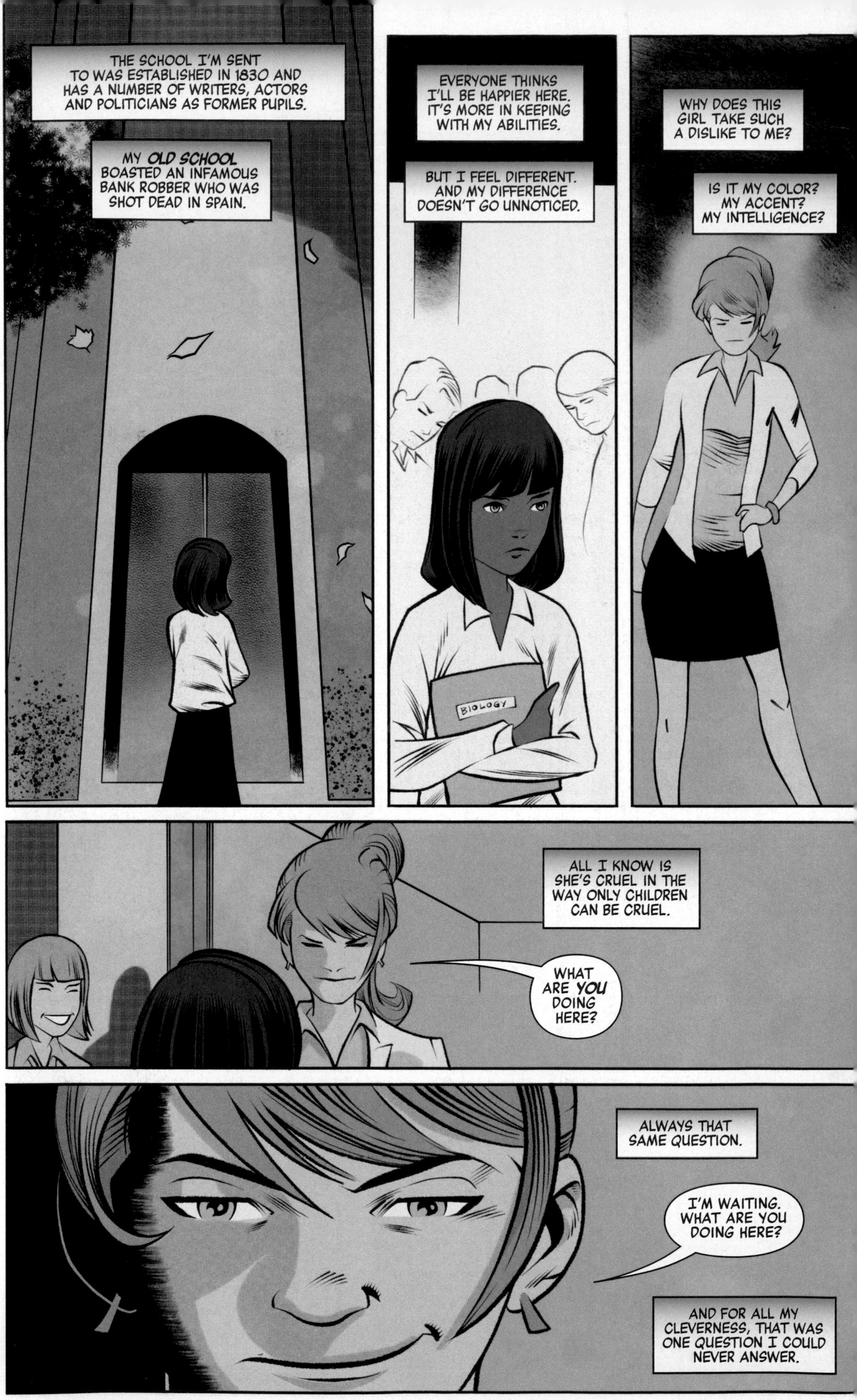
THE SCHOOL I'M SENT TO WAS ESTABLISHED IN 1830 AND HAS A NUMBER OF WRITERS, ACTORS AND POLITICIANS AS FORMER PUPILS.
MY *OLD SCHOOL* BOASTED AN INFAMOUS BANK ROBBER WHO WAS SHOT DEAD IN SPAIN.
EVERYONE THINKS I'LL BE HAPPIER HERE. IT'S MORE IN KEEPING WITH MY ABILITIES.
BUT I FEEL DIFFERENT. AND MY DIFFERENCE DOESN'T GO UNNOTICED.
BIOLOGY
WHY DOES THIS GIRL TAKE SUCH A DISLIKE TO ME?
IS IT MY COLOR? MY ACCENT? MY INTELLIGENCE?
ALL I KNOW IS SHE'S CRUEL IN THE WAY ONLY CHILDREN CAN BE CRUEL.
WHAT ARE *YOU* DOING HERE?
ALWAYS THAT SAME QUESTION.
I'M WAITING. WHAT ARE YOU DOING HERE?
AND FOR ALL MY CLEVERNESS, THAT WAS ONE QUESTION I COULD NEVER ANSWER.

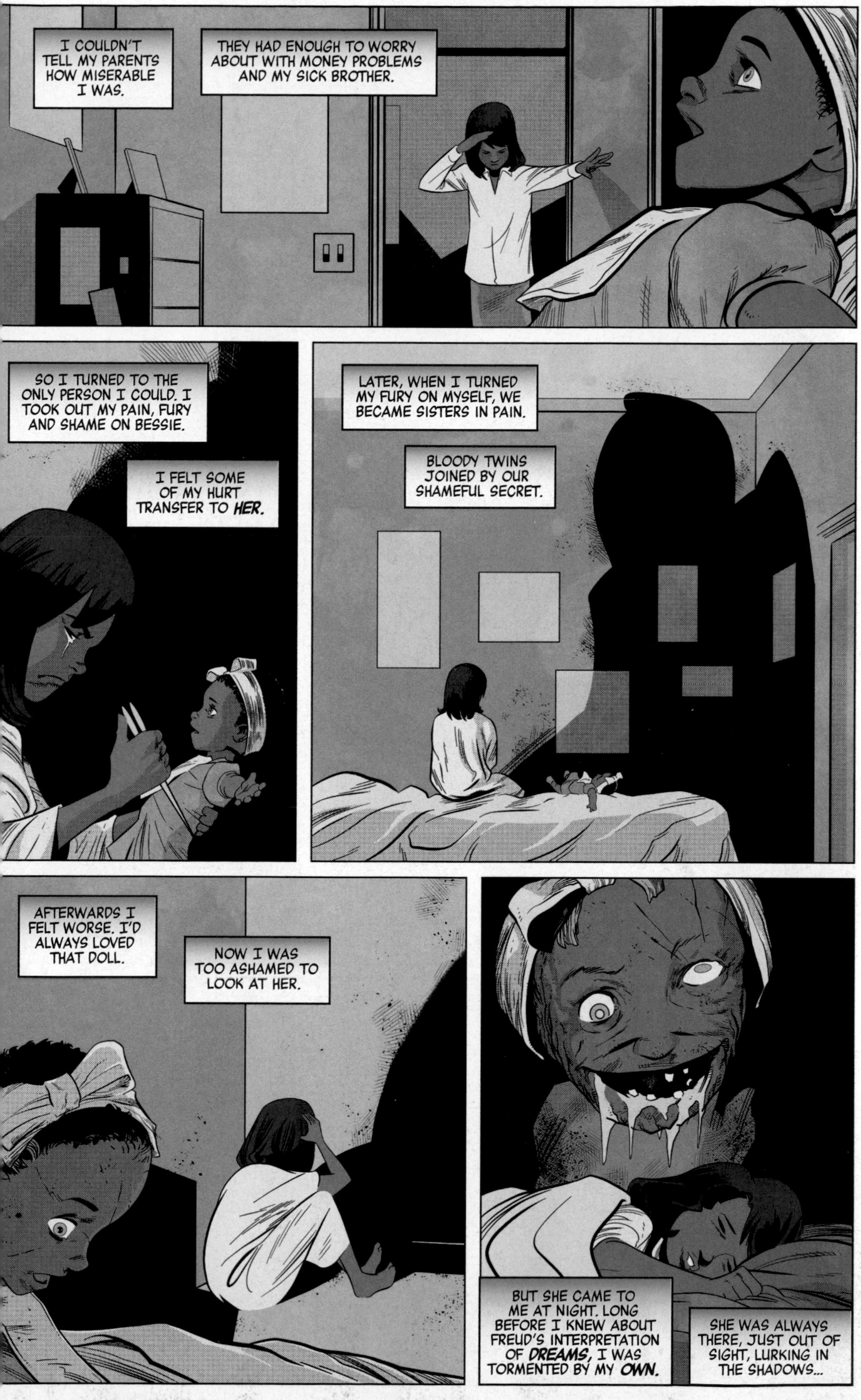
I COULDN'T TELL MY PARENTS HOW MISERABLE I WAS.
THEY HAD ENOUGH TO WORRY ABOUT WITH MONEY PROBLEMS AND MY SICK BROTHER.
SO I TURNED TO THE ONLY PERSON I COULD. I TOOK OUT MY PAIN, FURY AND SHAME ON BESSIE.
I FELT SOME OF MY HURT TRANSFER TO HER.
LATER, WHEN I TURNED MY FURY ON MYSELF, WE BECAME SISTERS IN PAIN.
BLOODY TWINS JOINED BY OUR SHAMEFUL SECRET.
AFTERWARDS I FELT WORSE. I'D ALWAYS LOVED THAT DOLL.
NOW I WAS TOO ASHAMED TO LOOK AT HER.
BUT SHE CAME TO ME AT NIGHT. LONG BEFORE I KNEW ABOUT FREUD'S INTERPRETATION OF DREAMS, I WAS TORMENTED BY MY OWN.
SHE WAS ALWAYS THERE, JUST OUT OF SIGHT, LURKING IN THE SHADOWS...

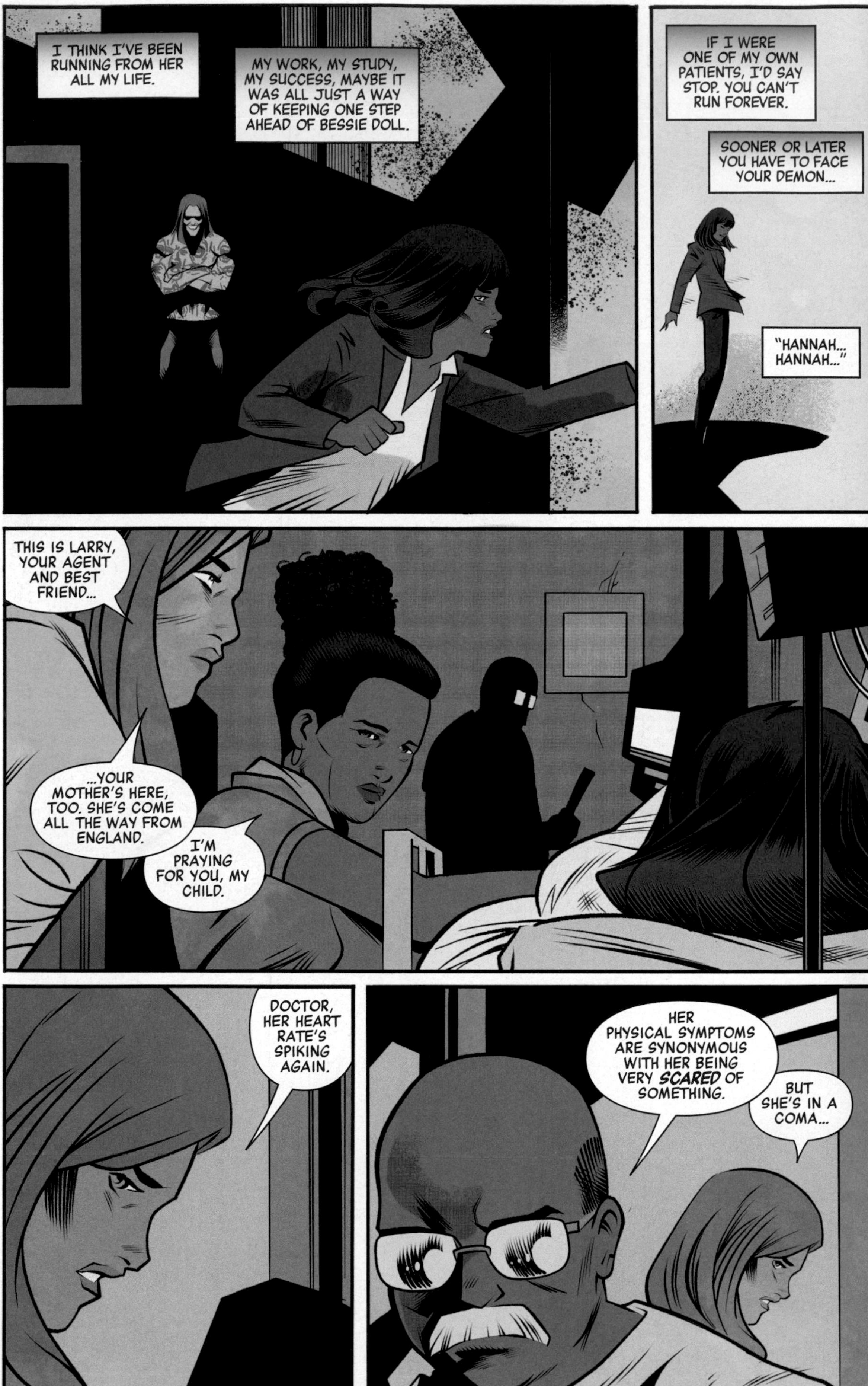
I THINK I'VE BEEN RUNNING FROM HER ALL MY LIFE.
MY WORK, MY STUDY, MY SUCCESS, MAYBE IT WAS ALL JUST A WAY OF KEEPING ONE STEP AHEAD OF BESSIE DOLL.
IF I WERE ONE OF MY OWN PATIENTS, I'D SAY STOP. YOU CAN'T RUN FOREVER.
SOONER OR LATER YOU HAVE TO FACE YOUR DEMON...
"HANNAH... HANNAH..."
THIS IS LARRY, YOUR AGENT AND BEST FRIEND...
...YOUR MOTHER'S HERE, TOO. SHE'S COME ALL THE WAY FROM ENGLAND.
I'M PRAYING FOR YOU, MY CHILD.
DOCTOR, HER HEART RATE'S SPIKING AGAIN.
HER PHYSICAL SYMPTOMS ARE SYNONYMOUS WITH HER BEING VERY SCARED OF SOMETHING.
BUT SHE'S IN A COMA...

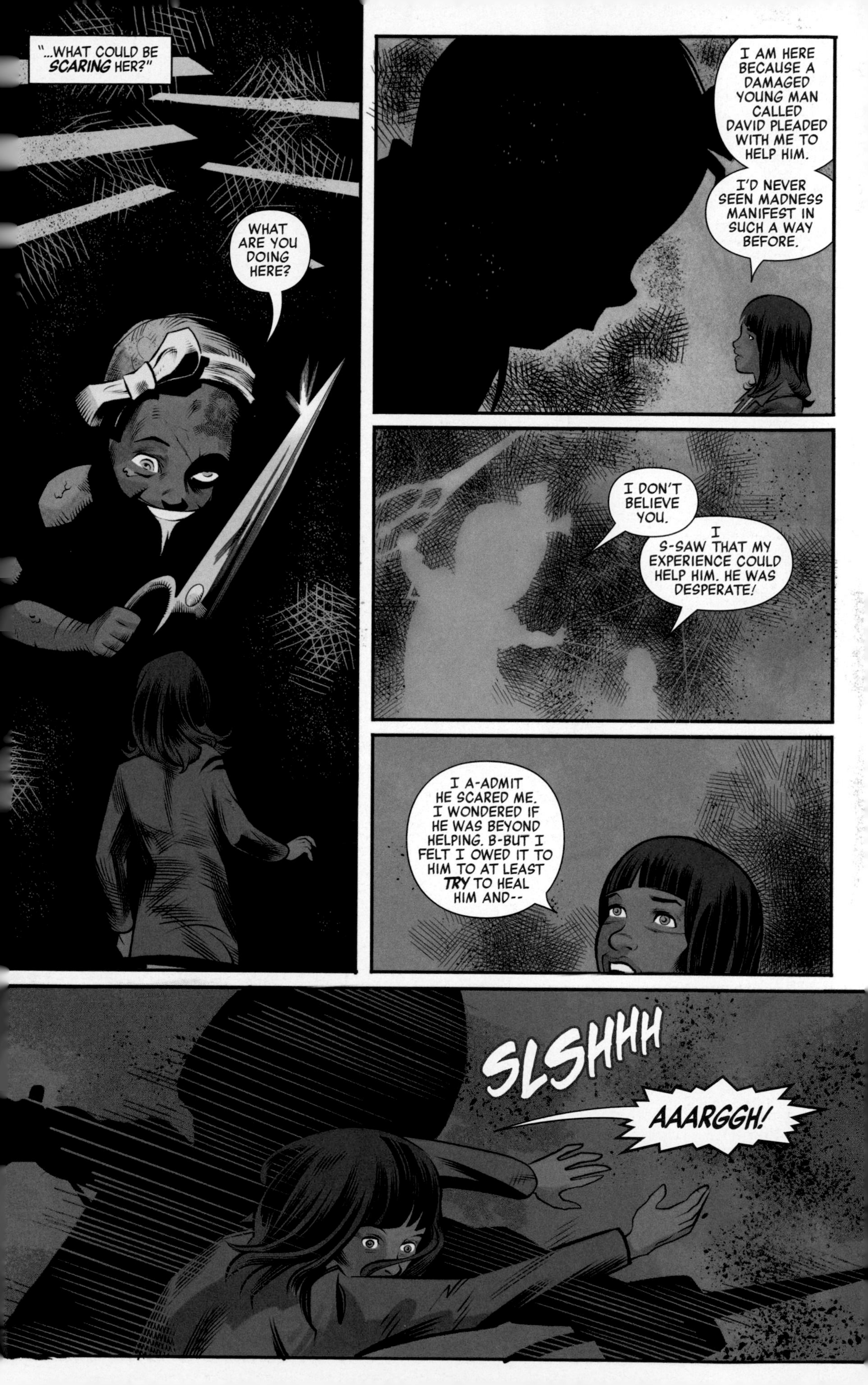
"...WHAT COULD BE SCARING HER?"
WHAT ARE YOU DOING HERE?
I AM HERE BECAUSE A DAMAGED YOUNG MAN CALLED DAVID PLEADED WITH ME TO HELP HIM.
I'D NEVER SEEN MADNESS MANIFEST IN SUCH A WAY BEFORE.
I DON'T BELIEVE YOU.
I S-SAW THAT MY EXPERIENCE COULD HELP HIM. HE WAS DESPERATE!
I A-ADMIT HE SCARED ME. I WONDERED IF HE WAS BEYOND HELPING. B-BUT I FELT I OWED IT TO HIM TO AT LEAST TRY TO HEAL HIM AND--
SLSHHH
AAARGGH!

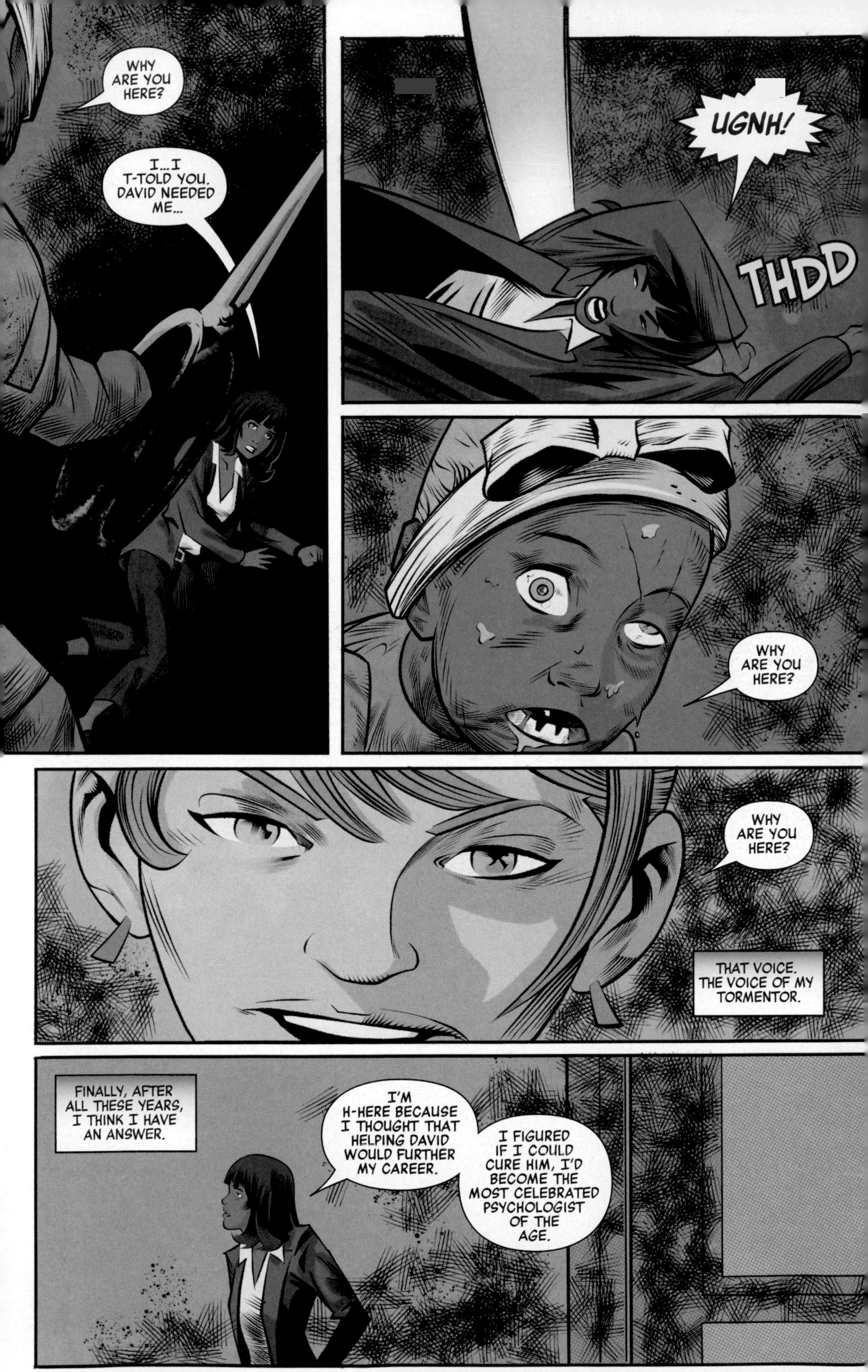
WHY ARE YOU HERE?
I...I T-TOLD YOU. DAVID NEEDED ME...
UGNH!
THDD
WHY ARE YOU HERE?
WHY ARE YOU HERE?
THAT VOICE. THE VOICE OF MY TORMENTOR.
FINALLY, AFTER ALL THESE YEARS, I THINK I HAVE AN ANSWER.
I'M H-HERE BECAUSE I THOUGHT THAT HELPING DAVID WOULD FURTHER MY CAREER.
I FIGURED IF I COULD CURE HIM, I'D BECOME THE MOST CELEBRATED PSYCHOLOGIST OF THE AGE.

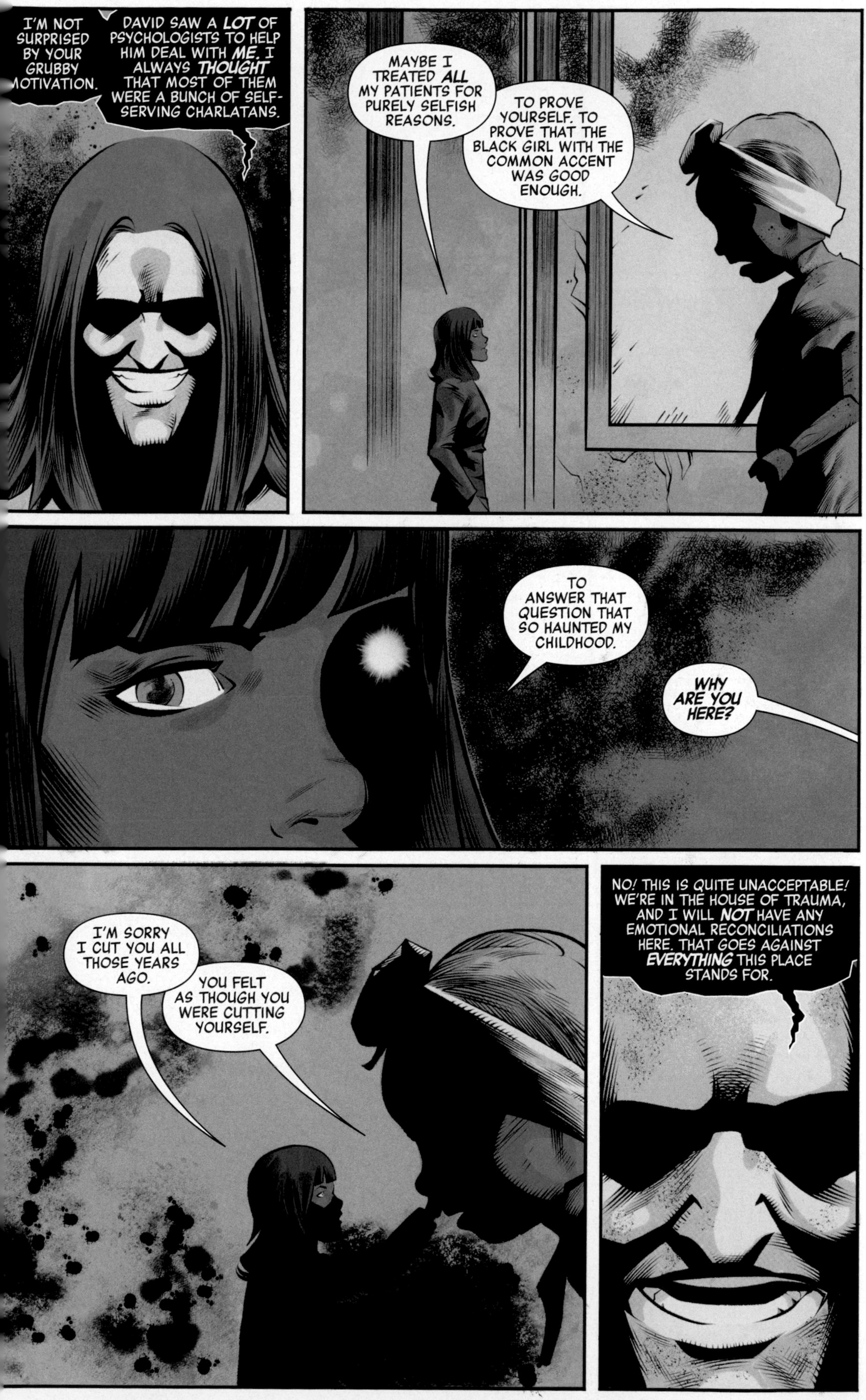
I'M NOT SURPRISED BY YOUR GRUBBY MOTIVATION.
DAVID SAW A LOT OF PSYCHOLOGISTS TO HELP HIM DEAL WITH ME. I ALWAYS THOUGHT THAT MOST OF THEM WERE A BUNCH OF SELF-SERVING CHARLATANS.
MAYBE I TREATED ALL MY PATIENTS FOR PURELY SELFISH REASONS.
TO PROVE YOURSELF. TO PROVE THAT THE BLACK GIRL WITH THE COMMON ACCENT WAS GOOD ENOUGH.
TO ANSWER THAT QUESTION THAT SO HAUNTED MY CHILDHOOD.
WHY ARE YOU HERE?
I'M SORRY I CUT YOU ALL THOSE YEARS AGO.
YOU FELT AS THOUGH YOU WERE CUTTING YOURSELF.
NO! THIS IS QUITE UNACCEPTABLE! WE'RE IN THE HOUSE OF TRAUMA, AND I WILL NOT HAVE ANY EMOTIONAL RECONCILIATIONS HERE. THAT GOES AGAINST EVERYTHING THIS PLACE STANDS FOR.

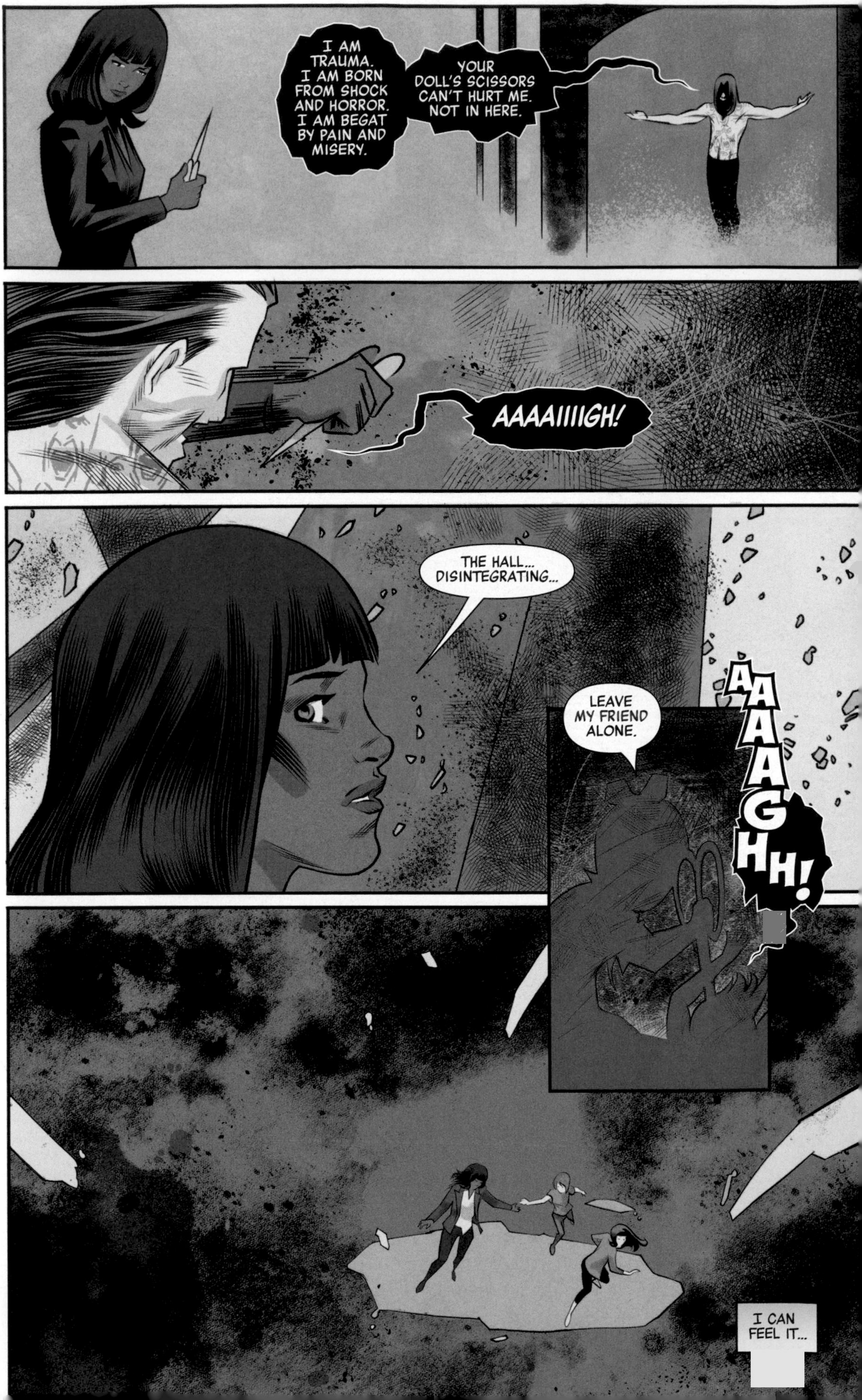
I AM TRAUMA. I AM BORN FROM SHOCK AND HORROR. I AM BEGAT BY PAIN AND MISERY.
YOUR DOLL'S SCISSORS CAN'T HURT ME. NOT IN HERE.
AAAAIIIIGH!
THE HALL... DISINTEGRATING...
LEAVE MY FRIEND ALONE.
AAAAGHH!
I CAN FEEL IT...

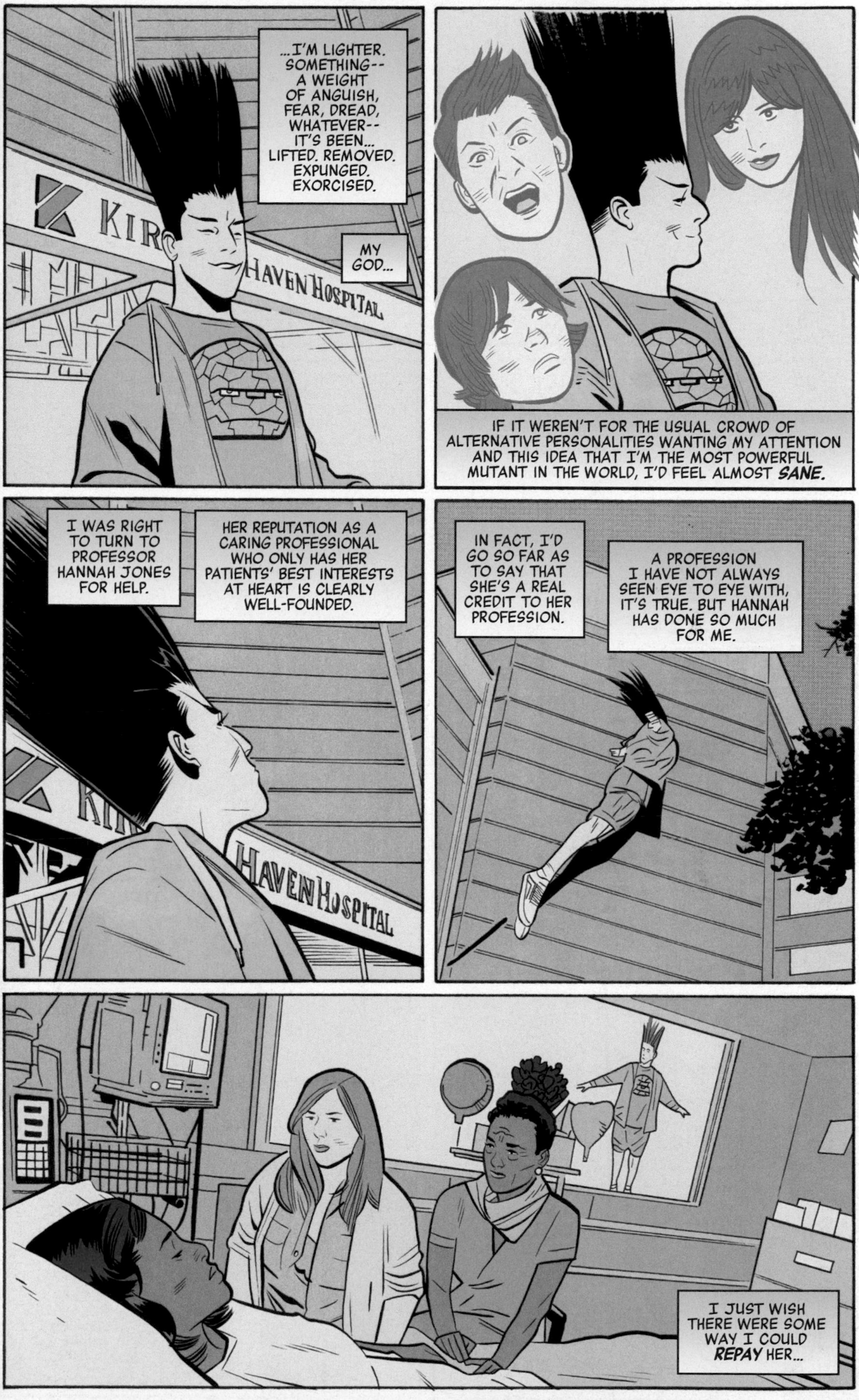
...I'M LIGHTER. SOMETHING-- A WEIGHT OF ANGUISH, FEAR, DREAD, WHATEVER-- IT'S BEEN... LIFTED. REMOVED. EXPUNGED. EXORCISED.
MY GOD...
KIR
HAVEN HOSPITAL
IF IT WEREN'T FOR THE USUAL CROWD OF ALTERNATIVE PERSONALITIES WANTING MY ATTENTION AND THIS IDEA THAT I'M THE MOST POWERFUL MUTANT IN THE WORLD, I'D FEEL ALMOST SANE.
I WAS RIGHT TO TURN TO PROFESSOR HANNAH JONES FOR HELP.
HER REPUTATION AS A CARING PROFESSIONAL WHO ONLY HAS HER PATIENTS' BEST INTERESTS AT HEART IS CLEARLY WELL-FOUNDED.
KIR
HAVEN HOSPITAL
IN FACT, I'D GO SO FAR AS TO SAY THAT SHE'S A REAL CREDIT TO HER PROFESSION.
A PROFESSION I HAVE NOT ALWAYS SEEN EYE TO EYE WITH, IT'S TRUE. BUT HANNAH HAS DONE SO MUCH FOR ME.
I JUST WISH THERE WERE SOME WAY I COULD REPAY HER...

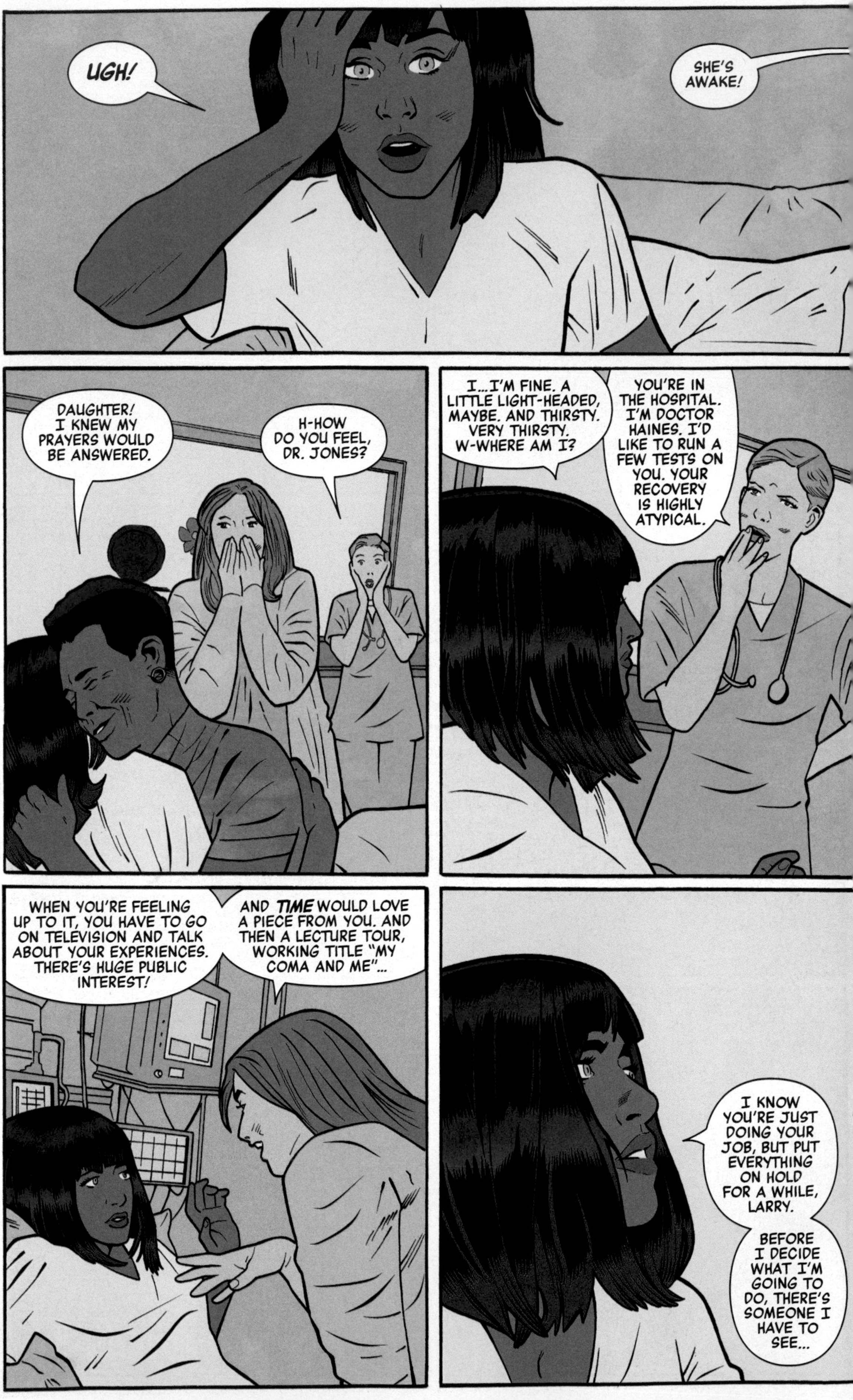
UGH!
SHE'S AWAKE!
DAUGHTER! I KNEW MY PRAYERS WOULD BE ANSWERED.
H-HOW DO YOU FEEL, DR. JONES?
I...I'M FINE. A LITTLE LIGHT-HEADED, MAYBE. AND THIRSTY. VERY THIRSTY. W-WHERE AM I?
YOU'RE IN THE HOSPITAL. I'M DOCTOR HAINES. I'D LIKE TO RUN A FEW TESTS ON YOU. YOUR RECOVERY IS HIGHLY ATYPICAL.
WHEN YOU'RE FEELING UP TO IT, YOU HAVE TO GO ON TELEVISION AND TALK ABOUT YOUR EXPERIENCES. THERE'S HUGE PUBLIC INTEREST!
AND TIME WOULD LOVE A PIECE FROM YOU. AND THEN A LECTURE TOUR, WORKING TITLE "MY COMA AND ME"...
I KNOW YOU'RE JUST DOING YOUR JOB, BUT PUT EVERYTHING ON HOLD FOR A WHILE, LARRY.
BEFORE I DECIDE WHAT I'M GOING TO DO, THERE'S SOMEONE I HAVE TO SEE...

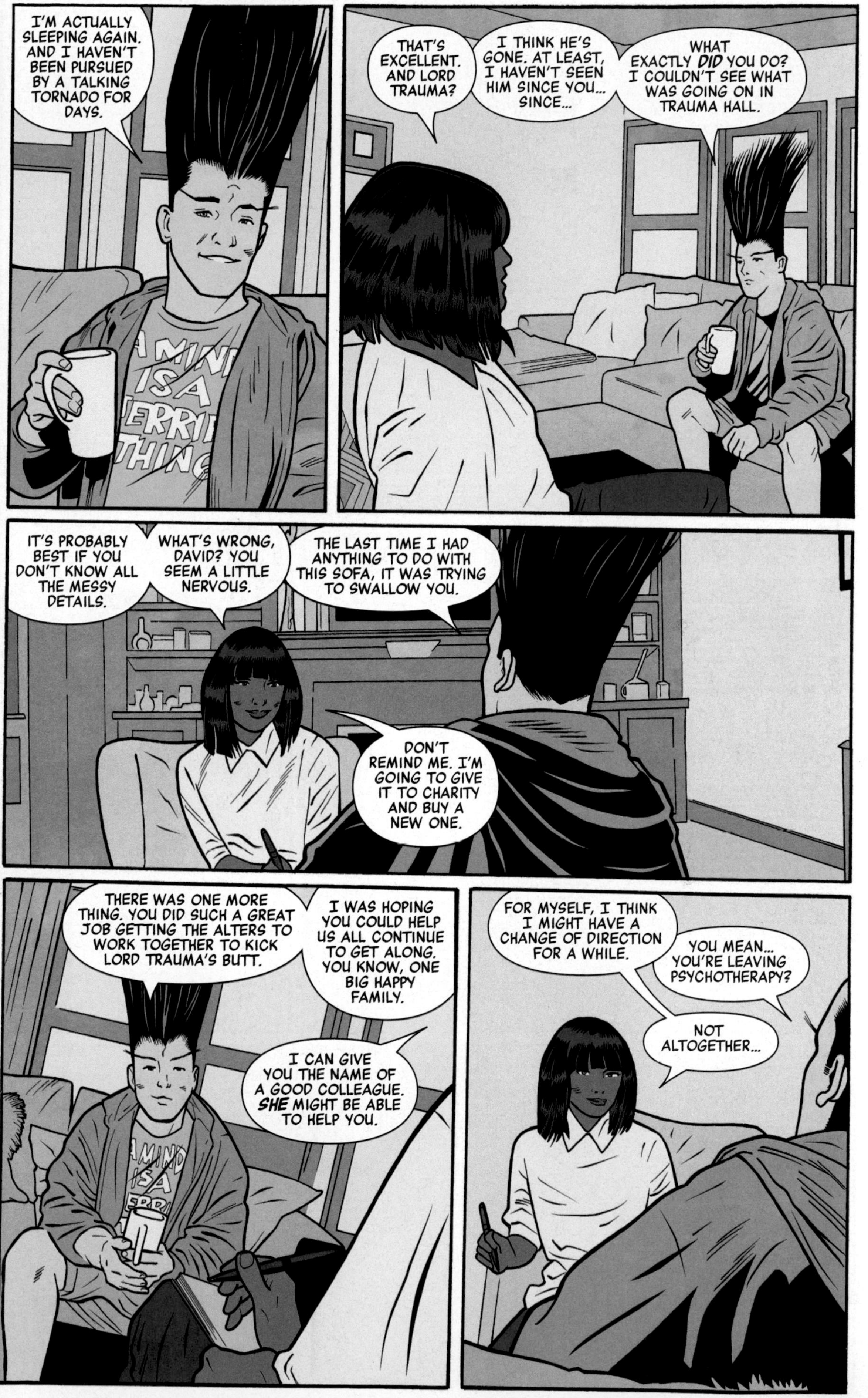
I'M ACTUALLY SLEEPING AGAIN. AND I HAVEN'T BEEN PURSUED BY A TALKING TORNADO FOR DAYS.
A MIND IS A TERRIBLE THING
THAT'S EXCELLENT. AND LORD TRAUMA?
I THINK HE'S GONE. AT LEAST, I HAVEN'T SEEN HIM SINCE YOU... SINCE...
WHAT EXACTLY *DID* YOU DO? I COULDN'T SEE WHAT WAS GOING ON IN TRAUMA HALL.
IT'S PROBABLY BEST IF YOU DON'T KNOW ALL THE MESSY DETAILS.
WHAT'S WRONG, DAVID? YOU SEEM A LITTLE NERVOUS.
THE LAST TIME I HAD ANYTHING TO DO WITH THIS SOFA, IT WAS TRYING TO SWALLOW YOU.
DON'T REMIND ME. I'M GOING TO GIVE IT TO CHARITY AND BUY A NEW ONE.
THERE WAS ONE MORE THING. YOU DID SUCH A GREAT JOB GETTING THE ALTERS TO WORK TOGETHER TO KICK LORD TRAUMA'S BUTT.
I WAS HOPING YOU COULD HELP US ALL CONTINUE TO GET ALONG. YOU KNOW, ONE BIG HAPPY FAMILY.
I CAN GIVE YOU THE NAME OF A GOOD COLLEAGUE. *SHE* MIGHT BE ABLE TO HELP YOU.
FOR MYSELF, I THINK I MIGHT HAVE A CHANGE OF DIRECTION FOR A WHILE.
YOU MEAN... YOU'RE LEAVING PSYCHOTHERAPY?
NOT ALTOGETHER...

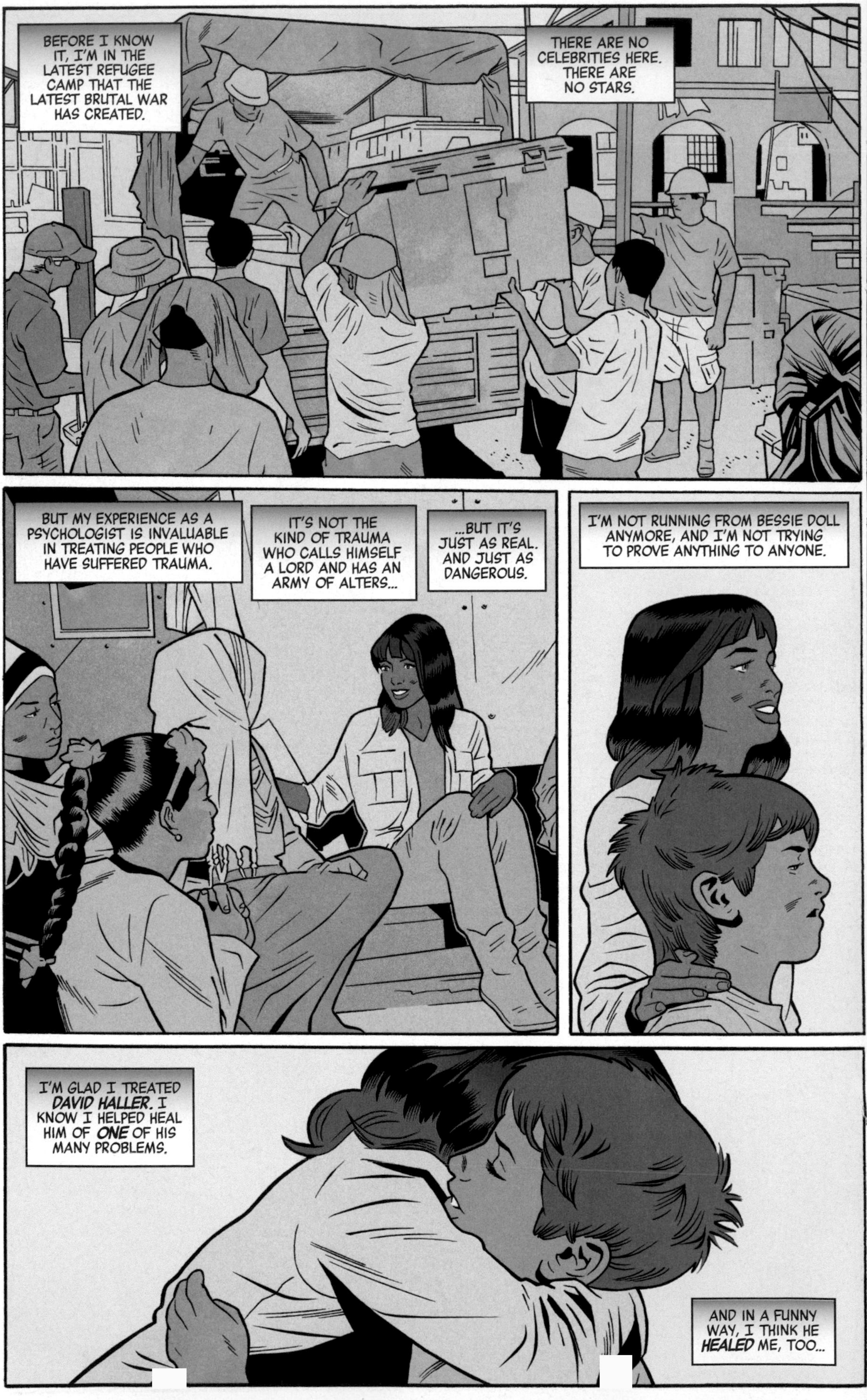
BEFORE I KNOW IT, I'M IN THE LATEST REFUGEE CAMP THAT THE LATEST BRUTAL WAR HAS CREATED.
THERE ARE NO CELEBRITIES HERE. THERE ARE NO STARS.
BUT MY EXPERIENCE AS A PSYCHOLOGIST IS INVALUABLE IN TREATING PEOPLE WHO HAVE SUFFERED TRAUMA.
IT'S NOT THE KIND OF TRAUMA WHO CALLS HIMSELF A LORD AND HAS AN ARMY OF ALTERS...
...BUT IT'S JUST AS REAL. AND JUST AS DANGEROUS.
I'M NOT RUNNING FROM BESSIE DOLL ANYMORE, AND I'M NOT TRYING TO PROVE ANYTHING TO ANYONE.
I'M GLAD I TREATED DAVID HALLER. I KNOW I HELPED HEAL HIM OF ONE OF HIS MANY PROBLEMS.
AND IN A FUNNY WAY, I THINK HE HEALED ME, TOO...

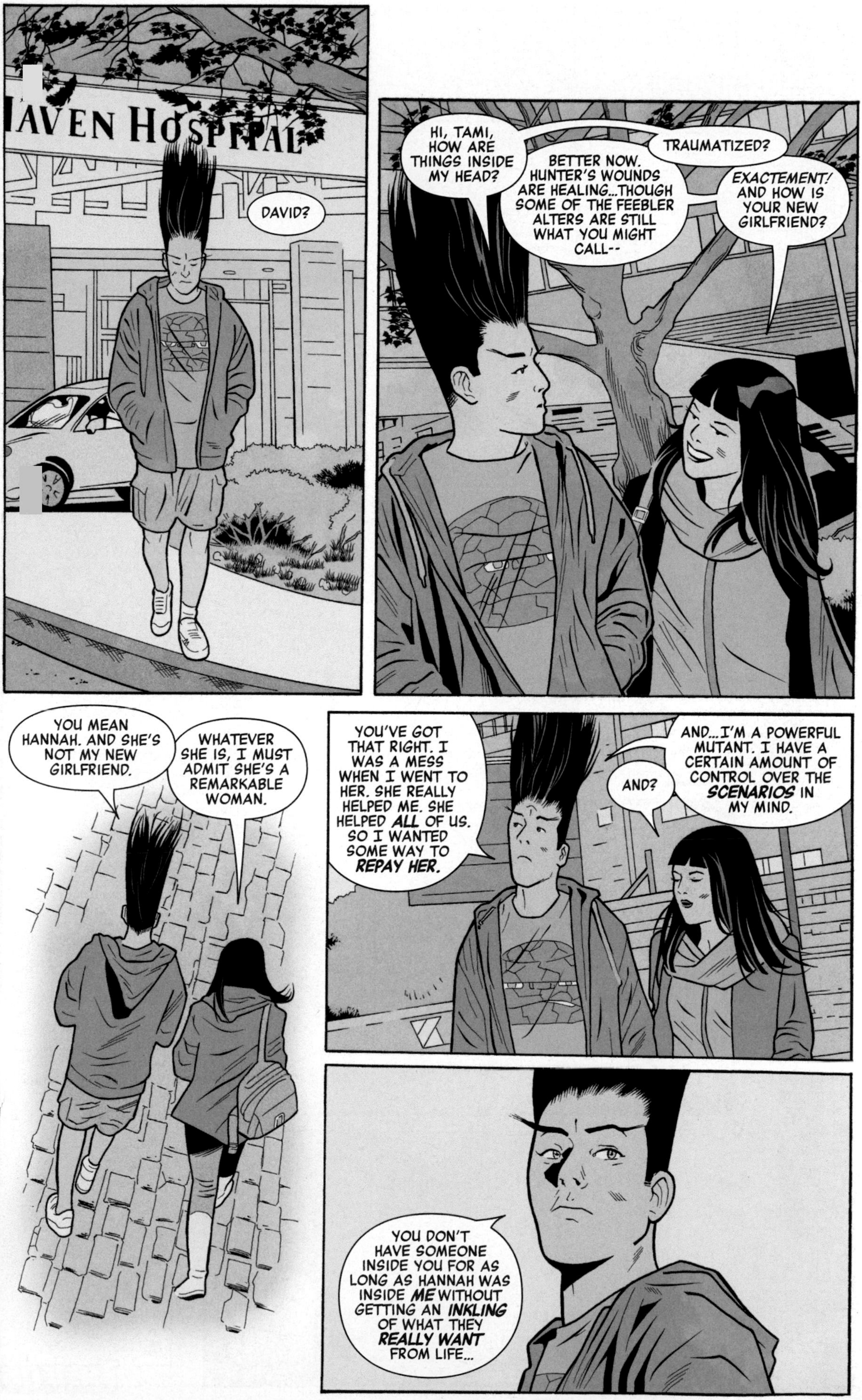

HAVEN HOSPITAL
DAVID?
HI, TAMI, HOW ARE THINGS INSIDE MY HEAD?
BETTER NOW. HUNTER'S WOUNDS ARE HEALING...THOUGH SOME OF THE FEEBLER ALTERS ARE STILL WHAT YOU MIGHT CALL--
TRAUMATIZED?
EXACTEMENT! AND HOW IS YOUR NEW GIRLFRIEND?
YOU MEAN HANNAH. AND SHE'S NOT MY NEW GIRLFRIEND.
WHATEVER SHE IS, I MUST ADMIT SHE'S A REMARKABLE WOMAN.
YOU'VE GOT THAT RIGHT. I WAS A MESS WHEN I WENT TO HER. SHE REALLY HELPED ME. SHE HELPED ALL OF US. SO I WANTED SOME WAY TO REPAY HER.
AND...I'M A POWERFUL MUTANT. I HAVE A CERTAIN AMOUNT OF CONTROL OVER THE SCENARIOS IN MY MIND.
AND?
YOU DON'T HAVE SOMEONE INSIDE YOU FOR AS LONG AS HANNAH WAS INSIDE ME WITHOUT GETTING AN INKLING OF WHAT THEY REALLY WANT FROM LIFE...

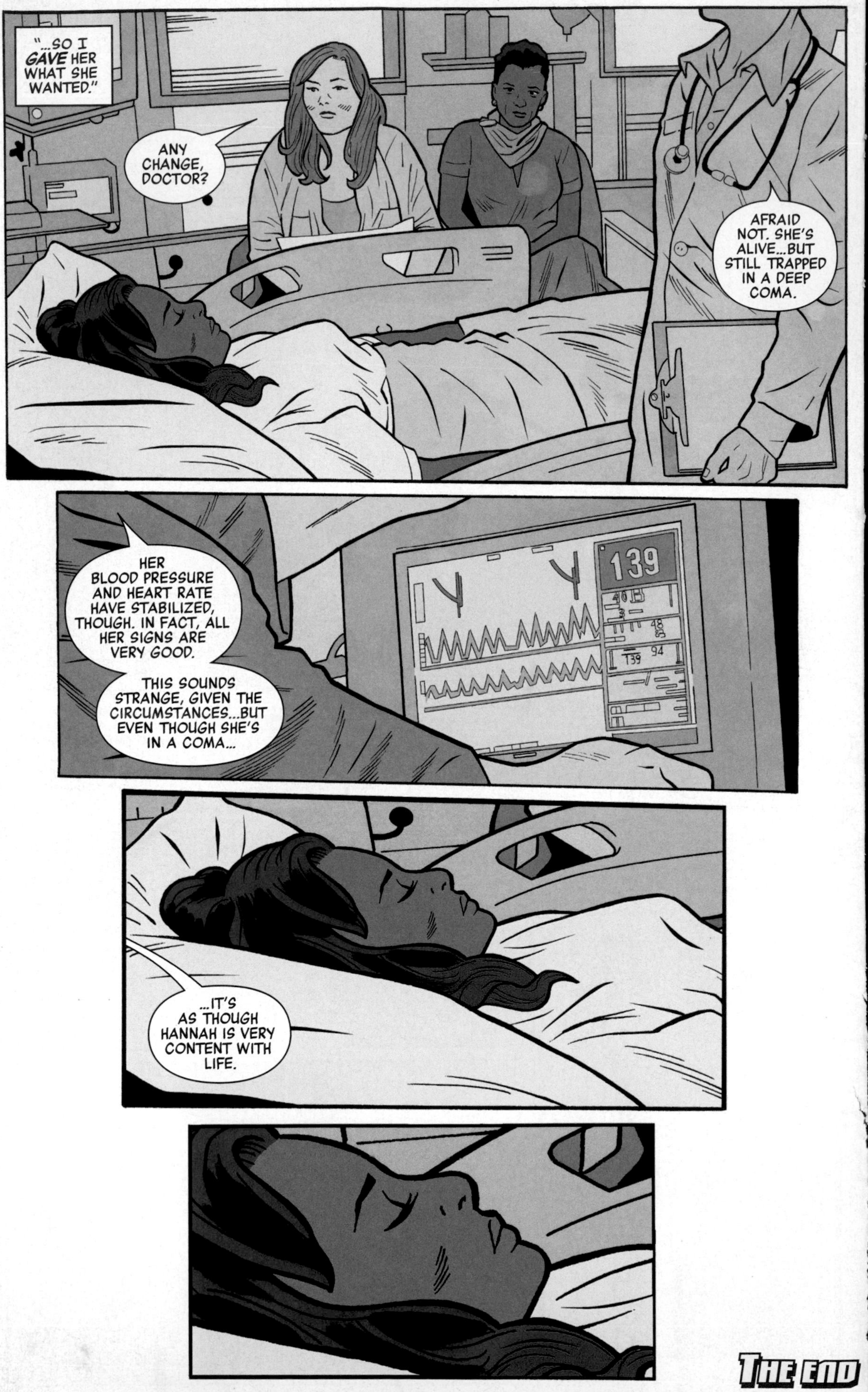
"...SO I GAVE HER WHAT SHE WANTED."
ANY CHANGE, DOCTOR?
AFRAID NOT. SHE'S ALIVE...BUT STILL TRAPPED IN A DEEP COMA.
HER BLOOD PRESSURE AND HEART RATE HAVE STABILIZED, THOUGH. IN FACT, ALL HER SIGNS ARE VERY GOOD.
THIS SOUNDS STRANGE, GIVEN THE CIRCUMSTANCES...BUT EVEN THOUGH SHE'S IN A COMA...
139
...IT'S AS THOUGH HANNAH IS VERY CONTENT WITH LIFE.
THE END

#1 VARIANT BY **BILL SIENKIEWICZ**

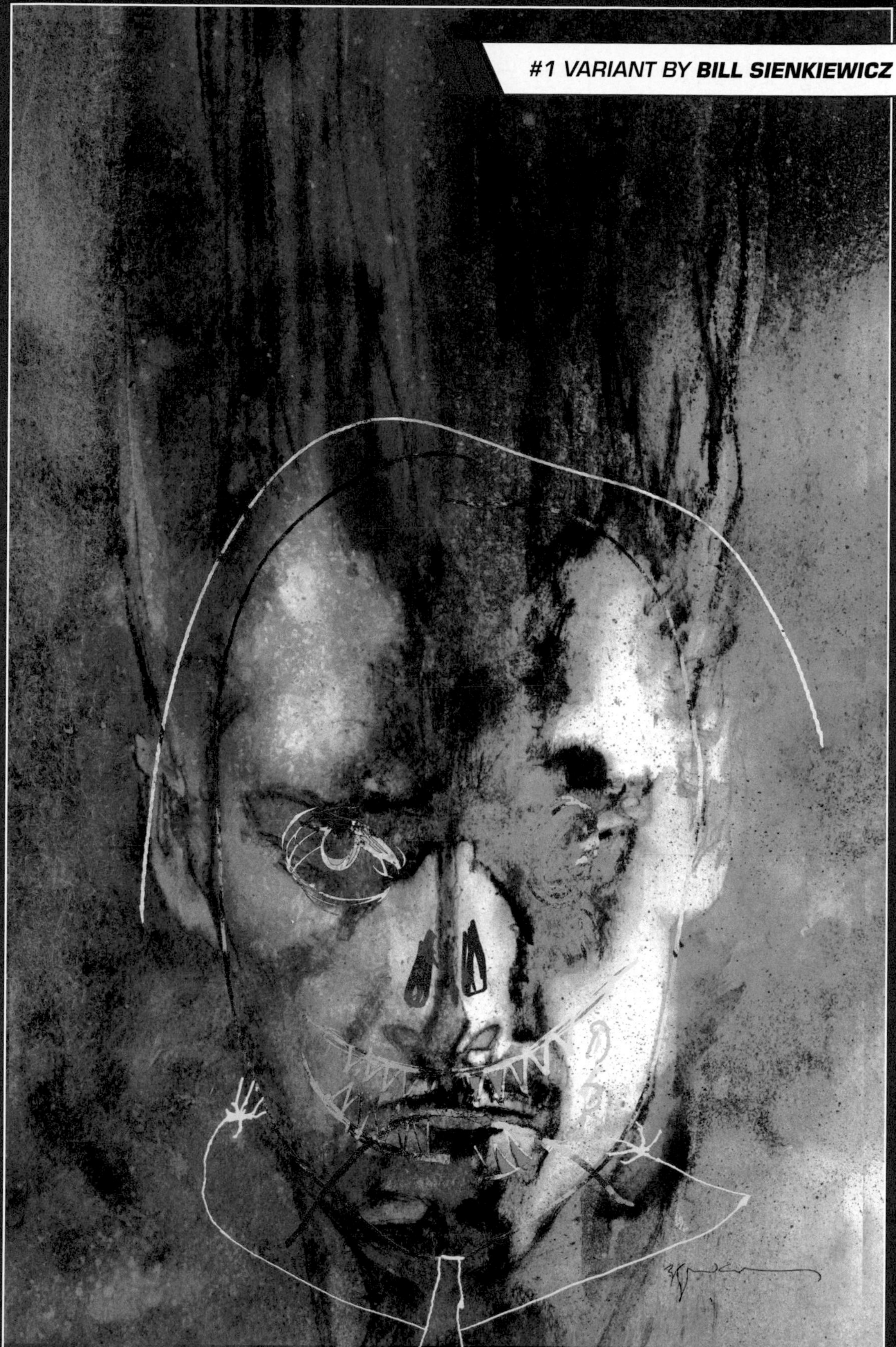

#1 VARIANT BY NIKO HENRICHON

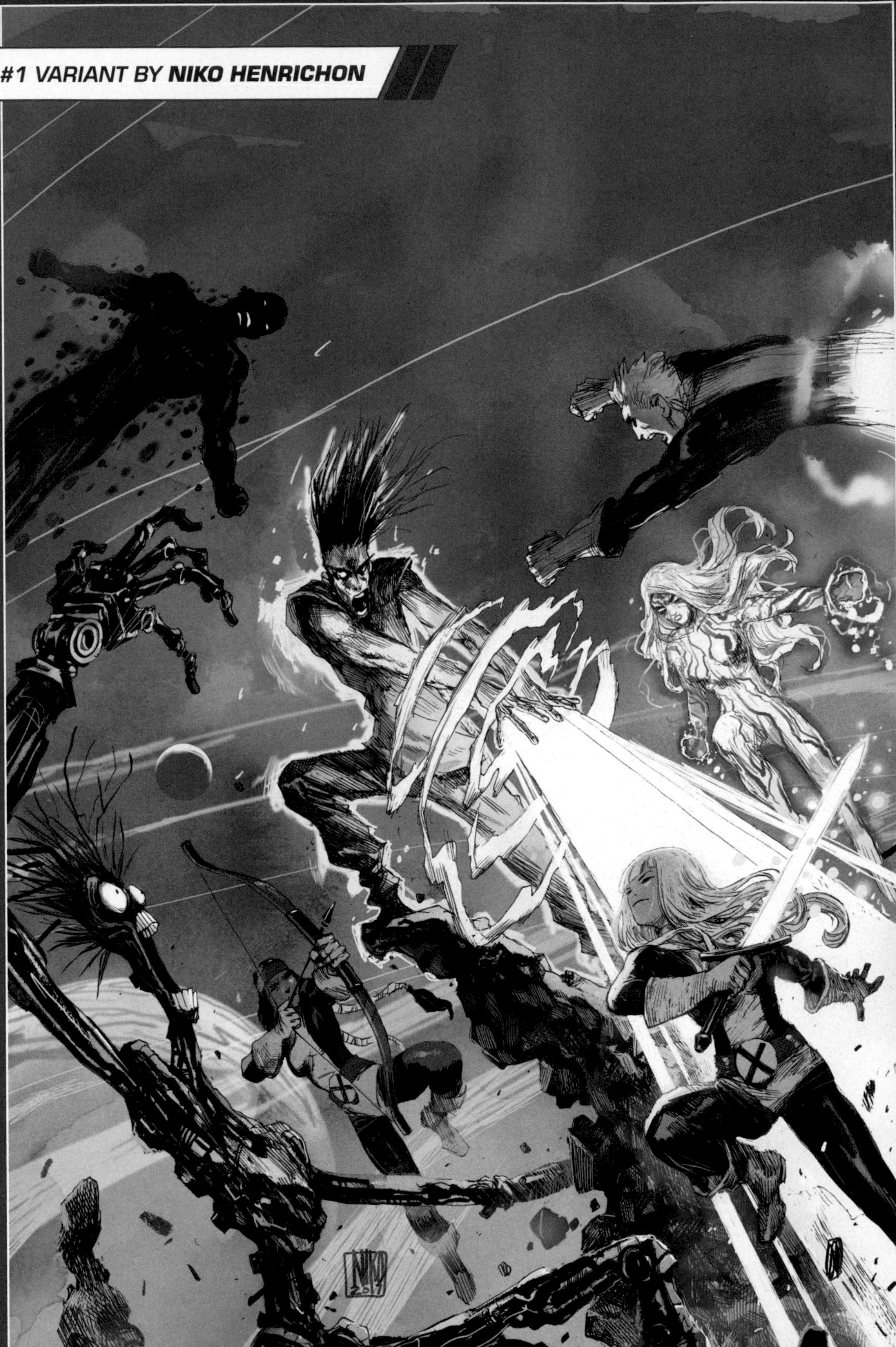

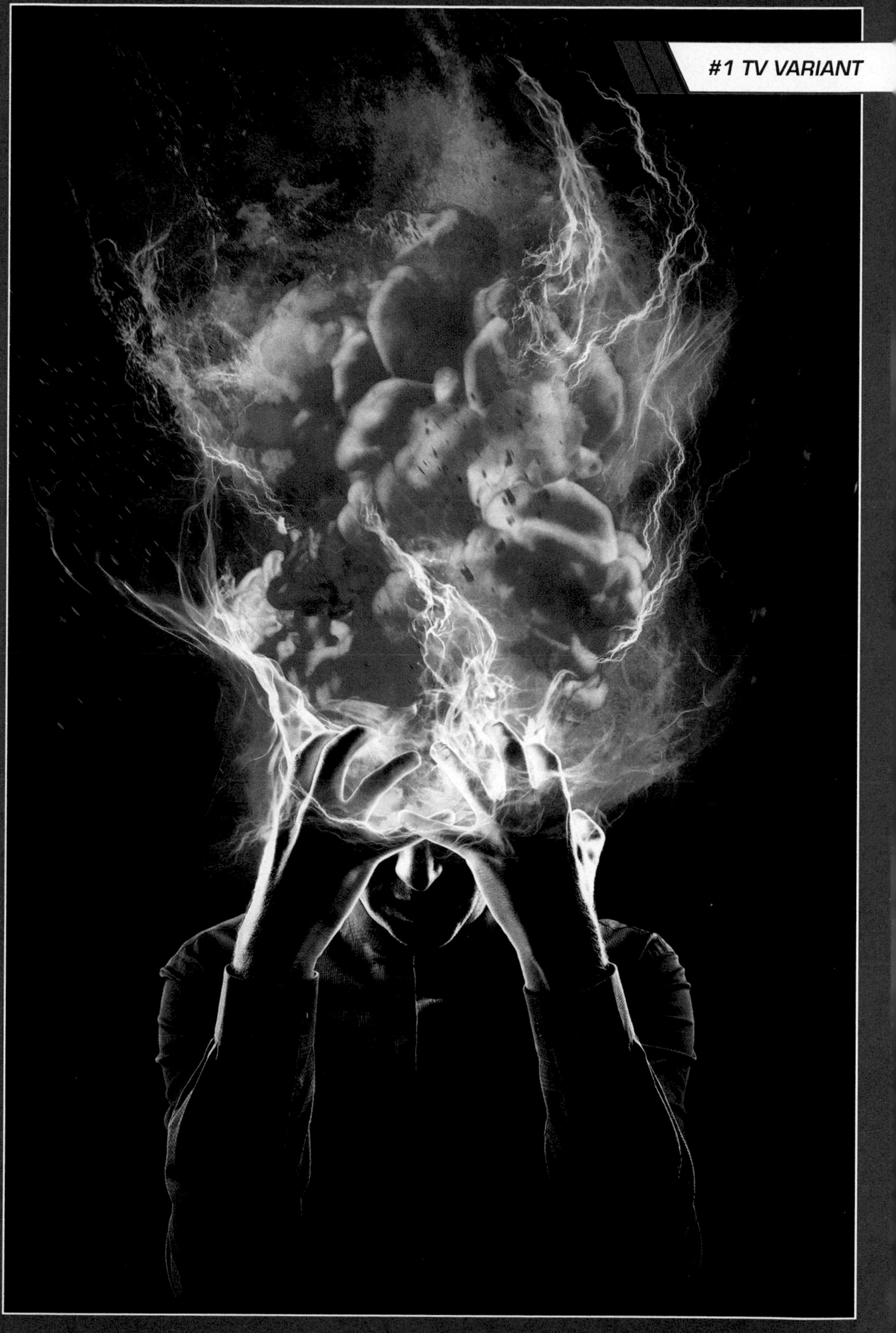
#1 TV VARIANT